Engaging the Line

Studies in Canadian Military History

Series editor: Andrew Burtch, Canadian War Museum

The Canadian War Museum, Canada's national museum of military history, has a threefold mandate: to remember, to preserve, and to educate. Studies in Canadian Military History, published by UBC Press in association with the Museum, extends this mandate by presenting the best of contemporary scholarship to provide new insights into all aspects of Canadian military history, from earliest times to recent events. The work of a new generation of scholars is especially encouraged, and the books employ a variety of approaches – cultural, social, intellectual, economic, political, and comparative – to investigate gaps in the existing historiography. The books in the series feed immediately into future exhibitions, programs, and outreach efforts by the Canadian War Museum. A list of the titles in the series appears at the end of the book.

CANADIAN WAR MUSEUM
MUSÉE CANADIEN DE LA GUERRE

Engaging the Line

How the Great War Shaped the Canada–US Border

Brandon R. Dimmel

UBCPress · Vancouver · Toronto

25 24 23 22 21 20 19 18 17 16 5 4 3 2 1

Printed in Canada on FSC-certified ancient-forest-free paper (100% post-consumer recycled) that is processed chlorine- and acid-free.

Library and Archives Canada Cataloguing in Publication

Dimmel, Brandon R., author
Engaging the line : Great War experiences along the Canada-US border / Brandon R. Dimmel.

(Studies in Canadian military history)
Includes bibliographical references and index.
Issued in print and electronic formats.

ISBN 978-0-7748-3274-8 (hardback). – ISBN 978-0-7748-3275-5 (pbk.)
ISBN 978-0-7748-3276-2 (pdf). – ISBN 978-0-7748-3277-9 (epub)
ISBN 978-0-7748-3278-6 (mobi)

Cities and towns – Canadian-American Border Region – History – 20th century – Case studies. 2. Border security – Canada – History – 20th century – Case studies. 3. Border security – United States – History – 20th century – Case studies. 4. World War, 1914–1918 – Social aspects – Canada – Case studies. 5. World War, 1914–1918 – Social aspects – United States – Case studies. 6. Canadian-American Border Region – History – 20th century – Case studies. I. Title. II. Series: Studies in Canadian military history

JC323.D54 2016 327.7107309'041 C2016-904964-7
C2016-904965-5

Canada

UBC Press gratefully acknowledges the financial support for our publishing program of the Government of Canada (through the Canada Book Fund), the Canada Council for the Arts, and the British Columbia Arts Council.

This book has been published with the help of a grant from the Canadian Federation for the Humanities and Social Sciences, through the Awards to Scholarly Publications Program, using funds provided by the Social Sciences and Humanities Research Council of Canada.

Publication of this book has been financially supported by the Canadian War Museum.

Printed and bound in Canada by Friesens
Set in Minion Pro by Marquis Interscript
Copy editor: Dallas Harrison
Proofreader: Alison Strobel
Indexer: Pat Buchanan

UBC Press
The University of British Columbia
2029 West Mall
Vancouver, BC V6T 1Z2
www.ubcpress.ca

Contents

Illustrations

Abbreviations

9–11	September 11, 2001
AL	American Legion
CBSA	Canada Border Services Agency
CBWG	Cascadia Border Working Group
CEF	Canadian Expeditionary Force
CPF	Canadian Patriotic Fund
DP	Dominion Police
DST	Daylight Saving Time
GAR	Grand Army of the Republic
GNR	Great Northern Railway
INS	Immigration and Naturalization Service
IODE	Imperial Order of the Daughters of the Empire
IR	Imperial Reserve
IWW	Industrial Workers of the World
LAC	Library and Archives Canada
MD1	Military District 1
MP	Member of Parliament
MPP	Member of Provincial Parliament
SSCA	South Surrey Conservatives Association
USDA	United States Department of Agriculture

Acknowledgments

I AM VERY grateful to a number of people for their help in completing this book. First of all, I must thank Dr. Jonathan Vance of Western University for his patience and guidance. Dr. Thomas Klug of Marygrove College in Detroit also offered an enormous amount of valuable assistance. I would also like to thank a number of archivists for their help, including Ryan Gallagher of Surrey Archives, Hugh Ellenwood of White Rock Museum and Archives, Michael Fish of Windsor Public Library Archives, and Janice Fairney of Charlotte County Archives. In addition, I would like to acknowledge the reference and librarian staff at D.B. Weldon Library, particularly David Murphy and Elizabeth Mantz. Dr. Miriam Wright of the University of Windsor also offered substantial guidance as this project progressed. Local historians John Cunningham and Doug Dougherty must be acknowledged for relating their intimate knowledge of the St. Croix Valley during and after my visit to the region in 2009. I am also indebted to the University of Western Ontario and the Government of Ontario for providing financial assistance necessary to pursue the research for this project.

Of course, the support of friends and family was also crucial in keeping this project moving forward. My greatest thanks go to Dorotea Gucciardo, Marian and Dale Creighton, Donald and Sylvia Dimmel, Larry and Jackie Dixon, Stephanie Dimmel and Scott McIntosh, Bruce and Donna Dimmel, and my parents, Richard and Laurie Dimmel. Without your support, this book would not have been possible.

Engaging the Line

Introduction

THE CANADA–US BORDER changed dramatically during the First World War. Prior to August 1914, the international boundary had been – for the most part – porous, a fluid zone of friendly economic and social interchange. After the outbreak of war, however, the border steadily transformed into a high-security surveillance area where citizens of Canada and the United States encountered the state like never before. For some Canadians, this change was necessary; after all, Canada was at war, and citizens needed to be protected against potential threats, such as the substantial German American population.

But for many residents of Canadian borderland communities – such as Windsor, Ontario, which shares the international boundary with Detroit, Michigan – these changes to the border during wartime were highly controversial. For generations prior to 1914, Windsorites had visited, on a daily basis, the ballparks, stores, and factories of Detroit. Now federal customs officers tasked with protecting the revenue of the dominion and Windsor's retailers discouraged locals from shopping in Detroit, where items such as clothing and jewellery were usually much cheaper. When boarding and leaving the ferries – which took locals across the Detroit River in an age before the Ambassador Bridge and Detroit–Windsor Tunnel (completed in 1929 and 1930, respectively) – Windsor residents could also expect to answer an escalating number of questions about their ethnicity, employment, and income posed by Canadian and American immigration officials. As for Windsor residents who joined the Canadian army, they were barred from crossing the border. Together these changes at the border served to strain long-running transnational social and economic relationships. It was a situation that concerned many residents of Windsor, who saw their region's vibrant border-crossing culture suffocated by the distant and previously unseen federal governments of the United States and Canada. By late 1916, many Windsorites took to writing letters to the local newspaper, the *Evening Record*, to express their mounting frustration: "Established residents of Windsor and Detroit understand each other thoroughly and mingle together in harmony," one Windsorite noted in a letter published December 5, 1916. "Respect is mutual. Friendship is self-evident. Hundreds of persons on this side cross to Detroit daily and find employment in the great city across the river." But that friendly interchange was now threatened, the writer thought. "It is only when outside influences are exerted that friction arises."[1]

These "outside influences" were not always so visible at the Windsor–Detroit section of the border or at other parts of the long Canada–US international boundary. In fact, at the turn of the twentieth century, few travellers faced any challenges as they attempted to cross from one country to the other. There were several reasons for this ease of crossing. First, Canada and the United States welcomed most travellers, especially white Protestant Anglo-Saxons born on the other side of the boundary. Industrialization of the North American economy was also a factor: in the Detroit River region specifically, growth of the area's automotive industry depended on access to a large pool of cheap labour, which an extranational neighbour could help to provide. Second, the state remained small at a time when the overwhelming attitude of North Americans was that the government that governed the least governed the best. Keeping that government small and taxes low meant limiting the number of customs and immigration officers on the government payroll. Meanwhile, most of those customs and immigration agents who did patrol the Canada–US border were hired to work in the communities in which they lived, and most tailored their inspections to the demands of the surrounding communities. In many border towns, the thinking was that having an open border helped rather than hindered the local culture and economy.

In 1914, this thinking was prominent in Windsor. Unlike many other communities in Canada (e.g., Ontario capital Toronto, where about one in every three city residents had been born in Britain), Windsor was home to as many Americans as Britons.[2] For years American investors had been establishing branch plants within Windsor city limits, thereby circumventing the Canadian government's high tariffs and gaining entry into the lucrative British market.[3] Windsor residents crossed each day to Detroit to work, shop, and take in baseball games or plays. Windsor schools were built using Detroit institutions as models – no surprise given that many of Windsor's young people flocked to Detroit high schools, colleges, and universities.[4] And this transnational movement was hardly one way, for thousands of Detroiters regularly visited Windsor's baseball parks, bars, restaurants, and horse-racing tracks. Facilitating such cross-border travel – and the evolution of a very visible border-crossing culture – were dozens of ferries capable of transporting thousands of passengers from one side of the Detroit River to the other in just a few minutes.[5] Waiting for these passengers were small teams of locally raised customs and immigration agents who, at least prior to the war, only weeded out travellers of an "undesirable" race (typically Asians and African Americans) or appeared to

FIGURE 1 Windsor's factory district in 1911. With American branch plants – such as Frederick Stearns and Company, a prominent pharmaceuticals firm – relocating to Windsor throughout the period, the population and economy of the border cities region boomed. *Source:* Southwestern Ontario Digital Archive.

be a danger to themselves or others. Most white Anglo-Saxon Canadians and Americans easily passed through inspection.[6]

The first threat to this border-crossing culture between Windsor and Detroit was the First World War. It also threatened similar relationships in other towns lining the nearly 9,000-kilometre-long Canada–US boundary. This book explores the impact of the First World War on border-crossing culture in three transnational communities, including Windsor and Detroit; St. Stephen, New Brunswick, and Calais, Maine; and White Rock, British Columbia, and Blaine, Washington. These communities all have one common characteristic: proximity to the border and an extranational neighbour. In addition, each case study represents a unique region along Canada's southern border, including the northeast (St. Stephen and Calais), central Canada (Windsor and Detroit), and the Pacific coast (White Rock and Blaine).

I first approached this project while studying for my PhD. I wanted to know how the intense nationalism aroused by the war affected "border-crossing culture," a term first used by historian Thomas Klug in a 2010 article titled "The Immigration and Naturalization Service (INS) and the Making of a Border-Crossing Culture on the US–Canada Border, 1891-1941."[7] Unfortunately, Klug

– whose study focuses on changing interpretations of the border-crossing experience along the American shore of the Detroit River – does not provide us with a clear definition of the term. Such a term is founded upon our definition of *culture*, an incredibly difficult word to define. One of the most accessible definitions comes from American-born intellectual Walter Lippman, who suggested that culture is "what people are interested in, their thoughts, their models, the books they read and the speeches they hear, their table talk, gossip, controversies, historical sense and scientific training." In other words, culture is "the climate of ... civilization."[8] Historian Jonathan Vance, author of *A History of Canadian Culture*, acknowledges that culture "is a tricky concept" that "can encompass almost everything that characterizes a society – the customs, modes of behaviour, beliefs, values, and social practices and structures."[9] Border-crossing culture, therefore, can be defined as the thoughts, customs, events, policies, speeches, gossip, controversies, and history surrounding the international boundary. As this book shows, for many residents of Canadian and American border communities, the international boundary was an omnipresent actor in the formation of local culture.

Few historians have examined how people living along the border reacted to the American and Canadian federal governments' attempts to better secure the boundary during the First World War. In the introduction to their collection of essays *Bridging National Borders in North America*, Andrew Graybill and Benjamin Johnson identify this gap in the scholarship and ask "did borders mean the same things to local residents of border areas as they did to national policymakers?"[10] A similar query was posed twenty-five years ago by geographers Victor Konrad and Lauren McKinsey, who asked "are there areas of public policy where Canadians and Americans sharing a particular border region actually have closer opinions than either group has with respective nationals?"[11]

This book attempts to answer these questions. It finds that Canadian residents of border communities who prided themselves on living within a peaceful, permeable border region before the First World War were most likely to resist attempts by the government (federal or provincial) to change how the border was administered during the war. In some cases, this meant protesting measures that prevented the easy movement of goods and people, and in other cases it meant objecting to the introduction of policies that indirectly affected border-crossing culture (e.g., the implementation of daylight saving time in 1918). The longer the social, cultural, and economic ties to an American border town, the more evident the opposition to "outside influences" or government efforts to enforce border controls in one form or another.

The history of borders, and especially the Canada–US border, represents a relatively new academic field. But the remarkable growth of transnational trade and transportation networks is drawing attention to these highly contradictory spaces. According to Melissa Gauthier and Fayuca Hormiga, whose work focuses on the movement of illegal goods across the US–Mexico boundary, borders "represent lucrative zones of exchange and trade, often illicit and clandestine."[12] This is precisely why borders fascinate us today. To put it succinctly, they are high-stakes zones – to challenge the border is to challenge the nation-state.[13]

Yet globalization is doing just that. Arguably, it is now more difficult (and certainly more expensive) than ever before for national governments to effectively monitor and patrol international boundaries. Authors such as David Kaplan, Emmanuel Brunet-Jailly, and Bruno Dupeyron have explored how Europeans struggle with the challenges posed by sharing a political and economic union while attempting to limit the transnational movement of violent radicals. "As national border-security policies attempt to enable security personnel to recognize dangerous individuals and substances, they must compete not only with the increasingly large market-driven flows of goods and people crossing borders and borderlands but also with the local culture and political clout of borderlands," Brunet-Jailly and Dupeyron write.[14] The United States faces a similar quandary when it comes to its southern border – although some of the nation's most influential corporations depend on the cheap labour provided by illegal immigrants, particularly those moving north across the Mexican border, many US citizens regularly express concern that these newcomers are threatening the economic and social stability of American neighbourhoods.[15]

These problems are not new. Europe has been struggling with the issues presented by permeable borders for centuries (and especially since the establishment of the European Union roughly two decades ago), while Americans and Mexicans have debated the border separating their countries since the nineteenth century. A fascination with these unique threats has translated into a growing historiography focused on European national boundaries and the US–Mexico border.

Interest in the Canada–US border, meanwhile, has been comparatively limited – particularly among American scholars. But in the period since completion of the Canada–US Free Trade Agreement in 1988 and the shocking events of 9–11, issues relating to the permeability of that border have become the focus of unprecedented discussion.[16] After American journalists and US officials erroneously pointed to the Canadian border as the entry point for the 9–11 hijackers, it became the subject of much debate. The idea that the Canadian border acts as a convenient crossing point for terrorists en route to the United States ironically turns the long-undefended border, once the pride of upper North Americans, into something distinctly *negative*.[17]

Although examining the Canada–US border is relatively new to many American historians, Canadian scholars have long debated its role in shaping the Great White North's economy and culture. One of the first studies of economic and social relations across the border was Goldwin Smith's *Canada and the Canadian Question.* Published in 1891, it discussed the extensive cross-border social and economic ties linking Canadians and Americans as well as the deep regional and cultural divisions within Canada.[18] Smith noted the role played by American capital in expanding Canada's nascent manufacturing sector as well as the widespread out-migration of Canadians to the growing United States.[19] Given the fluidity of the Canada–US border and growing tensions north of the border (particularly after the execution of Métis leader Louis Riel in 1885), Smith suggested that Canada could succeed only if it moved toward commercial or even political union with the more powerful United States.[20]

Smith wrote his book at a time when hundreds of thousands of Canadians were leaving Canada to live permanently in the United States. Historian Marcus Lee Hansen examined this movement in *The Mingling of the Canadian and American Peoples,* published in 1940. Hansen, who followed the southward migration of Canadians between the Revolutionary War and the 1920s, argued that in both the United States and Canada political affiliations were less important to a family than economic opportunities.[21] In other words, if a better-paying, more stable job was available south of the border, then few Canadians gave any thought to leaving their homeland for the United States. It was an attitude that encouraged migration and established a culture of permeability at the border and beyond.

Hansen's central message – that, for the average family, the decision to migrate across the border was personal and transcended national affiliation – is a prominent theme in several more recent texts on the migration of Canadians to the United States. Arguably, the two most comprehensive studies are Bruno Ramirez's *Crossing the 49th Parallel* (2001) and Randy Widdis's *With Scarcely a Ripple* (1999).[22] Ramirez studies the cross-border movements of French and English Canadians from 1900 to 1930 and finds that, in the Maritimes, people's permanent and seasonal movements were the results of an economy integrated with New England and based on lumbering, shipbuilding, and farming. In Ontario, conditions for migration (a cross-border regional economy) were similar but the destinations different: New York, Michigan, Ohio, and Illinois.[23] Meanwhile, in Quebec, land shortages forced many residents to seek permanent and seasonal employment in the rapidly expanding New England textile industry.[24] Ramirez shows that, at least until the early twentieth century, the natural barriers in northern North America ran north-south rather than east-west. Migrants gave little thought to national affiliation when they made these transitions; instead, they moved to whatever community offered them the most stable social and economic environments for their families.

In his analysis of Canadian migration to the United States between 1880 and 1920, Widdis takes the story a step further by examining the lives of migrants once they arrived in their new homes. He finds that several factors – including common language, religion, education, and economic outlook – led to the integration of Anglo-Canadians into American society "with scarcely a ripple."[25] At the same time, the integration of Anglo-Canadians was facilitated by their own lack of a cohesive identity; specifically, ethnic barriers separated English speakers who traced their lineages to Scotland, Ireland, Wales, England, or other parts of the British Empire.[26] This weakening of the Anglo-Canadian identity, Widdis suggests, contributed to their rapid integration into American society.

In response to this rapid out-migration – in addition to concerns about "manifest destiny" in the United States – in the 1890s Ottawa relaxed Canada's immigration standards (the idea being to replace outgoing Canadians with incoming Europeans).[27] In judging which men and women were best suited for life on the harsh Canadian prairies, the Liberal Party's minister of the interior, Clifford Sifton, abandoned traditional preferences for Britons and favoured any "stalwart peasant in a sheepskin coat with a stout wife." The new policy worked. The population of the Canadian west exploded over the next two decades, from 300,000 in 1896 to 1.5 million in 1914.[28]

As a result of these "lowered" immigration standards, Canada was much slower to implement immigration law at the international boundary than the United States. South of the border, anxiety over the growing immigrant population continued to rise. In the cities, rivalries among ethnic groups were more readily apparent as Slavs, Swedes, Poles, and native-born white Americans competed for the same jobs. There was no easy solution: while labour groups identified the influx as a source of competition that would drive wages and working conditions down while prolonging the average workday, employers sought out immigrants for the same reasons.[29] At the same time, most Americans, employers and employees alike, fretted about the arrival from Europe of paupers, criminals, prostitutes, the physically disabled, and the mentally unfit.[30] These people, they worried, would restrict America's economic growth by becoming expensive burdens on the state.

As Marian Smith shows in her article "The Immigration and Naturalization Service (INS) at the US-Canadian Border, 1893–1993," one of the first attempts of the United States to monitor immigrant traffic was the 1893 "Canadian Agreement" signed by the American government and Canadian transportation companies. The agreement, which received only tacit approval from Ottawa, allowed for American immigration officials to inspect US-bound Europeans leaving Canadian ports.[31] At the time, Ottawa made no effort to introduce a similar scheme to protect its own land and sea borders, meaning that immigrants arriving at Canadian ports of entry were not examined for medical or physical deficiencies.[32] Thus, as the American government moved quickly toward adopting a centralized border inspection apparatus in the late nineteenth century, Canada lagged behind.

But Ninette Kelley and Michael Trebilcock, in their book *The Making of the Mosaic*, find that that changed shortly after the turn of the twentieth century. Through the Immigration Acts of 1906 and 1910, the Canadian government clearly laid out which groups were considered desirable and undesirable while formalizing admission and deportation procedures.[33] The change of heart was a result of Canadians growing steadily more concerned that immigration from southern and eastern Europe was causing a spike in criminal activity.[34] In reality, the rise in crime was merely a side effect of Canada's rapidly growing population, but it was seen by many Canadians as a sign that immigration law was in desperate need of reform.[35] The result was that by 1910 both Canada and the United States had established federal immigration departments and placed immigration inspectors at most busy border crossings along the Canada–US boundary.

So what was the border-crossing experience like in the years just before the First World War? Klug tries to answer that question in his article, which shows how immigration law was put into practice by agents actually working at the border and what impact it had on the lives of daily commuters. For instance, in Detroit prior to the construction of the Ambassador Bridge (1929) and Detroit–Windsor Tunnel (1930), most travellers arrived in the Motor City by way of ferry, forming in long queues at the foot of Woodward Avenue along the Detroit River. This meant that a team of two or three officers faced an immense challenge picking out undesirables with hundreds of people pouring off a single ferry. The solution, INS administrators believed, was to force passengers to line up two abreast, forming manageable lines for inspectors. But that did not sit well with the travellers, as revealed by a Bureau of Immigration investigator who noted that the process "causes constant irritation and resentment" among ferry passengers and was "naturally productive of impatient and insulting remarks" launched at the inspectors.[36] Klug also reveals that immigration agents were members of the transnational Detroit River community and used their knowledge of local people and businesses to help distinguish between suspicious outsiders and regular commuters. In this way, Klug demonstrates that understanding the Canada–US border is not as simple as studying immigration policy or migration trends.[37]

This book is about that border, but it also concerns the impact of the First World War era on local communities straddling it. Not only did the war present

Canadian and American governments with a reason to protect their borders, but also it caused the citizens of both countries to rethink their place in the world. Patriotism and nationalism reached new heights in Canada as the nation underwent its "trial by fire," starting with the Second Battle of Ypres in April 1915. Canadian historians have established useful models for a study focused on the home front, but this is a recent phenomenon: for decades following the emergence of Great War literature in the 1930s, the focus was on the military side of the equation, first at the broad, strategic level and then eventually "at the sharp end."[38] Only in the past decade or so have examinations of home front Canada emerged, including Ian Miller's *Our Glory and Our Grief* (2002), Robert Rutherdale's *Hometown Horizons* (2004), James Pitsula's *For All We Have and Are* (2008), and Jim Blanchard's *Winnipeg's Great War* (2010). The collective message of these books – from Miller's study of Toronto's Great War to Blanchard's examination of wartime Winnipeg – is that every community had a unique wartime experience.[39]

But if each city, town, and county had its own war experience, they all shared a new relationship with the state. Invisible to most Canadians and Americans before the war, the government (both federal and provincial) established after August 1914 a real presence in people's day-to-day lives. Today Canadians' extensive and comparatively intimate relationship with the state can be seen in our payment of income taxes, our use of passports, and the evolution of a visible international boundary presided over by customs and immigration officials. All of these measures were either introduced or widely expanded during the Great War era.

To date, a number of books have examined how the citizen-state relationship developed in the United States during that era. In *Uncle Sam Wants You,* Chris Capozzola reveals how obligations to the local community – including family, church, employer, and school – were all subsumed under obligations to the state during wartime. According to Capozzola, the war initiated a visible transition in which the citizen looked beyond the immediate locality when identifying a community of like-minded people.[40] A similar message can be found in Craig Robertson's *The Passport in America,* which shows how the expansion of the passport system during and after the First World War helped to fuse once disparate local and national communities. According to Robertson, the process of regulating the passport and the border-crossing experience marked an important transition away from a time when the government remained "a stranger in the lives of its citizens."[41]

Studies of Canadians' evolving relationship with the state during the First World War remain rare. Jeffrey Keshen has examined the emergence of Canada's censorship network in *Propaganda and Censorship during Canada's*

Great War, and Gregory Kealey has examined the rise of state surveillance in a series of articles, including "State Repression of Labour and the Left in Canada, 1914–20." Unfortunately, a comprehensive study of this topic remains absent from the historiography.[42]

There are similar gaps in the historiography dealing with changes at the Canada–US border during the twentieth century's early years. With the exception of Klug, no scholar has yet examined how changes to border security affected border-crossing culture in communities located along the international boundary. This study, one of the first of its kind, focuses on the Canadian side of the boundary. It shows that the Great War's emphasis on efficiency, patriotism, and protection of Canadian citizens put great strain on border-crossing culture. It finds that those people who protested radical changes to the administration of the boundary were members of communities – such as Windsor and St. Stephen – that could trace their cross-border ties to the period well before the development of immigration law and, later, the outbreak of war. These were the communities where border-crossing culture survived and was even enhanced by the war. In comparison, the vast majority of White Rock's first settlers arrived as immigration law was implemented in the twentieth century's first decade. Furthermore, prewar attitudes toward cross-border liquor trafficking and Asian immigration on Canada's west coast helped to dictate rather different conceptions of the border.

These findings rely heavily on primary research, including municipal council minutes, archival files (e.g., diaries, correspondence, and oral interviews), and, in large part, newspapers, including the *Semiahmoo* (later *Surrey*) *Gazette, British Columbian, Blaine Journal, Windsor Evening Record, Detroit News, Detroit Free Press, Saint Croix Courier,* and *Calais Advertiser,* among others. These newspapers were not only the primary source for local, national, and international news during this historical period but also a forum that allowed members of the community to express their opinions through letters to the editor. Each of these newspapers included at least an editorial section, and the *Windsor Evening Record, Detroit Free Press,* and *Saint Croix Courier* included sections where letters to the editor were published. Studying these letters and editorials helped me to uncover multiple viewpoints from within the wider population.

In addition to newspapers, this study uses municipal council minutes to investigate the operations of local governments. These records reveal some of the major concerns of local citizens; for example, the protest by Windsor City Council against the Ontario provincial government's ban of Sunday newspapers from Detroit in 1916 reveals that heated letters to the *Windsor Evening Record* on the subject were representative of a majority of the people.[43] Where possible, I have used city council minutes and other source materials to verify and supplement reports in the local newspapers.

Also of use was correspondence between local immigration inspectors and Canadian Superintendent of Immigration W.D. Scott. Correspondence found on microfilm reels acquired from Library and Archives Canada includes general memoranda between Scott and the various officers in charge at White Rock, Windsor, and St. Stephen.[44] These records outline the challenges facing officers stationed at the border before and during the war, including the search for undesirables and enemy aliens from Austria-Hungary, Bulgaria, and Germany. The latter task proved to be particularly troublesome since so few of the travellers from these countries looked any different from their Canadian or American counterparts. The correspondence reveals that patrolling the border was by no means an easy job during the war; not only were officers expected to weed out undesirables and enemy aliens from a flood of permanent and temporary travellers, but also they were paid a low wage and constantly criticized by their superiors, who found easy scapegoats in their front-line agents for policy failures.

Although I investigate a number of different themes in this study, I have attempted to keep the structure simple. The book proceeds through three separate case studies, investigating first Windsor and Detroit, then St. Stephen and Calais, and finally White Rock and Blaine. Each case study examines the extent of a border-crossing culture before the war, the war's impact on this culture, and finally local reactions to changes to the border's administration during the war years. A conclusion provides a comparative examination of the different regions studied and a brief look at each of the border communities in the years after the war.

This book marks a meeting point between two vibrant and continually evolving historical fields focusing on Canada's Great War and the Canada–US border. Because of the conflict's important place in Canada's journey toward nationhood, interest in the Great War remains high. My hope is that this study provides an important contribution to the growing body of literature on the Canada–US border and helps us to better understand an important period in North American history.

Part 1
Windsor, Ontario, and Detroit, Michigan

DETROIT WAS FOUNDED in 1701 by a charming Gascon adventurer named Antoine Laumet de Lamothe Cadillac. He named the city for its geography, *de troit*, or "the strait," which linked Lake Erie with Lake St. Clair and Lake Huron. Cadillac was an unscrupulous tradesman who sold brandy to the nearby Indigenous peoples against the wishes of local chiefs and Jesuit priests. He dealt with fur smugglers, ignoring the strict regulations placed on the fur trade by his superiors in Paris. Cadillac cared nothing for rules – his goal was to use the Detroit River to dominate the trade of all goods across the Great Lakes. He saw this river not as a line between empires but as a tool that could be used to enhance his own power and prestige.[1]

In time, many residents of the Detroit River region would embrace this attitude, dismissing the idea that geography should restrict, rather than enhance, the region's economic and cultural development. As the following chapter demonstrates, a unique transnational relationship between Windsor and Detroit was not spawned by the Great War but merely evolved during these years. The seeds for a border-crossing culture had been planted generations earlier, starting with the French *habitants* and *voyageurs* who made the Detroit River frontier their home. Through war and revolution, these original families, as well as the British, American, and European settlers who joined them much later, maintained positive relations with their friends and kin across the river.

Initially, the challenges facing Cadillac's company must have seemed ominous: almost 1,000 kilometres from the safety of Montreal, their presence in the *pays d'en haut* (or "upper country") could have been conceived as an obscene gesture made against their traditional enemies in the Great Lakes region, the powerful Five Nations Confederacy. But, surprisingly, the gamble paid off: a period of peace with the Five Nations during the early eighteenth century allowed the town to flourish, its population increasing substantially in that first decade.[2] Their years along the St. Lawrence were visible as the settlers made homes for themselves in this new land; the local economy that emerged was heavily influenced by the seigneurial system of Quebec, with farmers cultivating long, narrow plots running great distances back from the river. The demand for riverside lots soon led settlers to spill over the river onto the opposite shore, into what would later become Windsor and surrounding Essex County.

Crossing the river was no great hardship; the French used their sturdy canoes to move from shore to shore. Occasionally, the river would freeze over, allowing travellers to cross by foot.[3]

Throughout the eighteenth century, the Detroit River region continued to grow, partly because the area remained comfortably isolated during both the Seven Years' War and the American Revolution.[4] For practical purposes, little changed for Detroiters after the Treaty of Paris in 1783; Britain maintained control of the city along with several other strategically vital forts in the northwest.[5] As a result of the Jay Treaty in 1794, however, the redcoats finally left Detroit, retreating to Fort Amherstburg in British territory.

Britain's abandonment of the city represented the first divergence of character between Detroit and the area that would later become Windsor. Many of the French and English residents of the town who preferred life under the Crown followed the redcoats across the river and were replaced by a significant contingent of New Englanders pushing west. Although the presence of the French in Essex continued to be considerable throughout the first part of the nineteenth century, in Detroit their numbers would soon be overwhelmed by Americans and later Germans, Poles, and Irish.[6]

But these changes came slowly. In the early nineteenth century, both Windsor and Detroit remained very French.[7] Those living on the Canadian shore continued to share a much closer relationship with their Detroit neighbours than with residents of distant York (later Toronto) or London, primarily because communicating with or visiting these latter communities meant travelling hundreds of kilometres through unbroken wilderness. The immense distance between Windsor and other villages in Upper Canada, in addition to the region's French-speaking heritage (80 percent of its 4,000 settlers traced their heritage back to the St. Lawrence Valley), meant that the area was considered rather distinct, even isolated, from the rest of the colony.[8]

These factors concerned colonial administrators as tensions mounted with the Americans during the first decade of the nineteenth century, and it was unclear whether the French Canadians of the Detroit River region would fight in the event of war. Indeed, in the eyes of many of these French-speaking people, there was little incentive to do so. They identified with neither Britain nor the United States, viewing both as alien empires based on cultures distinct from their own.[9] In the event of war, it remained unlikely that the people of Essex would casually dismiss a century of good relations with their neighbours in Detroit in order to protect Britain's holdings in Upper Canada.[10]

The American invasion of Essex County and the Western District began in July 1812.[11] US Brigadier-General William Hull, perhaps sensing weakness among the poorly trained and ill-equipped militiamen standing between Detroit and

York, decreed in a proclamation spread throughout the district that "no white man found fighting by the side of an Indian will be taken prisoner" and that "instant destruction will be his lot."[12] The result was that, by mid-July, an officer of the Essex militia complained that half his men had abandoned their posts and returned home. It remains unclear whether this action was motivated by Hull's threat, the need of militiamen to care for their crops, or both.[13]

Regardless, the American commander and the men serving under him failed to keep their promise that they would not harass the people of Windsor. Twice they occupied Essex County during the war, and in both instances they looted the personal property of locals. Horses, flour, lumber, furs – all were grabbed up by American troops during their stays in the Windsor region, first over the summer of 1812 and again after the defeat of York in April 1813.[14] For their part, Americans living in Detroit during its siege, capitulation, and occupation in August 1812 were embarrassed and embittered by the British victory. They were further enraged by the January 1813 Frenchtown massacre, when British officers allowed their Aboriginal allies to slaughter a group of wounded American prisoners.[15]

The hardships brought on by the War of 1812 reinforced the Jay Treaty in making the Detroit River a meaningful boundary, but over time hard feelings dissipated. First, in Essex County, much of the blame for the hardship brought on by the war was lumped on the British, who had failed to supply locals with the tools and training needed to make an effective defence possible. Indeed, from the beginning, the colonial administration acted as though the entire region between the Detroit River and London was expendable.[16] Second, many of the Americans who attacked and looted Essex homes during the war were not Detroiters but militiamen recruited in Kentucky.[17] In other words, rarely was it a familiar face that wandered off with the last of the grain or firewood in the middle of the night. And third, in many communities across the Michigan Territory and Upper Canada, blame for the war fell on opposing governments, not the people living under them.[18] After all, it was not an event in Detroit or Essex that had sparked hostilities but the squabbles of two distant governments, mostly over the subject of American neutrality and sovereignty at sea – issues not close to the hearts of the settlers of Detroit and Essex County.

Border troubles returned to the county in 1866 with the arrival of the Fenian threat.[19] The Fenians, a well-funded organization of Irish Americans, sought the independence of their homeland from Britain through the occupation of British North America. Today their scheme sounds ludicrous, but by no means was Canada prepared at the time to repel an invasion. Its militiamen could be kept from their farms for only a few weeks at a time and, like the general population, were thinly spread out across a vast territory. Unlike the Fenians, many of whom had served under the Union flag during the US Civil War, the Canadian militiamen were poorly trained and had little combat experience. Canadians, then, were rightly afraid of what might happen if the Fenians succeeded in breaking through at two or more points along their frontier.[20]

But the Fenian threat largely failed to disturb relations between Windsor and Detroit; indeed, throughout these tense years, ferries continued to cross the river at regular intervals. This led to one particularly anxious morning when it was reported that a ferry carrying pious Detroiters to Windsor for a religious festival was, in fact, filled with Fenians. The town shut down in a matter of minutes, and local men prepared to repulse the attack. The boat was turned around before it could dock – no doubt greatly annoying the many peaceful pilgrims on board.[21]

The Fenian threat represented a few brief moments of excitement in an otherwise tedious period for residents of Essex County. In comparison to Detroit, economic progress remained sluggish. Completion of the Sault Ste. Marie, Michigan, canal allowed Lake Superior iron and copper to flow into Detroit, fuelling the expansion of several manufacturing industries in the 1850s, including steel production, brewing, tanning, and sawmilling.[22] Meanwhile, in Windsor and Essex County, the absence of effective transportation routes prevented most residents from rising out of abject poverty.

That finally changed with the completion of several important transportation links, notably the American-owned Great Western Railway in 1854, which connected these communities with Hamilton, London, Niagara Falls, and Toronto. Importantly, it also brought Windsor and Essex County into a rapidly evolving American manufacturing zone between Michigan and New York. As other rail lines were extended to the county, Windsor became the primary marketplace for the region's bountiful agricultural harvest.[23]

The Great Western Railway had an immediate impact on settlement in Essex County. Windsor's population rose steadily after completion of the line, from just 300 in 1846 to nearly 5,000 two decades later. Construction of the line created a demand for labourers to lay the track, while the need for rail ties helped to expand the region's lumber industry. The business of moving people and goods became lucrative for Essex County, through which thousands of settlers would pass en route to the burgeoning industrial metropolises of the American Midwest.[24]

Soon after the railway was completed, the Detroit River's steamship business grew to meet the demand for transportation across the waterway.[25] Not until the interwar period of the twentieth century would a bridge and tunnel be constructed to facilitate such heavy traffic, but the ferry companies were capable of moving people across the border. The first ferries were little more

FIGURE 2 The Detroit River, seen here in 1900, would become an increasingly busy place as Windsor and the Motor City boomed during the first half of the twentieth century. *Source:* "Water Front, Detroit, Mich." c. 1900, http://www.loc.gov/item/det1994021211/PP/.

than commercial canoes; in the 1820s, François Labalaine used just such a craft to transport pioneers from one side of the river to the other, listening for the sound of his wife's four-foot-long tin horn as the indication that passengers were ready on the Canadian side.[26] Later in the decade, Captain John Burtis tried his hand at the trade with the river's first horse ferry. As the horse walked along in an enclosed space, it drove the boat's propellers. Onlookers said that it looked like "a large cheese box on a raft," which might explain why Burtis reported a deficit of $378.67 after his first year on the river.[27] In the 1830s, steam replaced horse power as the fuel of choice, and the number of ferries traversing the river increased steadily. By the late 1860s, three ferries were in operation, two working 6 a.m. to 6 p.m. shifts, another working from 6 p.m. to 11 p.m., meaning that transportation was available all but seven hours a day. In the 1880s and 1890s, Detroit companies produced several enormous ferries to handle the growing load of passengers, none bigger than the *Columbia*, which could carry 3,500 people in a single trip.[28] It was a cheap and convenient ride, and in the early 1890s a one-way ticket cost just a few pennies.[29] Ice was rarely a factor since the Detroit River was so fast flowing that complete freeze-ups of the area between downtown Windsor and Detroit occurred only a few days each year.[30] By 1914, at least twenty-two different ferries were operating at different points along the Detroit River, with passenger totals surpassing 40,000 on busy holidays, such as the Fourth of July.[31] The ferries' names (two were called *Olive Branch*, one *Alliance*) and appearance (many boats, such as the *Essex*, flew the Union Jack, Red Ensign, and Stars and Stripes together) indicate just how important these vessels were to the development of a border-crossing culture in the nineteenth century.[32]

Although most travellers used the ferries to cross the Detroit River, many of the commercial and industrial goods moving between Windsor and Detroit went underneath the dividing waterway via the Michigan Central Railway Tunnel. Completed in 1910, the 8,390-foot tunnel helped to fuse the economic relationship between the two border communities and drew Windsor deeper into the industrial sphere of the rapidly growing American Midwest.[33]

But it was not just transportation and communication that contributed to Windsor's development in the late nineteenth century. Equally important was the federal Conservative Party's National Policy, introduced in the late 1870s. Based on three main platforms, including railway construction, populating the west, and high tariffs, it was designed to stabilize the national economy and protect Canadian manufacturers from US competition. To avoid the policy's high tariffs, US companies established separate operations, called branch plants, north of the border.[34] Because of Windsor's proximity to the border and Detroit, branch plants became a crucial part of its economic development in the late nineteenth century. By the 1880s, several major Detroit companies had established operations across the river, including pharmaceutical firms Parke-Davis and Stearns.[35] By 1914, the number of American branch plants operating in Windsor, population 20,000, would be twenty-six, a greater per capita rate than any other medium or large city in Canada.[36] The war did little to prevent American businesses from streaming into Windsor, and by 1920 the Border Chamber of Commerce estimated that, of the city's 206 manufacturing concerns, "practically all ... represent American capital and enterprise."[37]

The most important of these American-owned plants was Ford Canada, incorporated in 1904.[38] Henry Ford, who had opened Ford Motor Company in Detroit only a year before, hoped to circumvent the Canadian government's strict tariff restrictions and gain access to the British market. After being approached by Windsor's Gordon McGregor, manager of the unprofitable Walkerville Wagon Works facility, Ford decided to use the site as a base of operations. He had several reasons for establishing a plant in the Windsor region. First, it was close to Detroit (and McGregor, who would become the new company's general manager, would later consult Ford on a regular basis for advice on labour issues and production).[39] The proximity meant that a significant

FIGURE 3 The Ford Motor Company of Canada, established in Walkerville in 1904, just a year after Henry Ford opened Ford Motor Company in Detroit. Although annual profits were initially low (just over $4,000 in 1906), by 1914 they were well in excess of $1 million. *Source:* "Ford Motor Co. Factory," June 1914, http://www.loc.gov/item/det1994022188/PP/.

contingent of the company's early managers were Detroiters, while most of Ford Canada's design and engineering expertise came from across the river.[40] Second, Windsor had many of the same geographical advantages of Detroit, being positioned along the main water route of the Great Lakes in addition to five major railways.[41] And third, Ford liked McGregor: the latter had shown considerable initiative by approaching the Detroit manufacturer, and his family pedigree – his father had been a prominent businessman, mayor of Windsor, and Member of the Provincial Parliament – also reflected well on the young entrepreneur.[42] Ford also recognized that the Wagon Works facilities were suitable for an assembly operation, that Windsor was rapidly becoming an industrialized city with several companies that could take on support contracts, and that there was significant interest in the project from various Windsor investors.[43]

From there, the Detroit River region's automotive industry evolved at a dizzying pace.[44] Within five years, several other prominent automotive manufacturing concerns emerged in the region, including Maxwell (later incorporated by Chrysler), General Motors, Buick, and Oldsmobile. All of these companies would have impacts on Windsor in some form or another (opening plants there or hiring Canadian "day labourers" to work in Detroit facilities), but none would have both the economic and the cultural impacts of Ford.

At first, Ford Canada's achievements were modest. The company's first automobile, a Model A, rolled out in late October 1904 to the applause of just seventeen employees.[45] In 1906, the company produced 101 vehicles with profits of just over $4,000. Since sales of the company's more luxurious models, such as the Model B and six-cylinder Model K, were low, Ford Detroit began working on a car that would be cheap, reliable, and easy to repair. The result was the Model T, unveiled in 1908 (but not produced in Walkerville until mid-1909). It came in a single colour (black), had few of the creature comforts of the Model B or K, and certainly had nothing approaching the extravagance of the Oldsmobile or American Benz. But at $975, it was half the price of the Cadillac ($1,850) and the Toronto-built Russell ($1,950). Despite not starting work on the Model T until the summer, in 1909 Ford Canada built 458 of them, smashing the previous year's production record of 327.[46] By 1912, Ford Canada's earnings were over $1 million.[47]

Ford's impact on the border cities – which before amalgamation in 1935 included Windsor and the surrounding municipalities of Ford City, Sandwich, Walkerville, and Ojibway – was widespread. In December 1912, an Essex County bylaw created the municipality of Ford City, encompassing the Walkerville plant. As the company grew, so did Ford City, quintupling in population over a two-year period.[48] Growth was so rapid that the municipality experienced a housing shortage so intense that the company sought permission to house its workers in tents outside the factory walls.[49]

Despite these issues, more people flocked to Ford – and for good reason. The company not only paid well (four dollars a day by 1915 or twice the industrial average), but Henry Ford also showed a genuine interest in the welfare of his employees.[50] A July 1914 baseball game between single and married Ford men at Put-in-Bay represented the first of many pleasure activities funded by management.[51] Although McGregor ran the Canadian operations, by 1914 Henry Ford was clearly the face of business and culture in the border cities.[52]

Throughout the mid to late nineteenth century, Windsor's proximity to and economic dependence on Detroit facilitated the development of unique social relationships and a distinct border-crossing culture. Vital services regularly brought members of these communities together. In 1857, they were linked by submarine telegraph cable and, twenty-three years later, by telephone exchange. Windsor relied on Detroit's fire protection service to quell blazes until the 1880s.[53] Throughout this period, Windsor families sent their children to Detroit art and music colleges.[54] During the summer months, Americans and Canadians met for picnics at various island parks along the Detroit River, including Bois Blanc (later Bob-Lo), Sugar Island, and Belle Isle.[55]

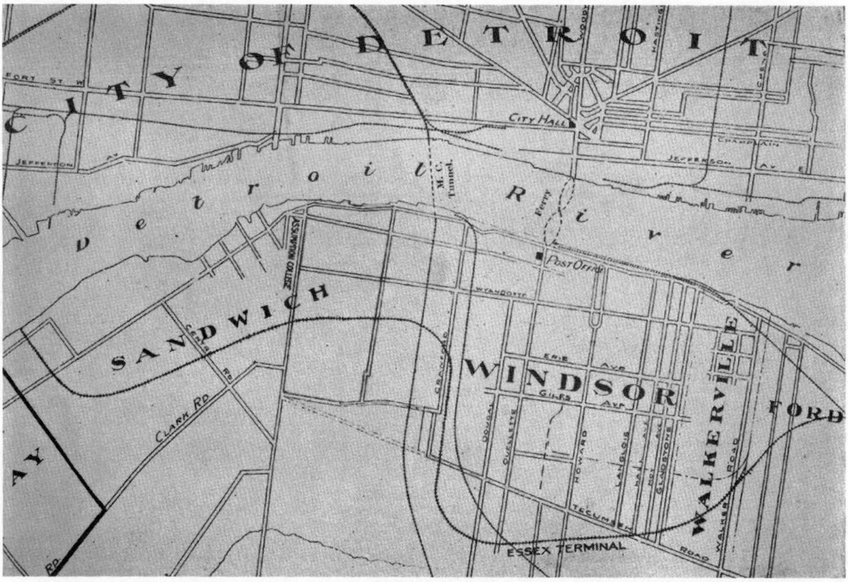

FIGURE 4 A map of Windsor and the rest of the border cities – including Ojibway, Sandwich, Walkerville, and Ford City – in 1913. By the start of the war the following year, roughly 20,000 people lived in the area. *Source:* Southwestern Ontario Digital Archive.

Windsor and Detroit also shared similar ethnic characteristics during the prewar period. Today "Motown" is one of the most segregated cities in North America, with racial tensions between whites and African Americans lingering for generations after riots in the 1940s and 1960s.[56] But in 1910 the American border city was markedly white.[57] According to that year's census, native-born white Americans accounted for 65 percent of the total population, followed by Germans (9 percent), Canadians (9 percent), Britons (4 percent), and Russians (4 percent). African Americans represented just 1 percent of Detroit's population, and just ninety-nine people of Asian and "other" descent lived within city limits.[58] Windsor was similarly white in the period leading up to the war, though it possessed considerably fewer Germans and more Britons (10 percent).[59] But it was by no means a British city; as in Detroit, the vast majority of people living there were native born.[60] Just as 9 percent of Detroiters claimed Canada as their place of birth, so too roughly the same percentage of Windsorites reported being American born. Residents of Windsor and Detroit also attended similar religious institutions; on the Canadian side, most were Roman Catholic (34 percent), with Methodists, Anglicans, and Presbyterians accounting for the remaining churchgoers.[61] In Detroit, heavy immigration by Poles and Irish in the nineteenth century also made Roman Catholicism that city's predominant faith during the Great War era.[62]

In distinguishing Windsor from other cities in Ontario, it is worth comparing some of these findings with Toronto, Ontario's most populous city and economic and political capital. According to the 1911 census, nearly one-third of Toronto's population hailed from the British Isles, about three times the number found in Windsor. Less than 60 percent of Toronto's residents had been born in Ontario, considerably lower than Windsor's 76 percent.[63] In comparison to Toronto, roughly three times the number of Windsorites reported having been born in the United States. Windsor was also home to many more French Canadians, who accounted for nearly one-fourth of the city's total population (4,113).[64] Their presence in the city directly affected its religious breakdown, with Roman Catholics forming the dominant religion. In comparison, Catholics represented just 13 percent of Toronto's churchgoers, the majority of whom attended Anglican (31 percent) or Presbyterian (20 percent) services on Sundays.[65]

Essentially, in the early twentieth century, Windsor's demographics more closely resembled those of Detroit than those of the provincial capital. In large part, this was the result of late-nineteenth-century conceptions of the state and the international boundary in the Great Lakes region. In the search for better jobs and farmlands, residents of Ontario and the American Midwest treated the international boundary in much the same way that we might treat a provincial or state line. The absence of a border protection scheme contributed to this conception of the boundary as an imaginary divide and would have an enormous influence on perceptions of immigration regulations during the First World War era. (In comparison, travellers eventually settling in fiercely pro-British White Rock would admit to having never felt entirely comfortable while living under the Stars and Stripes.)

Whether they crossed the international boundary for business or pleasure, for the long term or a daily excursion, the people of Windsor had become accustomed to life along a permeable border by the turn of the twentieth century. Without knowing it, they were about to enter a period that would challenge this tradition. Rising concerns about racial purity and competition in the labour market would lead to the implementation of immigration inspection stations all along the border, from the Maritimes and New England to the Pacific Northwest. By 1910, both countries had agents stationed at regular intervals along this immense frontier. At first, the inspections were relaxed, and most Canadians and Americans passed through without difficulty. But the war changed that. It aroused new ideas about the border and what crossing it represented. For Windsorites, the act of going to Detroit to work, shop, grab the Sunday newspaper, or take in a game of baseball suddenly had unexpected consequences. For some members of the local community, this made sense. When the home country is at war, one should support it, they said, even if that only meant frequenting Windsor rather than Detroit businesses. For others, these kinds of official and unofficial restrictions were strange, unwelcome, and unnecessary. These members of the border cities community would continue to advocate closer relations with the people and businesses of Detroit and to oppose any legislation that disrupted traditional cross-border lifestyles. In some cases, this position brought them into conflict with Canadians from outside the immediate region, people whom they attacked as "outsiders" who did not understand the economic and social circumstances of the Detroit River region. In Windsor, the question of border security would become the basis for a war at home between these opposing factions.

1
"Brothers Once More"
Relations between Windsor and Detroit

THE SUMMER OF 1914 was an exciting time in the border cities region encompassing Windsor, Walkerville, Sandwich, Ford City, and Ojibway. A late-June provincial election was preceded by stirring political orations across Essex County. The central issue was bilingual instruction in Ontario schools. Regulation XVII, which the James Whitney Conservatives had passed only two years earlier, restricted French instruction to just a single hour each day. It was legislation that did not sit particularly well with local descendants of French *voyageurs* and *habitants*. When ballot counting was completed on June 30, the Liberals – who had promised to reverse or greatly alter Regulation XVII – stood defeated by a landslide, sending just twenty-six representatives to the provincial assembly compared with the Conservatives' eighty-three.[1] But in Essex County, the story was different. In each of the region's ridings, the Liberals had emerged victorious. An estimated 10,000 people poured into the streets of Windsor to celebrate the local victory, even as the party floundered elsewhere. The air was filled with the smell of burning brooms, which people swung haphazardly above their heads.[2]

It was not just their political affiliations that set the people of Essex County apart from the rest of Ontario in 1914. As the province, indeed the country, struggled through a recession that year, the economy of Windsor and the surrounding border cities boomed. For a three-year period between July 1911 and July 1914, at least one manufacturing facility per month opened within the immediate region, many of them American owned.[3] As a result, the mood in Windsor was clearly jubilant during the balmy summer days of 1914. Ford Canada threw open its doors to locals and tourists alike, offering daily tours of the technological wonders within the factory's walls.[4] The company also reduced the prices of its vehicles at the same time as it introduced higher wages for employees.[5]

The development of a prosperous cross-border economy translated into the extension of transnational culture in 1914. That summer Windsorites mingled with Detroiters for Fourth of July celebrations, largely because so many Windsor residents worked across the river.[6] By eleven in the morning, the dividing waterway was overflowing with ferries. Automobiles, most decorated with both the Union Jack and the Stars and Stripes, navigated through throngs of jubilant people intoxicated with both sheer excitement and Canadian Club whiskey.[7]

FIGURE 5 A bird's-eye view of downtown Windsor – and the bustling Detroit River waterfront – in 1914. On average, hundreds of thousands of travellers crossed the border using the river's many ferries each month. *Source:* Southwestern Ontario Digital Archive.

Thousands of Detroiters travelled to Windsor, too, where they enjoyed drinks and frog leg dinners at the Canadian city's riverfront hotels. Immigration and customs officers were overwhelmed by the flood of traffic, the *Evening Record* reporting that agents were "ready to testify that nearly two-thirds of the city of Windsor helped Detroit celebrate the Fourth of July." For the most part, locals passed through inspection without much trouble.[8]

In contrast, the border cities' Dominion Day festivities were hardly boisterous. On July 1, 1914, most of Windsor's residents deserted their city (and country) in favour of American island resort destinations along the Detroit River. The Windsor Knights of Columbus organized a trip to Tashmoo Park, a holiday playground in Algonac, Michigan. About 2,000 members of the Baptist and Lincoln Road Methodist churches put together an excursion to Sugar Island, also Michigan territory. Another 3,000 Windsor residents visited the Canadian amusement park on Bob-Lo, or Bois Blanc Island, but Belle Isle, part of Detroit and considered the "coolest and closest beauty spot," was the "Mecca" for most Canadian residents of the border cities that Dominion Day. Activities included swimming, baseball, fat man races, and cracker-eating contests.[9]

Many of the Detroiters who visited Windsor in the summer of 1914 headed for the Canadian border city's horse-racing tracks. At a July 16 event, an estimated

800 automobiles and 15,000 people, many of them patrons from Detroit, descended on the local track.[10] Throughout the war, several new venues would open, notably the Devonshire and Kenilworth tracks, their success heavily dependent on Detroit patronage.[11] This traffic would be facilitated by the introduction of larger ferries designed specifically to handle passengers with automobiles. In July, the *Essex* was unveiled; although it was by no means the first ferry capable of transporting automobiles, it was the first specifically designed with that purpose in mind. According to the *Evening Record*, it could handle nineteen cars on a single journey.[12]

Horse racing was just one of several sports that brought Windsorites and Detroiters together during the summer months. Baseball was also incredibly popular in these communities, with both cities contributing teams to Detroit's amateur leagues. For Windsorites, going to these games was a communal experience: fans met at the ferry docks at a set time and then proceeded to Detroit's Garry Park ball diamond.[13] For many Windsor-based players, managers, and fans, Detroit clubs set the bar.[14] Most games in the border cities drew crowds of up to 200, but matches between elite Detroit and Windsor clubs could bring out 500 fans.[15] Helping to fill the stands were promotions that saw ticket prices waived for women, making the ballpark a place to meet members of the opposite sex.[16]

The extent of cross-border social and economic relationships in Windsor and Detroit made it hard to tell that this was the site of several intense military skirmishes during the nineteenth century. Locals sometimes made light of these former tensions, suggesting that many Windsorites no longer identified with those conflicts or their legacies. In a July 1914 editorial, *Evening Record* journalist M.R. Winters (clearly no historian) wrote that

> just about 100 years ago this time, [the] United States was pounding the thunder out of old John Bull on the battle field and the result was that George Washington and his coworkers built up a pretty nifty little nation ... Not content with trimming [the British] on the battle field in the conflict of 1812, the Americans kept up the work by ripping things to pieces on the sport field and those who swore allegiance to his majesty King George V and his Union Jack were wearing dismal looks until recently.[17]

Beyond using the War of 1812 as a source of humour, Winters's suggestion that the British were "pounded" in the conflict is rather unorthodox commentary considering most traditional Canadian accounts of the fighting.[18] There is also no mention of local contributions to the war effort, including the August 1812 sacking of Detroit or the subsequent American occupations of Essex

County. The account is hardly an incisive political editorial, but it does shed light on how some locals, many of whom were French Canadian or American, viewed the area's British connection in 1914.

Unique and highly localized interpretations of Canadian-American relations were again visible during preparations for the Anglo-American Peace Centenary, a continent-wide celebration of 100 years of cordial relations between the United States, Britain, and Canada. As one of the busiest border crossings in North America by 1914, the Windsor–Detroit corridor was considered an important landmark for the upcoming festivities. Although the First World War would dramatically reduce the scope of the centenary, during the summer of 1914 Detroiters and Windsorites agreed that the construction of a transnational tunnel would be the most appropriate way to commemorate a century of peace between the two communities.[19] When war was declared in August, local members of the Canadian Peace Centenary Association were in the process of petitioning business leaders for financial support.[20] The idea of an underground tunnel linking Windsor and Detroit would be revived again shortly after the war as members of these communities sought appropriate ways to commemorate the Allied victory. Unfortunately, funding troubles prevented such a plan from coming to fruition until 1930.[21]

Whereas peace celebrations aroused considerable passion along the Detroit River before 1914, interest in the military remained low. After dissipation of the Fenian threat in the late 1860s, militia enlistments fell off considerably among residents of Essex County. The threat posed by Louis Riel and the Métis in the South Saskatchewan River valley in 1885 partially revived interest in the militia, culminating in creation of the 21st Essex Regiment of Infantry that June. But the rebellion was crushed long before any local men were required, and enlistment again subsided. Training thereafter was principally for the purpose of parades, such as the celebration associated with the incorporation of the City of Windsor in 1892. Interest in the military was briefly revived again in 1899 when sixteen local men were sent to South Africa to help Britain quell the Boer uprising, two never returning home.[22] The fourteen local soldiers who did eventually return to Windsor were greeted by throngs of supporters, a banquet in their honour, and the gift of new gold watches. But again the martial spirit dissipated. Not even the proliferation of a global arms race between imperial rivals Britain and Germany could arouse interest in the 21st Regiment, by then renamed the 21st Essex Fusiliers. In fact, enlistment was so low that officers practising manoeuvres were reduced to using toy soldiers and outdated maps when carrying out mock battles.[23] Local uninterest in the military was reflected in Windsor's newspaper, which rarely focused on tensions in Europe. In July 1913, the *Evening Record* dismissed the idea of a "German Menace," determining instead that Germany was unlikely to initiate a war because it had "enough troubles at home to keep her busy."[24]

As was the case across Canada, assassination of the Austrian archduke in late June 1914 did not arouse fears in Windsor of a world war.[25] Although the issue shared front-page space with the provincial election campaign when first reported by the *Evening Record*, in the weeks that followed interest in European sabre rattling waned.[26] In fact, it was nearly a month before Windsor's newspaper again reported on the Balkan tensions, and even then no one seemed to know what impacts they might have on Canadians. The *Evening Record* speculated that war would be limited to Austria-Hungary, Serbia, and perhaps Russia.[27] Windsorites were told by government officials that any conflict fought in eastern Europe was unlikely to alter the day-to-day routines of people in Canada.[28] Reports on the troubles in Ireland suggested that, if Canadian troops were needed anywhere, it was there, not in continental Europe.[29] Finally, on July 30, just days before Britain's declaration of war, the *Evening Record* insisted that Kaiser Wilhelm II was "bent on preserving peace."[30]

August 1 brought news to the contrary. Only days before, Austria-Hungary had demanded that Serbia, which it accused of having had knowledge of the plot against Archduke Ferdinand, heir to the Hapsburg throne, hand over the assassins or face an invasion. Such an ultimatum was an open dismissal of Serbian sovereignty and left little room for negotiation. Indeed, Austria-Hungary wanted war. Since its 1908 annexation of Bosnia-Herzegovina, territory that many Serbs thought belonged to a Greater Serbia (or Yugoslavia), tensions had steadily mounted between the two countries. The assassination presented Franz Josef, Austria-Hungary's emperor of sixty-six years, with an opportunity to quell that opposition.[31]

Austria-Hungary announced its declaration of war on Serbia on July 28. Two days later Tsar Nicholas II of Russia began the mobilization of his country's massive army. The move was seen as an act of aggression by Austria-Hungary and its powerful ally, Germany, which declared war on Russia on August 1. Because of a twenty-year-old alliance between Russia and France, the French army was also mobilized.[32] Fully expecting this development, the Germans immediately initiated plans for the invasion of their long-time rival to the west. The manual for this ambitious strategy, the decade-old Schlieffen Plan, called for a pincer attack on Paris that would result in French capitulation. Once that was complete, the Germans could shift troops back east in order to brush off the massive but cumbersome Russian army. It was a challenging move even for a technologically advanced and well-trained fighting force.[33] Diplomatically, it had the undesirable effect of ushering the British Empire (and most significantly the Royal Navy) into the war, which seventy years earlier had agreed to protect "little" Belgium from its much bigger neighbours. Britain responded to the invasion with an ultimatum of its own, and when Germany failed to change its course the empire and its dominions were at war. The date was August 4 – little over a month after the assassination of Ferdinand.[34]

By law, Canada was obligated to fight in 1914. Although Confederation had made it a self-governing dominion in 1867, its external affairs remained under British control until the signing of the Statute of Westminster in 1931. For many English Canadians, this was a moot point. The motherland was threatened, so Canada should be ready to defend it, they said.[35] Even in Quebec, where fifteen years earlier French Canadian nationalists such as Henri Bourassa had firmly opposed helping Britain in its war with the South African Boers, few stood against Canada's mobilization in August 1914. As the pressure for men to enlist mounted in 1916, Quebecers steadily gravitated toward a different position, but in the late summer of 1914 they appeared to be ready to answer the call – as long as it remained just a call rather than conscription.[36]

Remaining on the outside looking in was the United States. According to historian James Stokesbury, to Europeans Americans were a "peculiar breed," which might help to explain why the British, French, Russians, Germans, and other belligerents ignored the enormous human cost of the American Civil War.[37] Despite the country's variety of ethnic groups, most of them European in origin, Americans as a whole showed little interest in supporting either the Allies or the Central Powers in August 1914. Perhaps this was because, as the *Detroit Free Press* indicated, America was so diverse. Made up of Germans, Britons, Slavs, and French alike, it meant that joining either side could lead to a new civil war at home.[38]

As the rest of the world prepared for what was supposed to be a short war, its end expected by Christmas 1914, Americans recalled Shiloh, Antietam, and Gettysburg. W.A. Shryner, an Indiana man recently returned from a year in Europe and passing through Detroit, remembered seeing powerful armies and citizens hysterical with nationalism – a fatal combination in his judgment. "From all I could see there is not the slightest chance of it being anything but a long drawn-out struggle of extermination," Shryner noted in a letter to the *Detroit News* on September 2, 1914. "It will take a long time to bring Germany to her knees. The thousands who are about to be slaughtered haven't the least idea what it is all about, but they have been taught race hatred until they believe it is a holy cause."[39]

Windsor's newspaper did not escape these influences and likewise dreaded a British declaration of war. An *Evening Record* editorial three days before that announcement suggests that Windsorites might have been reluctant to join a

FIGURE 6 A view of the ferry from Ouellette Street in 1913. This photograph was taken for the *Evening Record*, Windsor's main newspaper before and during the war. *Source:* Southwestern Ontario Digital Archive.

European conflict: "Any call for troops in Canada will be received in a spirit of opposition to the cursed militarism that is a blot on twentieth century civilization." The newspaper did not see war as a way for the country to prove itself worthy on the world stage but predicted that it would negatively impact Canada by killing its best men:

> This is the time for sober thought. Reflect on the horrible consequences of participating in a war that really does not concern us. Consider the frightful sacrifice of life that would be made needlessly ... It would be a stupendous folly to send a Canadian contingent abroad to face hardship and death in opposing one or more nations with whom we have no quarrel.[40]

In Toronto, there was no such wavering at the offices of the *Globe*. On August 3, it insisted that, "if it means war for Britain, it means war also for Canada. If it means war for Canada, it means also the union of all Canadians for the defence of Canada, for the maintenance of the Empire's integrity, and for the preservation in the world of Britain's ideals of democratic government and life." The *Globe* insisted that Prime Minister Robert Borden could be "confident that the Canadian people are not only loyal to their obligations, but soberly and resolutely ready to do their solemn duty as citizens and as a nation." For the *Globe,* the war represented a way for Canada to finally eliminate its regional and ethnic differences. "In the day of testing the voice of Canada will be one voice," the paper declared.[41]

But in Windsor the *Evening Record*'s messages about the conflict strongly resembled anti-war sentiment in Detroit. In early August, the *Detroit News* interviewed University of Michigan professor James B. Angell, who referred to the approaching conflict as an "impending slaughter."[42] The newspaper drew direct comparisons between this new war and the American Civil War. With Detroit preparing to hold the Grand Army of the Republic (GAR) national convention in late August, these bitter memories were not far from the surface.[43] "So great was the destructiveness when the map had an area of about 1,000,000 square miles and when much less than 2,000,000 men were engaged at any time," the *Detroit News* noted. "What will the conditions be when 13,000,000 fighting men with longer range guns of every sort, and with railways and improved highways, and thousands of motor vehicles besides railway cars to rush them about[?]"[44]

The rhetoric was similarly disparaging over at the *Detroit Free Press.* "The period of waiting is over. The die is cast. War is on in Europe and humanity is about to take part in the most terrible conflict of all history," the *Free Press* proclaimed, adding that the United States must avoid participating at all costs: "For the present we have but one course, absolute neutrality. This is too cosmopolitan a nation, its very fibres are too indiscriminately drawn from all the peoples fighting, to permit us to lean to one or another of them."[45] Windsor's residents might have recognized that these issues posed a significant threat to a local population similarly divided among various ethnicities, including people of British, American, and French Canadian heritage.[46]

Since Germany's declaration of war on Russia on August 1, Windsorites waited anxiously to hear Britain's plans. Finally, on the night of August 4, Detroiters brought word that Britain too was at war. Carried over the river by hundreds of American workers and newsboys, Detroit newspapers bearing the British declaration were dispersed across the Canadian city late that evening. Men and women alike fought to get their hands on the first copies of the *News* and *Free Press,* among others.[47]

Soon an excited though apprehensive atmosphere descended on the city. Members of the local 21st Essex Fusiliers, led by Major S.C. Robinson, were joined by hundreds of British-born citizens in Windsor's streets. Locals declared their support for Britain in its time of need and condemned the kaiser. "Germany is just like a man who gets into a fight, loses his head and hits everybody in sight," shouted Harry Rush, a Windsor bank manager, as he snapped up one of the first Detroit papers. "Yes, and England will slip one over on the emperor's haw for getting so gay," replied the newsboy. The exultant crowd bellowed out the lyrics to "Rule Britannia" and "God Save the King."[48]

Americans, too, were prevalent in what the *Detroit News* described as a "war-mad" scene in Windsor. Many of them were young men who pressed Major Robinson to sign them up right away. Some boasted of their military experiences in South Africa, Cuba, or the Philippines. Robinson, in no way prepared for an onslaught of Windsor or Detroit volunteers, promised the American boys that they would be put to use. "If these Americans pass the necessary requirements, there is no reason why they should not be accepted in our regiments," he told the *News*. "Many Americans enlisted with us during the Boer War and they made good and valiant soldiers."[49]

But even as throngs of Detroit and Windsor residents celebrated Britain's declaration of war, others in the Canadian border town questioned their countrymen's willingness to fight for the British Empire. Although the *Evening Record* revealed that hundreds of Windsor men of all ages would "don a redcoat, strap on their equipment, and take their rifles and go into the unknown parts of Europe in defence of the British flag and England," it also noted the existence of a considerable contingent who "look upon the local redcoats as a joke, [and] laugh when they hear that the men of the city are willing to go to the front."[50]

In the days after Britain's declaration of war on August 4, the *Windsor Evening Record* continued to lament the coming bloodshed. Like the *News* and *Free Press* across the river in Detroit, the *Evening Record* seemed to be convinced that the war would not be over by Christmas, nor would Canada escape a long list of casualties. As a possible solution to this problem, the newspaper turned its attention to eugenics, the preservation and proliferation of the more "desirable" classes and races in society – usually healthy, tall, and muscular white Anglo-Saxons.[51] "At the time of the Napoleonic wars magnificent specimens of manhood were killed off in large numbers, leaving weaker and smaller men at home to re-people the continent of Europe," the *Evening Record* noted.

> It is appalling to contemplate the future of the human race if wars are to continue, destroying those who are mentally and physically fit and leaving behind the unfortunates who may suffer from lunacy, epilepsy, tuberculosis, and all the ills that flesh is heir to ... If it is impossible to get along without wars, the nations of the world might better agree to draw their armies from the insane asylums and epileptic hospitals.[52]

The *Evening Record*'s admission that such a plan would produce "a funny war" but protect the "best type of men" represented reasoning clearly distinct from those who fully supported Canada's participation in the conflict. To those who saw the war as an opportunity for Canada to demonstrate its value on the world stage, the military required the best and brightest to ensure that the Canadian Expeditionary Force (CEF) would succeed where others failed. Generally speaking, this was one of the reasons that First Nations people, African Americans, Asian Canadians, and those with even marginal physical and mental health issues (let alone insanity and epilepsy) were refused outright by the military until the recruiting situation became desperate in 1916.[53] The suggestion by Windsor's newspaper that these kinds of men bear the brunt of the fighting indicates that it did not necessarily believe that military accomplishments would benefit Canada internationally or domestically.

However, for every Windsor man and woman who hated the idea of the war, there were at least as many willing to sacrifice their money, time, and lives in support of it. Windsor recruiters had little trouble finding recruits in August and September 1914, when hundreds of men from both the Canadian border city and the American border city enlisted for active service overseas. Initially, enlistments in Windsor were low, with just twenty-five men joining up on August 5. The *Evening Record* that day indicated that some local men were afraid to enlist before the defeat of the Germany navy, which many people believed would prevent Canadian troops from safely crossing the Atlantic. But by Saturday evening the number of local recruits had increased nearly fourfold, to ninety-three, and on Tuesday, August 11, one week after the British declaration of war, nearly 200 men had signed on. Of the 197 who were a part of this first wave, 87 listed Windsor as their place of residence, 49 said Detroit, and another 29 hailed from Walkerville. Just three of the earliest recruits listed Ford City, the site of the Ford plant, as their home, and only eight listed the wider Essex County as their place of residence. The *Evening Record* estimated that one in four of these first recruits was British born, considerably lower than the 6:10 ratio of British born to all other recruits recorded across the rest of Canada.[54] The newspaper also reported that the majority of the forty-nine Detroiters originally hailed from England, Scotland, Wales, or Ireland.[55] The next day these new recruits, many of them without uniform, paraded through Windsor. An estimated 25,000 people, many visitors from Detroit, came out to see and cheer them. "Never in the history of the city has such a crowd turned out," the *Evening Record* reported. "The demonstration was a fitting tribute to the men who have offered their all in the call to arms."[56]

Over time, local support for the war effort eroded the anti-war sentiment of August 1914. Certainly, there was no shortage of local men willing to offer their services for the war effort.[57] This was in line with recruiting across the country, initially substantial. In fact, recruitment was so high in Canada that recruiters weeded out all but the healthiest of Anglo-Saxon men; rejections came to those missing fingers or toes, those under 5'3" in height, those with slight physical or mental illnesses, and those with uncompromising wives who would not let them go overseas. Pay for a private was $1.10 per day, about equal to that of a junior clerk and far more than a farmhand's wage.[58] Helped in large part by its proximity to the border (across which many American professional soldiers and adventurers would come), Windsor's recruiting for service overseas did not struggle until 1916, about the same time that most other municipalities in Canada experienced similar problems.[59]

Windsor women showed their support by joining the city's most prominent imperialist organization, the Imperial Order Daughters of the Empire (IODE), and the local branch of the Red Cross Society.[60] At the IODE's first meeting on August 11, 1914, regular and prospective members appeared in such numbers that the Windsor Armouries could barely house them all. Asked by the local military authorities to help raise money for a newly unveiled hospital ship fund, the women responded with donations ranging from fifty cents to five dollars.[61] After three days, the fund's total stood at $185.50 – roughly $4,000 today.[62]

Although many Detroiters remained committed to President Woodrow Wilson's policy of neutrality during the war's first two and a half years, they did contribute to both the recruiting and the fundraising efforts in Windsor. In March 1915, members of the Women's Union of Detroit's Forest Avenue Presbyterian Church donated nine surgeons' gowns, fourteen hospital nightshirts, seventy eyepads, 400 abdominal pads, and surgical linens to Windsor's chapter of the IODE.[63] Detroit women also helped Windsorites to raise money for the war effort, such as in April 1915, when singers from the American city performed at a patriotic tea put on by Windsor's St. Andrew's Church.[64] Detroit's St. Andrew's Hall, home to the city's St. Andrew's Society, supported dozens of Canadian families through contributions to the Canadian Patriotic Fund (CPF).[65] In November 1916, Detroit hosted an Allies Bazaar that raised money for women and children affected by the war.[66] The Canadian display featured grain and maple leaves laid over the Union Jack and drew attention from Americans and Canadians alike.[67] Of particular interest to the Detroiters were Canadian recruiting posters included in the display; although they were not put there to be sold, Americans offered as much as twenty-five dollars for each one.[68]

Although recruiting statistics showing the number of Canadians, let alone Americans, enlisting in particular military districts remain imprecise, it is clear that many Detroit men enlisted in Windsor prior to the US declaration of war in 1917. As early as March 1915, the *Evening Record* reported the deaths of three Detroit men killed while serving with the CEF, all having enlisted in Windsor.[69] On a single day during the brutal Battle of the Somme in 1916, five Detroit men, presumed to have enlisted with the 99th Battalion in Windsor, were wounded in action.[70]

Some Americans who enlisted in Windsor joined local battalions such as the 99th or, later, the 241st Essex and Kent Scottish. But others joined the 97th Battalion's American Legion (AL), a special contingent established within the Canadian Expeditionary Force to recruit US citizens. The American Legion recruited across Canada but had particular success in Windsor, where recruiters such as Sergeant "Pop" Emery, a former member of the Seventh United States Cavalry and a veteran of the Spanish-American War, worked hard to convince visiting Americans that they should join the Allied war effort.[71] Emery and other AL recruiters had keen eyes for finding potential recruits; in the summer, they often staked out Windsor's horse-racing tracks, handing out recruiting pamphlets to men of military age as they walked through the facility's gates. The strategy worked best on those men who lost their money betting on the ponies, such as Chicago resident George Clarke, who decided to enlist after gambling away $2,000. In July 1916, the *Evening Record* noted that "recruiting literature distributed at the gates of the race track [has] brought forth a large number of men," suggesting that Clarke was not alone.[72]

Regardless of the battalion that they joined, Americans – especially Detroiters – comprised a key part of recruiting in Windsor. In the opinion of the *Evening Record,* this made the Canadian border city "the most fruitful recruiting ground in Ontario," particularly as the number of enlistments in Canada slowed in 1916.[73] That summer Windsor began recruiting for the 241st Scottish Borderers Battalion, which sought to attract locals with a distinctive uniform featuring the Highland kilt. The strategy had only marginal success in drawing out Windsor's Scots, but it did attract a substantial number of Americans.[74] When an estimated 12,000 Windsorites and Detroiters poured into the streets of Windsor to bid farewell to the unit as it shipped out in April 1917, Mayor Charles Tuson paid special tribute to the Americans, who comprised 27 percent of the battalion's strength.[75]

Because Windsor's military authorities had so little trouble finding recruits for overseas service during the war's early stages, local men were not pressured to join the ranks – meaning that the conflict failed to have a significant impact on the region's border-crossing culture. Until conscription became imminent in 1917, Detroit and Windsor sports teams regularly engaged in matches, just as they had prior to Britain's declaration of war in August 1914. News of these games filled the sports section of the *Evening Record;* for example, in March

1915, it reported on the stunning victory of the Windsor Rovers soccer team, which defeated a number of Detroit squads to capture the Michigan State Soccer League championship.[76] Windsor and area amateur baseball teams – such as the Walkerville Crescents and Windsor Wanderers – continued to make regular appearances in Detroit, while horse racing drew tens of thousands of Americans across the border during the summer months.[77] But there was more to the sporting interaction between Windsorites and Detroiters than just baseball and horse racing during the period of American neutrality: residents of both communities regularly came together for a wide variety of sports, from lawn bowling to horseshoe tossing to dog shows.[78]

Just as they had done prior to the war, Windsorites also attended the many theatrical productions put on across the border, at facilities such as the Garrick, Cadillac, and Lyceum Theatres.[79] Detroit and Windsor preachers and musicians continued to move back and forth across the line to perform, while organizations such as the St. Andrew's Society often sought entertainers from the other side of the river for their meetings.[80] All that interaction among Windsor and Detroit men and women fostered some particularly intense personal relationships, and the Great War era saw a number of cross-border marriages.[81]

As the war progressed, the nature of this cross-border social relationship did change. As Canada moved toward conscription in 1917, Windsorites who at one time had been willing to look the other way when young men joined sports teams instead of the military were no longer so accommodating. In January, news that a group of Windsor men were trying to organize a hockey team to play in Detroit received a vitriolic response from the *Evening Record*, which noted that "public opinion will support ... giving no consideration to any request from these un-military young men, who are more concerned about chasing a hockey stick than in assisting to chase the Huns."[82]

Hockey was hardly the only sport affected by increasing pressure on men to enlist. Entrance of the United States into the war in April seriously reduced the number of Americans making their way to Windsor's horse-racing facilities. In response, all three race tracks closed in July 1917, with no plans to reopen until the war was over.[83] Baseball was also affected – few games were played in 1917 between Windsor and Detroit men of military age, which forced locals to attend high school games.[84]

The official US policy of neutrality also brought tensions to the Detroit River border region as the conflict progressed. In January 1917, the editor of the *Windsor Evening Record* criticized America for "deserting" Canada by continuing to pursue neutrality, even as German submarines attacked Allied sea vessels carrying US citizens.[85] Then, in late March, the *Evening Record* congratulated Austin Hoy, an American man, for reportedly sending a telegram to President

Wilson formally protesting US neutrality. According to Windsor's newspaper, Hoy, whose mother and sister had died when the *RMS Laconia* was torpedoed by a German U-boat in late February 1917, planned to join the Canadian army.[86]

But neither conscription nor US neutrality dramatically reduced interaction between Windsorites and Detroiters during the war. In fact, the American entry into the conflict in 1917 brought the communities together on multiple occasions during the war's last two years, even in circumstances in which such interaction was officially outlawed. On learning that the president had asked Congress for a declaration of war on Germany, the *Evening Record,* which only weeks earlier had criticized America for its neutrality, expressed elation. Calling the decision "a powerful blow for democracy," when it became known that Congress would approve of the request, the *Evening Record* predicted this to be the turning point in a long and brutal war.[87] "It is recognized that the genius, energy, and money of the United States should be directed toward ending the war with blows that can be dealt quickly," the newspaper insisted.[88]

News that the United States had joined the Allied cause spread rapidly throughout the Canadian community. Letters to the *Evening Record* suggested celebrating the event by finally building that bridge between the two communities.[89] Windsor Anglican Reverend D.W. Collins declared the American declaration of war "the greatest event in the history of the human race," adding that Canadians and Americans were "brothers once more, fighting side by side against a common enemy."[90] Days before, the *Evening Record* reported that "practically the entire population" of the city joined several thousand Detroiters in a massive parade winding its way through the Canadian border community to celebrate the event. Leading the procession were men dressed as Uncle Sam and John Bull, followed by the Windsor Boy Scouts, the 241st Battalion, members of the Canadian Engineers, and several American soldiers from Detroit. Starting at the local Armouries, the parade wound down Ouellette Avenue and was "heartily cheered" all the way. Later that evening many of the parade's participants and onlookers crossed to Detroit, where they joined 2,000 residents of that city in a march down Woodward Avenue.[91]

For days, the partying engulfed both cities, particularly Detroit. So determined were members of Windsor's 241st Battalion to participate that they went across the boundary despite being specifically warned against doing so. There they were treated like royals by their American friends, who bought the Canadians drinks and cigars. Unfortunately, the fun came to an end later that week when the troops were rounded up by a sergeant-major who promptly threw them in the "clink."[92] "There they remain like Napoleon in exile, dreaming of past glory," noted the *Evening Record,* "but no doubt heartily agreeing with the spokesman of the expedition who said, 'It was worth it.'"[93]

FIGURE 7 Residents of Windsor distribute Camel cigarettes to American soldiers as they pass through in 1918. *Source:* Jonathan Vance.

In April 1917, the people of Detroit anxiously waited to see what impact their doughboys would have on the fighting. In the meantime, they lived vicariously through their Canadian neighbours, inviting Windsor politicians and military officials to participate in civic events and to speak before Detroit-based organizations such as Sons of the American Revolution.[94] Detroiters felt a special connection to the CEF and cheered wildly when it defeated the Germans at Vimy Ridge in early April. "Accounts of the achievements of the Canadian soldiers at Vimy ridge and beyond it send thrills through the ears of American readers, particularly through the hearts of those of us who live near the border," noted the *Detroit Free Press.* "They are our fellow Americans, in the larger meaning of the expression, and they are pointing out the road to honor and fame which the soldiers of the United States may later have opportunity to tread."[95] Later in the war, Detroiters would organize a pyrotechnical display of the Canadian victory at Vimy for the Michigan State Fair.[96]

As the war entered its final year, the people of Detroit and Windsor continued to work together to help advance the Allied cause. British and Canadian military recruiters set up shop in Detroit's Cadillac Square.[97] In April 1918,

Windsor Mayor Charles Tuson and returned veterans of the CEF marched alongside Detroit Mayor Oscar Marx and American recruits in a parade organized to raise money for the US city's third Liberty Loan campaign.[98] Windsor residents also organized a special Citizens' Welcoming Committee to provide cigarettes and reading material to American troops passing through the Canadian city en route to the front.[99] Within two weeks, the committee had accumulated 16,000 cigarettes and postcards, some of which were distributed to the Americans at a special ceremony attended by the Duke and Duchess of Devonshire in June 1918.[100] Speaking before a huge crowd in Windsor, the duke turned to Detroit's mayor and proclaimed that the American entry into the war had given the British "renewed confidence" when "our chances of victory looked dark indeed."[101]

Windsor's celebration of the growing bonds between Canada and the United States continued in the summer of 1918. In fact, Windsor hosted its own Fourth of July celebration that year, with locals making visiting US soldiers the honoured guests at several special events. First, a group of 1,000 doughboys were, in the words of the *Evening Record*, "given a royal reception" by the hundreds of citizens gathered at Windsor's train station. The soldiers – most hailing from Montana and Nevada – returned the favour by joining the Windsorites in singing the Canadian national anthem. By the time the doughboys departed, they had been loaded down with thousands of cigarettes and stamped postcards courtesy of Windsor's Welcoming Committee.[102] Detroit residents returned the favour by treating Windsor and area veterans of the Canadian Expeditionary Force to a late July picnic on the banks of Lake St. Clair.[103]

To the relief of all, the war would be over in five months. On the morning of November 11, 1918, word reached Windsor that an armistice had been signed. In response, exuberant men, women, and children took to the streets, following the 21st Regiment band, Victory Bond salesmen, Knights of Columbus, Oddfellows Club, Boy Scouts, and decorated automobiles in parades throughout the city. Workers left factories for the day, some waving around crude effigies of Germany's deposed kaiser.[104]

In Detroit, the scenes were similar – bands belted out "Over There," though such patriotic airs were barely audible among the cheers of the crowd gathered at Campus Martius and City Hall.[105] Onlookers noted that it seemed as if only streetcar drivers stayed at their posts, the remainder of Detroit residents shirking work and flooding into the streets to welcome the long-awaited peace accord.[106] A week later Detroit's mayor and council issued a formal invitation to Windsor City Council to take part in a massive Thanksgiving weekend International Victory Pageant in the American metropolis. Promising to contribute $1,000 from the city's own coffers, Windsor City Council unanimously agreed

FIGURE 8 American doughboys passing through Windsor in 1918 fill out postcards from residents. *Source:* Jonathan Vance.

to participate.[107] When the Detroit Common Council declared Armistice Day a legal holiday three years later, Canadian veterans and residents of Windsor were invited to join their American counterparts in a parade winding its way through the streets of the US border city.[108]

The war ended in the Detroit River border region much as it had began, with Americans and Canadians coming together to mark the occasion. This does not mean that residents of both Windsor and Detroit supported the war effort at all times; in fact, in the early stages, residents of each city approached the conflict with a great deal of caution. In Detroit, which hosted the national convention of the GAR in 1914, there were lingering memories of the incredibly costly American Civil War. Unlike many citizens of the various Allied nations, Detroiters did not foresee a short conflict but saw intense national rivalries and advancing military technologies as evidence that a long and brutal war would follow. In Windsor, the editor of the *Evening Record* was similarly concerned about where the war would lead Canada, though as the conflict progressed the newspaper, like most of the citizens of Windsor, threw its support behind the war effort.

Eventually, many Detroiters threw their support behind the Allies as well. Detroit men joined the CEF, and Detroit women contributed to patriotic fundraising campaigns in Windsor. Then, with the US declaration of war in 1917, the two communities came together on several occasions to celebrate the advancement of a local and transnational bond forged through shared economic, cultural, and military exploits.

Of course, the war did present a new challenge to this relationship in the form of increased border security. As the war progressed, the border's permeability was steadily eroded, a process that started with pressure to buy goods locally and then advanced to the imposition of a passport system that forced Windsor men of military age hoping to cross the line to acquire an unprecedented amount of documentation. How Windsorites reacted to these changes, introduced by a number of sources, serves to demonstrate just how important the border's permeability was to them during the war.

2
"Part and Parcel"
Administering the Windsor–Detroit Border

IN JULY 1914, Windsor's chief customs collector, Dr. J.A. Smith, desperately petitioned local residents for help managing a flood of cross-border traffic. The problem, according to Smith, was that the thousands of Detroiters coming across the border to visit Windsor's horse-racing tracks were creating a backlog of travellers at the international boundary.[1] The solution, Smith believed, involved Windsor travellers working with their local customs inspectors to balance the traffic throughout the day. "If the merchants and manufacturing men bring their goods across the river in the morning they will save themselves and the customs officers a lot of work and time," Smith said in a plea published by the *Windsor Evening Record.* "With the large number of automobiles coming across to the races, a horse and wagon has great difficulty getting on the boats and many merchants have been delayed two hours in bringing their goods across."[2]

By 1914, the international boundary between Windsor and Detroit had emerged as a major border-crossing area. Thousands travelled across the line to find work on farms and in factories during the first decade of the twentieth century. Many would make this trip across the border only a few dozen times during their lives, whereas others would do so on a daily basis, having established homes for themselves on one side of the line and using the efficient ferry system of the Detroit River to access employment or entertainment across the boundary.[3]

As the following chapter shows, Windsorites were willing to make many sacrifices during the war, but refraining from professional and leisurely visits to Detroit was not one of them. Eventually, Windsor residents protested against government legislation designed to restrict movement across the boundary. The language used in these protests reveals that many Windsorites believed that they were part of a unique transnational community that needed to be maintained during times of both peace and war.

This was partly revealed by Windsorites' reluctance to defend the border once war was declared. Even with a German American population of 44,000 in Detroit, Windsorites expressed little fear that their city would become a target for enemy aliens living across the river, and as a result little was done to ensure that no such attack would occur.[4] Few local men enlisted with the

FIGURE 9 Looking west along Pitt Street – one block south of the Detroit River – in 1914. At the time, the area was a curious mixture of hotels and factories, an indication of Windsor's haphazard development before and during the First World War. *Source:* Southwestern Ontario Digital Archive.

21st Regiment, the local militia unit that sought to bolster the city's home defence after the declaration of war. Even when newspaper reports in November 1914 suggested that German American Detroiters were plotting to blow up important facilities in Windsor, including a munitions factory and the Hiram Walker whiskey distillery, the 21st Regiment remained unpopular.[5] "There are hundreds of young men going around the streets today who would not volunteer to go to the front and now they refuse to volunteer to defend their own city," lamented one officer of the 21st Regiment in late November 1914. "We are right here on the border and if anything should happen in Canada it will be right along here." For the sake of comparison, the *Evening Record* pointed to Ontario centres London and Toronto, which, the newspaper insisted, had each received its fair share of home defence recruits.[6]

For its part, the Canadian government took reports of a German plot against Windsor in late 1914 far more seriously. Less than two weeks after the declaration of war in August, Ottawa began investigating German activity in border areas, even sending investigators to live in Detroit and Buffalo.[7] Secret agents were placed in these American communities by October and began reporting back later that month. An agent known only as F.R.J. was posted to Detroit, where he regularly visited popular German establishments, including the German American Hall on Monroe Avenue and the Heinz Café on Grand River Avenue. But he found that most of Detroit's Germans scoffed at the idea of launching a raid on nearby Canadian communities.[8] In fact, at many German establishments, F.R.J. was surprised to find proprietors and customers not particularly interested in the war at all.[9]

As fall turned to winter in 1914, the 21st Regiment still struggled to arouse much interest in home defence; those who enlisted wanted to go adventuring overseas, while the rest saw little threat from their neighbours across the river. In desperation, the 21st Regiment tried several different schemes to entice Windsor men to join, from persuading local manufacturing concerns to lay home defence recruits off last to creating a sports committee that organized various events among troops and Windsor and Detroit athletic clubs.[10]

But these strategies were only marginally successful. Part of the problem was that the militia department refused to provide funding for the arming and equipping of a home guard unit, the responsibility resting on municipalities.[11] Detroiters did not always help the effort either: in a well-attended address titled "Problems of Alien Population of Detroit" before the Windsor Literary and Scientific Society in early December 1914, Detroit pastor Earl R. Rice told listeners that "there is no reason to fear a German invasion," arguing that the German people were "desirable citizens" unlikely to cause trouble for Canadians.[12]

But the events of June 21, 1915, changed local perceptions of Detroit's German Americans, at least temporarily. Early that morning a jarring explosion rocked the border cities. A large section of Walkerville's Peabody plant, which had been producing uniforms for several months for the British military, was reduced to rubble by a timed explosive. Hours later it was discovered that a second bomb had been placed in the Windsor Armouries. Attached to a timer, the device had mysteriously failed to detonate. Had it worked properly, the bomb might have decimated Windsor's primary recruiting station and killed the new recruits sleeping inside.[13]

Windsorites were understandably shocked by the attack. Their mayor, Arthur Jackson, admitted to having received a letter warning that attempts would be made to destroy buildings in Windsor and the surrounding area but had dismissed it. "I considered it nothing more than a joke at the time," Jackson admitted to the *Detroit Free Press,* adding "but I handed it to the provincial police for what it was worth."[14] Across the river, the *Free Press* called for calm. "The conclusion of some of the people over the river that the dynamiting attempts were the result of a general organized plot hatched in Detroit by German-American citizens is not to be accepted even as a well-considered theory in the absence of positive proof."[15]

FIGURE 10 The Peabody factory in 1913. Two years later, while producing uniforms for the British military, it would be bombed by a group of Detroit-based German Americans. Their trials would last throughout the war. *Source:* Southwestern Ontario Digital Archive.

In the ensuing days, the Canadian government scrambled to investigate the bombing. Markings on the sticks of dynamite found in the Armouries pointed federal agents to Detroit-based manufacturers.[16] Dumbstruck law enforcement officials found dynamite all over Windsor, from the Gramm Motor Truck Company to the Invincible Machine Company, firms that had only recently received lucrative contracts from the British army. It was the Invincible Machine discovery that led to a major break in the case when a German American watchman working there admitted to having placed the dynamite at the Peabody plant.[17] He was arrested and prosecuted locally, his trial and those of his later apprehended accomplices lasting throughout the war.[18]

For a time, the attack put Windsorites on edge. The sight of airplanes flying overhead caused consternation that summer, some locals expressing fear that they were being piloted by Germans intending to drop bombs on the Sandwich jail, thereby setting the Peabody attackers free.[19] In September 1915, the sight of a large biplane led one frightened man to the Windsor Armouries, where he proclaimed that the plane was German and insisted that members of the 21st Regiment shoot it down immediately. (The guards, aware of the flight, calmly assured the man that the pilot was not a German but a Windsor resident on his way to the Michigan State Fair.[20]) Two weeks later residents of Sandwich were alarmed to hear that local Chief of Police Alois Master had received a phone call warning that Detroit-based Germans were storing dynamite nearby. Thankfully, it was soon revealed that the call had been the work of a practical joker.[21]

These kinds of scares – particularly those involving aerial bombardments – were hardly exclusive to Windsor and appear to have had a limited impact on relations between Windsorites and Detroiters.[22] Although Windsorites came to recognize US-based German sympathizers as a legitimate threat to public safety in the period after June 1915, even as the trials of those German Americans found responsible for the Peabody plot progressed, Windsorites constantly resisted attempts by the government to secure the border. Despite the obvious threats to their safety from across the international boundary, the people of Windsor continued to press for relaxed immigration and customs policies during the war's remaining years. Doing so would bring them into conflict with the provincial and federal governments as well as residents of other cities in Ontario.

Prior to August 1914, the concept of honouring one's duty to one's country rarely entered into casual border-crossing experiences at the Windsor–Detroit section of the Canada–US border. Not only did Windsorites work and play in Detroit in 1914, but also many of them purchased items, including clothing and jewellery, that were cheaper there than in Windsor. The *Evening Record*'s advertising section reflected this trend: Detroit businesses, including Kline's fine clothiers, Heyn's Bazaar, the Henry Blackwell Company, and Luscombe's shoe store enticed Windsorites with their one-dollar hats and two-dollar shoes.[23] Some firms, such as Steeve's Jewelry Store, openly addressed the price differential between Windsor and Detroit businesses. "Windsor people are always in our store," its July 24, 1914, ad declared. "The reason is that we give them better jewelry values than they can get at home ... For years this store has always been the jewelry buying place for Windsorites."[24]

Indeed, for years customs collections reflected the steadily growing cross-border business between Windsor and Detroit. In the mid-nineteenth century, Windsor's customs collectors were remunerated based on the amount of business conducted at the port, being paid one-third of the total revenue. In 1840, that meant that the city's first collector, William Hands, had an annual income of £1,795. Had such a system of payment been left in place, Windsor's collectors in the mid-twentieth century would have been very rich (collections in 1938, for instance, amounted to $20 million).[25] Much of the growth of customs collections in the Windsor–Detroit corridor occurred during the pre–Great War era. During 1898, collections totalled just $260,933, but between January and May 1913 alone they surpassed $3.8 million (roughly $80 million today).[26]

However, these statistics are misleading for one important reason: generally speaking, smuggling was accepted behaviour in the Canadian border city. In some cases, this meant helping undesirable groups, such as Chinese labourers, in crossing the border, but most often it involved material goods.[27] Events surrounding the Easter holiday weekend in 1915 demonstrate how ingrained smuggling had become in Windsor's border-crossing culture. Because of the superior variety and prices offered in Detroit, many Windsor women chose to do their Easter shopping across the border in late March 1915. But standing in their way on the morning of Friday, March 26, was visiting customs inspector Martha White – later dubbed "the lady searcher" by locals. Over the course of six hours, White (along with an unnamed female assistant), to the shock and dismay of most, searched an estimated 1,200 Windsor women returning from Detroit – hardly standard procedure at a border crossing where women were rarely searched. The result was chaos, both at the ferry docks and across the city. By mid-afternoon, the customs office "looked like the women's section of a large department store," the *Detroit Free Press* reported. Strewn across the floor were dresses, skirts, blouses, hats, and shoes from some of Detroit's most popular clothiers. White also acquired a long list of household items, including tables, benches, chairs, various kitchen utensils, and even several baby carriages. Many put up quite a fight: "Women screamed in hysteria and fought with the officers," noted the *Free Press.*[28] Others openly wept in front of White, fearing that they would be arrested. Some could not afford the duty and in desperation called husbands and boyfriends to help them out of trouble.[29] When they eventually got home, many women got on the phone to warn their friends about the lady searcher. "I called up a friend of mine who I thought was going over to purchase some articles, with the intention of warning her," one Windsor woman told the *Evening Record.* "She did not need the advice, however, as she had been phoned by three different friends, warning her."[30]

It took little time for Windsor residents to voice their disapproval of the government's decision to send in the lady searcher. On the day of the inspections, angry Windsorites told the *Detroit Free Press* that the action would hurt the incumbent Conservative Party's already fragile support base in the region.[31] Essex North Conservative MP Oliver J. Wilcox faced a flood of protests from Windsor residents following White's visit. Seeing a riding held since 1908 slipping away, Wilcox denied any knowledge of the decision to send in the lady searcher and pledged to investigate the matter fully. In the meantime, he sided with angry Windsorites. "While the laws must be obeyed, there should be a line drawn on small purchases," Wilcox said. "There are many people working in Detroit, and they consider they have a right to spend their money in that city." For his part, customs collector Dr. J.A. Smith assured *Free Press* readers that no political party was to blame and said that the inspections were part of a customs department agenda that went far beyond Windsor.[32]

Whereas some people thought that White's visit was related to an upcoming (but eventually delayed) 1915 federal election, others simply blamed Windsor's merchants. "If the merchants of this city have been responsible for women customs inspectors coming here from Ottawa and searching all women coming from Detroit, they will wait a long time before I buy any more from them," one Windsor woman told the *Detroit News.*[33] The next day reports from Detroit suggested that housewives in Windsor were united in their belief that the city's merchants were to blame for the inspections. The suspicions went deep. Some pointed to the rumoured existence of schemes put in place by Windsor furniture businessmen to prevent locals from buying baby carriages in Detroit. According to these rumours, if a man or woman went into a Windsor furniture shop and inquired about a baby carriage but did not buy one, his or her name would be recorded and distributed among all Windsor merchants (who kept in close contact via the Windsor Retail Merchants Association). If the man or woman appeared with a baby carriage within the next few weeks, but no Windsor merchant reported having sold such an item, his or her name would be reported to customs officials, who could confiscate the carriage if it was found to have been smuggled across the border.[34] Of course, these schemes remained the stuff of rumours. More telling might have been a *Detroit Free Press* interview with the lady searcher herself in which White admitted that there should be some protection in place for Windsor's merchants, losing thousands of dollars in revenue to Detroit businesses through cross-border shopping.[35] That comment alone seemed to indicate that, if anyone had made a request that the government send a female customs agent, it had been the 130 members of the Windsor Retail Merchants Association. For their part, Windsor merchants denied having requested that the customs department send White, but they did tell the *Evening Record* that it was their collective belief that Windsor residents should spend their money at home during wartime.[36]

Regardless of whom was to blame, the message from most Windsorites, no matter their political leaning, was that the lady searcher should be kept far away. One of the most direct protests on behalf of Windsorites came four days after the inspections took place. In a letter to the *Evening Record,* Windsor resident Robert Timms lashed out against the "senseless" and "irrational" inspections. "It was ill-advised, even if it did add a few hundred dollars to the customs coffers," Timms wrote. Pointing to the huge number of city residents who went to work in Detroit each morning, he noted that "Windsor is, except politically, part and parcel of the city of Detroit."[37]

Not everyone agreed with this sentiment. Other Windsorites thought that those who worked in Detroit (popularly known as "day labourers") owed nothing to the American city or its merchants. And like the Windsor Retail Merchants Association, they argued that Windsorites had a duty to spend their money at home during wartime. "Mr. Timms appears to think that those who earn their living in Detroit but reside in Windsor should spend part of their wages where they are paid," wrote Windsor resident T.D. Niven in a letter to the *Evening Record*. "Mr. Timms' suggestion involves three faults – it would defraud the Dominion revenue, it would tend to impoverish the home town, and it is unpatriotic in a general sense. I hope to see Mr. Timms in better business than seeking to sap the morality of his compatriots."[38]

Clearly, there was a divergence of opinion in Windsor over where city residents should spend their money during wartime. Protests against shopping in Detroit were couched in patriotic rhetoric, whereas those who defended the practice pointed to Windsor's economic dependence on Detroit as justification for spending hard-earned cash across the border. This latter group, which appears to have represented the majority of Windsor residents, wanted the federal government to keep agents such as White as far away from the border as possible. They cared little about the impacts of shopping in Detroit on Windsor merchants or dominion revenue (and, until the introduction of income tax in 1917, the bulk of the federal government's income came through customs collections).[39] There were already Canadian customs agents working in Windsor, including at least one woman, and they were doing a fine job in the eyes of most locals. Fines and duties were low and strip searches like those imposed by White rare.[40] These agents, unlike White, lived in the city where they worked and tailored the intensity of their inspections to local demand. They recognized the importance of a cross-border economy to the majority of Windsor residents.[41]

Debates of this kind were visible again during the fall of 1916, when the Toronto-based Lord's Day Alliance convinced the Conservative provincial government to pass the Lord's Day Act, enforcing by law that Sunday would remain a day of rest. On the surface, the act's main tenets – that people in Ontario should not work on a Sunday – bothered few Windsorites. But it was one small part of the legislation, that barring the distribution of American newspapers in the province on the Sabbath, that proved to be troublesome. This policy frustrated and annoyed many residents of Windsor, who had come by this point in the war to rely on Detroit's enormous Sunday periodicals (often sixty pages or more in length) for news from the front. After all, Windsor's own *Evening Record* was prevented from operating on Sundays, leaving what was considered an unacceptable gap in the amount of war information available to locals.

Reaction to the Lord's Day Act, which first had an impact on the distribution of American newspapers in Windsor during November 1916, was distinctly negative. In an editorial on November 17, the *Evening Record* slammed the barring of Detroit and Chicago Sunday newspapers because it feared that such a move would be seen as offensive by Americans and discourage them from enlisting in the CEF at Windsor. "More will come if we do not antagonize our American cousins," the *Evening Record* pleaded. Windsor's newspaper went on to characterize the legislation as a "slap in the face" against Americans and demanded that Ontario's attorney general repeal the legislation in order to "maintain the high degree of friendship that prompts courageous men of the United States to fight for a flag other than their own."[42]

A reply to this outrage came from Toronto's William M. Rochester, general secretary of the Lord's Day Alliance. His response, however, did little to calm anxieties over the Lord's Day Act and instead served to aggravate residents of the border community further. "The merit of these papers cannot reasonably be said to be the late war news they furnish," Rochester wrote in a letter published by the *Evening Record*. "The war, however, makes a convenient plea for the maintenance of a privilege which has been long enjoyed in your city." Rochester also emphasized the importance of remaining loyal to the government by not questioning such legislation. "It is ... not a question of whether the attorney-general acted judiciously, but whether he did his duty. If the latter, he should have the support of all loyal citizens."[43]

Subtly calling into question the loyalty of Windsorites did not sit well with the editor of the *Evening Record*, who shot back days later: "Mr. Rochester will have a difficult time trying to convince fathers and mothers who have sons at the front that the merit of Sunday papers 'cannot reasonably be said to be the late war news they furnish.'" The *Evening Record* then called into question Rochester's own patriotism: "Prussia looks to be the proper country for Mr. Rochester to move to. No doubt he would be right at home there."[44]

At the same time that Windsor's newspaper suggested that Rochester move to Germany, its council formally outlined its own opposition to the provisions of the Lord's Day Act. It emphasized the distinctiveness of Windsor and asked for special consideration in the matter of Sunday newspaper distribution: "This Council respectfully submits that the recent order preventing the circulation of said newspapers on Sunday be reconsidered and so modified as to meet the special conditions existing in Windsor and its vicinity and that a copy of this resolution be sent to the proper authorities. Carried unanimously."[45]

Windsor's Board of Trade also opposed the Sunday paper ban, one of its members grumbling that "we might as well be living in Siberia."[46] Conservative MP Oliver J. Wilcox offered a negative opinion of the legislation, too, telling the *Detroit Free Press* that "I see no reason why citizens of the border towns should be deprived of their Sunday reading."[47]

Despite the widespread protest, a response from the provincial government was not forthcoming.[48] After two weeks, the government had still not responded to the pleas of Windsor City Council, the Board of Trade, or MP Wilcox that the legislation be reviewed. At roughly the same time, Rochester appeared before the Detroit Pastors' Union to seek assistance in keeping American newspapers out of Windsor.[49]

The provincial government's refusal to amend the Lord's Day Act, combined with the activities of Rochester, served to fuel Windsorites' frustration with the newspaper ban. Timms, who had spoken out against the lady searcher in 1915, argued in a letter to Windsor's newspaper that conditions were different in Toronto and Windsor and that these distinctions needed to be considered when devising provincial legislation such as the Lord's Day Act.[50] Windsor's newspaper also continued to fight the Sunday paper ban, arguing that it would annoy and offend Detroiters (though neither the *Free Press* nor the *News* appeared to indicate this) and in doing so hurt cross-border relations. Importantly, the *Evening Record* suggested that the provincial government failed to understand the border-crossing culture of the Detroit River region. "Established residents of Windsor and Detroit understand each other thoroughly and mingle together in harmony. Respect is mutual. Friendship is self-evident," the *Evening Record* noted on December 5. "It is only when outside influences are exerted that friction arises."[51]

As the Sunday newspaper ban stretched into 1917, frustrated Windsor residents formed so-called Sunday Paper Clubs.[52] The idea was simple: schedules were drawn up, and each Sunday a different man would take the ferry to Detroit, where he would purchase enough newspapers for all of his neighbours. It worked for a few weeks – until the sight of so many normally law-abiding Windsor men toting around sacks of Detroit newspapers became impossible for local law enforcement officials to ignore. As the police reluctantly began to discourage the practice of forming paper clubs, the *Evening Record* expressed its disappointment: "At present the matter rests. The police have the names of the offenders. If Emperor Wilhelm Rochester decides that they must be prosecuted why – well they must be prosecuted, that's all."[53]

Despite the determination of Windsor residents to have the Lord's Day Act altered or overturned, the ban on American Sunday newspapers would remain in place throughout the war. And while time passed, and attacks by

Rochester and the *Evening Record* became less frequent, the matter remained highly charged. Months later Rochester released a special pamphlet on the subject of Sunday newspapers in which he targeted the people of Windsor by insinuating that their demands for special consideration under the Lord's Day Act put them at odds with their countrymen. "To have restored to them a privilege which for years they enjoyed contrary to law, the local petitioners seek to impose Sunday traffic in newspapers upon the whole dominion," Rochester wrote. "They ask Canada what they want only for themselves."[54] Disgusted with such remarks, the *Evening Record* yet again likened the work of Rochester's Lord's Day Alliance with German *Kultur* while emphasizing that such "oppressive domination" would continue to be circumvented by the determined people of Windsor.[55] Clearly, the *Evening Record* was willing to go to considerable lengths to protect the distribution rights of its primary competitors in Detroit.

Just as they despised customs searches and provincial Sunday newspaper laws, so too Windsor residents did not appreciate tightening immigration policies. Locals condemned the Canadian and American governments alike for imposing ever more stringent security measures as the war progressed, even though the Peabody bombing and subsequent trials of those involved demonstrated the existence of a clear and present danger to Windsor residents.

The job of a Windsor immigration inspector was by no means easy in 1914. Like its military department, Canada's immigration department was thoroughly unprepared for war. In Windsor, its weakness during the conflict was glaring for several reasons: the department was under incredible pressure to prevent enemy aliens from entering and leaving the country, even though the office was painfully understaffed; few Germans or Austrians looked much different from their Canadian- or American-born counterparts, making the job of preventing enemy aliens from entering or leaving the country virtually impossible; agents were poorly paid, and turnover was high; and, by the end of the war, the job of immigration inspector became a place for the government to put returned soldiers who struggled to find steady work elsewhere (with virtually no training and in many cases poorly educated, most veterans proved to be inadequate inspectors).

In 1915, there were twelve immigration agents stationed in Windsor, including Inspector-in-Charge J.S. Austin.[56] Despite increasing pressure on these men to keep out criminals and men and women with physical and mental health issues, the resources allocated to hiring and keeping particularly strong agents remained low.[57] In July, Windsor immigration officers sought an increase in their pay but were denied, Superintendent of Immigration W.D. Scott pointing out that, across the border in Detroit, inspectors were being asked to take a one-month leave without pay in order to reduce costs.[58] It was poor consolation, and throughout the period turnover remained high – primarily because of the position's low annual pay of $900 (less than $20,000 today).[59] Understaffing was also a problem: in November 1915, one Windsor resident wrote to the immigration department to complain that on at least eleven occasions between mid-September and mid-October the ferry dock immigration office had remained vacant during the early morning hours.[60]

Although understaffing remained a problem for immigration inspectors at Windsor throughout the war, Superintendent Scott frequently blamed inspectors themselves for such complaints. "Various members of the staff have been guilty of negligence, incivility and improper conduct and have displayed a lack of ordinary intelligence and judgment," Scott grumbled in a February 1916 letter to William Wallace Cory, deputy minister of the interior. Austin and the Windsor immigration officers drew particularly vitriolic commentary from Scott for allowing Albert Kaltschmidt, at that time the primary suspect in the 1915 Peabody plant bombing, to enter the country on multiple occasions.[61]

In response to the complaints, Scott assigned Special Investigating Officer Percy Reid to Windsor in early March 1916. Reid spent fifteen days at the ferry docks and made several key observations on the activities of immigration agents as well as the general atmosphere at the Windsor–Detroit border. During that time, it became clear to him that the problem was not necessarily the inspectors but the inspection process in place at Windsor. With an average of 340,000 people crossing the river on ferries one way every month in the summer (270,000 in the winter), the handful of inspectors faced an enormous challenge in weeding out undesirables coming into the city. Reid estimated that just two minutes passed from the moment a ferry's gangplank dropped to the time passengers walked by the immigration office's front door. "It means that every ten minutes from 250 to 300 passengers pass our inspectors," Reid wrote in his report. Besides all of this traffic at the ferry dock, inspectors were required to investigate freight traffic passing under the river via the Michigan Central Railway. As a result, Reid found that most people, including enemy aliens, entered Windsor with no more difficulty "than they would have in going from Hull to Ottawa." There was also no system in place to prevent enemy aliens from entering the United States, where they could find easy travel back to Europe and into the factories, farms, and armies of the Central Powers.[62]

In concluding his report on the situation in Windsor in March 1916, Reid recommended that a more capable officer be hired to replace Austin as inspector-in-charge, that three other officers be fired, and that at least two additional inspectors be hired immediately.[63] But this was a surprisingly tall order. By spring 1916, immigration authorities were having as much trouble finding

FIGURE 11 Prior to construction of the Ambassador Bridge (1929) and Detroit–Windsor Tunnel (1930), most people crossed the Detroit River and international boundary on ferries, like the one seen here in 1905. Many of these ferries flew both the Union Jack and the Stars and Stripes. *Source:* "Ferry Landing, Walkerville, Ont.," c. 1905, http://www.loc.gov/item/det1994018643/PP/.

men as the Canadian Expeditionary Force. With Windsor- and Detroit-based manufacturers hiring more and more workers at ever-higher wages, both cities experienced significant manpower shortages.[64] Local workers could choose their employers based on which ones offered the best pay and work environment. Even as pressure to keep a close eye on enemy aliens increased, the resources allocated to hiring new inspectors remained the same: $900 per year per inspector. It was hardly a terrible wage, but given the stress associated with the job, particularly during wartime, applications were not forthcoming.

In an effort to find new inspectors, Canadian immigration authorities altered their hiring protocols in late 1916. Rather than seek individuals with an above-average education and intellect – as proposed by Special Investigating Officer Reid in his March 1916 report – Ottawa turned to hiring returned soldiers as well as members of the local home defence force, in the process relaxing its previous standards. Despite personnel changes throughout the summer, people of German and Austro-Hungarian descent continued to move into and out of Windsor with ease.[65]

In November 1916, Scott inquired to Captain Paddon of the 21st Regiment about using several members of the militia to reinforce a desperately understaffed Windsor immigration office. Scott requested that these men be placed under the direction of the new inspector-in-charge, Orval Adams, while on duty at the ferry dock, with any enemy subjects apprehended turned over to immigration officials. Scott recognized that such a plan would face challenges – notably placing militiamen under the authority of an immigration inspector – but he was under intense pressure from Chief Commissioner of Dominion Police Sir Percy Sherwood to curtail the flood of enemy aliens across the Detroit River.[66]

By June 1917, returned soldiers and members of the 21st Regiment were aiding immigration inspectors at the border.[67] As summer turned to fall that year, Windsor, Walkerville, Sarnia, and Point Edward received guards from Military District 1 (MD1) headquarters in London, Ontario. These men were drilled on their duties and pertinent legislation, none more important than Order-in-Council PC 1433 (passed in May), which required all men of military age crossing the border to carry a passport. Once again the guards would be subordinate to the inspector-in-charge while nominally being under the control of a local military official. Clear instructions were made by Inspector-in-Charge Adams for these men to follow once they arrived.[68]

There was some hope that the number of enemy aliens and other undesirables making their way into Canada via Windsor would be reduced through the use of better-trained men. But that was not the case. By early December, Scott told Adams that he had been informed that men of military age who had been refused exemption from conscription and did not possess passports were being allowed to travel between Detroit and Windsor.[69] Initially, Adams defended his inspectors, telling his superiors that they were "taking every precaution to prevent any person evading the draft."[70] But complaints about the military guards persisted. In late December 1917, a soldier was found drunk on duty, and Adams continued to face difficulty in navigating the local military hierarchy in order to have such situations properly addressed. The immigration authorities were constantly searching for a way to have their inspector-in-charge given direct control over the Military Police, but it was never granted by the 21st Regiment or MD1 headquarters.[71]

In 1918, a slew of new problems complicated the system of placing returned troops and militiamen in Windsor's immigration office. The most troubling issue arose early in the year regarding allegations that Military Police had been taking bribes from local men eligible for conscription but desperate to get across the border to Detroit.[72] One federal inspector claimed to have "positive evidence that soldiers employed on the inspection of persons leaving Canada at the Windsor and Walkerville Ferry Dock had accepted funds or presents for a non-enforcement of the [PC 1433] regulation and had permitted men ... to leave Canada who should not have been allowed to leave."[73] The anxiety created by these rumours compounded a *Detroit Free Press* report in March that estimated at least 200 draft evaders living in Windsor, dangerously close to the US border.[74]

That was enough for the immigration department, which again changed its strategy for patrolling the international boundary with Detroit. Although it continued to use returned soldiers to inspect men and women entering Canada, for the purpose of investigating men of military age (or "Class 1") leaving for the United States, the department turned to Canada's fledgling federal security service, the Dominion Police (DP).

Prior to the Great War, Canada lacked an official intelligence agency. Aside from the federal government's commissioning of limited intelligence work on the Irish Fenian Brotherhood in the 1860s, there had been little demand for such a service. That changed with the outbreak of war in 1914. A force created earlier out of the Royal Northwest Mounted Police for the purpose of providing intermittent security services, such as the protection of public buildings, saw its responsibilities expanded considerably. Officially, the Dominion Police were tasked with registering and interning enemy aliens as well as securing the border, but they were not used in the latter capacity at Windsor until the last year of the war.[75]

DP officers first reached the border cities in the spring of 1918. The immigration department feared that their presence would create tensions with the official inspectors since the DP, like the Military Police, were not under the sole authority of Windsor's inspector-in-charge. Furthermore, unlike most of the Canadian immigration inspectors posted to the Detroit River in August 1914, they were not locals.

In barring the passage of men of military age, the DP had an immediate impact. In mid-March, the *Detroit Free Press* reported the arrest of several draft evaders living in Windsor, including a few hauled away from three local dance halls on a Saturday night.[76] The arrests and investigations created a stir in the border cities, but more was to come: DP Captain Asa Minard told the *Detroit Free Press* that he believed there to be at least 100 Windsor draft evaders living in Detroit who would be brought back, by force if necessary, over the coming months.[77]

By April 1918, the Windsor immigration office, aided by returned soldiers and Dominion Police, was finally beginning to make headway in preventing enemy aliens and draft evaders from travelling across the Detroit River. All men wishing to visit Detroit for work or play were required to show some form of documentation to both American and Canadian immigration authorities. For residents of Windsor, the entire border-crossing experience had changed dramatically since 1914, when immigration authorities limited their interrogations to visible and undesirable racial groups, criminals, prostitutes, and people with obvious mental and physical illnesses. Now a fifth-generation Anglo-Saxon Windsor resident with family living in Ypsilanti and a job in downtown Detroit could expect the same kind of attention. All of this, of course, was designed to ensure that Canadian men of military age did their duty and to keep the people of Windsor – by that point witnesses to the work of Detroit-based enemy terrorists – safe from German American raiders and saboteurs.[78]

But Windsorites hardly welcomed the changes, repeatedly protesting the use of force at the border. This was not a new phenomenon – when it was decided shortly after the war began that uniformed Windsor recruits should not venture across the border, the *Detroit News* inquired about the necessity of such measures. "This seems to go considerably beyond the proprieties of neutrality," the *News* insisted. "Many of the troops about Windsor have relatives in Detroit whom they visit, but even if they have no such incentive there is not the slightest reason why they should be barred from visiting Detroit as long as they conduct themselves properly."[79] For their part, Windsorites protested the use of force by American immigration agents in August 1916, when officials roughly handled a woman claiming to be on her way home to Detroit after having finished her shift at a Windsor cigar factory. Windsor onlookers were disturbed by the incident, many of them protesting her treatment to the American inspectors and later the local newspaper.[80]

Immigration inspections at the border became more frequent and more intense as the United States prepared to enter the war in April 1917. It introduced an eight-dollar head tax early that month; although Windsorites who had resided in Canada for over a year were exempt, the measure still aroused indignation on the Canadian side of the line.[81] Even so, the tax did not prevent new Canadians from visiting the United States. After three months, American immigration authorities told the *Detroit Free Press* that approximately $20,000 had been raised through the head tax alone, most of the income coming from Windsor-based aliens working in the US border city.[82]

On April 6, 1917, the United States declared war on the Central Powers. When word reached Windsor, local soldiers immediately petitioned the federal government for permission to celebrate the occasion alongside their American neighbours in Detroit. Washington approved, but in Windsor local military authorities found Ottawa unwilling to cooperate. Frustrated, the *Evening Record* blamed the "long process of unwinding red tape."[83] Although members of Windsor's 241st Battalion were disappointed with the federal government's decision to bar their passage to Detroit for the celebration, many went anyway, joining thousands of Windsorites for the Saturday-night festivities.[84] These members of the battalion left for Detroit the previous Wednesday, and not until the weekend were they finally rounded up by the military authorities.[85]

As a result of the American entry into the war, some locals expected that regulations at the border would be relaxed. After all, the US policy of conscription, approved by Congress on May 18, 1917, presumably would stop the flow of Canadian "slackers" over the boundary.[86] Instead, the federal government – determined to reverse a trend that saw recruiting dip from 30,000 enlistments per month in January 1916 to 5,000 per month in April 1917 – tightened its stranglehold on cross-border movement with Order-in-Council PC 1433.[87] Initially, this meant that men aged eighteen to forty-five travelling to the United States required a temporary permit (valid for three days) bearing name, age, and nationality. Eventually, however, every Canadian man of military age was required to carry a passport, which would include all of the above personal information in addition to a photograph.

PC 1433 was not particularly well implemented in Windsor. Unknown to most Windsorites, the order-in-council was invoked quietly on the night of May 24 and put into practice the following morning at 5:30. Thousands of Windsor men, who had crossed to Detroit with minimal inspection the day before, were now required to have a temporary card that few knew existed. Once it became known that such documentation could be acquired through Windsor's inspector-in-charge, the immigration office was flooded with angry and frustrated day labourers facing the possibility of missing work. Men rushed the office with such desperation that the glass on the door was shattered amid the chaos. Within hours, the store of 600 temporary cards had been exhausted, leaving scores of men anxious to get across the river out of luck.[88] Although rush orders were sent to local printers for new cards, Inspector-in-Charge Orval G. Adams and his team were forced to turn deaf ears on men pleading that they would be punished severely by employers for not getting to work on time.[89] Even for those inspectors who dealt with Windsor's cross-border labourers on a daily basis, the anger and frustration of the crowd were startling. "I never before had any idea how important to Detroit business life the citizens of Windsor really are," one officer told the *Evening Record.* "To hear some of them talk, one would think that they are holding down bigger jobs than the president of the United States."[90]

Many Windsorites lashed out at the federal government's new requirements for crossing the border. The *Evening Record* referred to the measures as "iron clad," the process leaving the city in a state of "confusion, causing loss of time and money to thousands of Windsor and Walkerville residents who work in Detroit." Windsor's newspaper was equally dismayed by the requirements associated with the passport system (to be finalized and introduced by June 1), which would require a cross-border day labourer to renew his application at the immigration office once a month.[91]

The *Evening Record* was not alone in expressing bewilderment with the passport system. Windsor's mayor, who had seen the chaos at the immigration office on the morning of May 25 first hand, sent a telegram to Prime Minister Robert Borden protesting the government's ignorance of Windsor's cross-border economy when implementing the passport measure. Given such a slapdash approach to realization of the scheme, the $2,500 fine and threat of five years of imprisonment for violation also struck the mayor as draconian.[92]

Many Windsorites underestimated the determination of the immigration authorities in enforcing the passport scheme, some forsaking the process of acquiring proper documentation on the assumption that inspectors would recognize them and allow them to pass. Over the coming weeks, such hopes were dashed.[93] In early June, a 21st Regiment band member with plans to perform in Detroit was barred from crossing the border despite being a well-known member of the community and having shown his passport to the immigration authorities on several previous occasions. A Windsor onlooker who chose to remain anonymous expressed confusion and frustration with the tightening border controls. Drawing comparisons to the work of American immigration authorities in Detroit, he noted that "conditions are worse here now than they ever were at the other side of the river."[94] Windsor's newspaper remained critical of the process as well, noting how men returning from Detroit were "indiscriminately jammed" into the "stuffy" and "poorly lighted and poorly ventilated" immigration office, where they were intensively examined by inspectors. On the weekend of June 8, 9, and 10, these checks were led by Travelling Inspector D.H. Reynolds and several assistants hailing from outside the Windsor region – as such, the *Evening Record* criticized them for being "unfamiliar with the local situation and local conditions."[95]

Although many Windsorites thought that the passport scheme went too far and came too quickly, it did have the desired effect of convincing some locals to join the manpower-starved Canadian Expeditionary Force. Windsor recruiters reported having a busy few hours on the morning of May 25, signing on an additional sixty-nine recruits at a time when five or six might be enlisted in a period of several months.[96] Many men probably saw the writing on the wall: conscription was coming, and the government was willing to do just about anything to make it a success. However, of equal importance was the fact that Windsorites continued to dismiss threats to the border from Detroit, with just four men joining the city's 21st Regiment (snidely referred to by many locals as the "21st Safety First") after an exhaustive province-wide home defence campaign that ended in late May.[97] It represented the poorest showing of any municipality in Ontario, demonstrating that, though the federal government believed that tightening the border was important in protecting the people living there, most Windsorites thought much differently.[98]

Despite new reports of German American terrorist schemes against Windsor and other Canadian cities in early 1918 (from bomb plots to invasions), opposition to strict immigration controls mounted throughout the spring and summer.[99] Many of the complaints were directed at the Dominion Police, who had recently appeared at the border to reinforce the official immigration inspectors and Military Police, the latter considered largely incapable and in some cases even corrupt. Locals found the DP, most of whom were from outside the Windsor region, not only overly disruptive in their inspections but also arrogant and melodramatic. "It is really funny to watch the procedure," noted the *Evening Record*, "when a Dominion officer, in civilian clothes, throws back his coat lapel, like a stage detective, and points to the badge of authority on his vest."[100] Shortly thereafter, Windsor's newspaper half-heartedly noted that the only way to get around the suffocating red tape at the border might be to join the two countries together once and for all.[101]

In June, Windsor's political leaders took up the matter. In a note to the Canadian immigration authorities in Ottawa, members of Windsor City Council asked "if the department cannot at this time make arrangements for a less rigid enforcement of the immigration rules at the border," adding that

> the very friendly relations that now exist between Canada and the United States were brought about largely by the friendly relations and social intercourse that ha[ve] always prevailed by the residents of the border municipalities and we would ask that an Inspector be sent here to report to your department as to how much more rigid the immigration law is enforced in Canada than it is in the United States.[102]

Superintendent of Immigration W.D. Scott's response to this letter has been lost, but Scott probably assured Windsor's council and citizens that the tighter immigration controls were there to protect the people of the border cities. Still, council's insistence that changes be made to the operations of the immigration office indicates that the *Evening Record* was not complaining on behalf of a minority.

One last episode in 1918 revealed Windsor's insistence that its border-crossing culture be maintained at all costs, even during wartime. In April, the federal government, at the insistence of the Canadian Railway Board, instituted daylight saving time (DST). After the American government implemented DST earlier in the year, Canada's railway companies complained that trains were having to wait an hour before crossing into the United States, in order to maintain published schedules.[103] Across much of the country, the measure was readily adopted – except in Windsor, where its council voted ten to one against DST. This was because most of Detroit's businesses remained on Eastern Standard Time, and council, under considerable pressure from cross-border day labourers in Windsor (not wanting to wake up one hour earlier for work), thought that the adjustment would cause too much confusion with Detroit.[104]

But not everyone agreed that a break should be made with the government in order to maintain ideal business relations with Detroit. Speaking before the Chamber of Commerce, Windsor merchant Clarence Smith declared that the government's order should be complied with, arguing that "Windsor is a Canadian city ... Let us stand behind the government as a matter of patriotism."[105] Over the coming days, the federal government applied its own pressure, forcing Windsor and area banks, courts, and government offices to make the adjustment to DST. In response, Walkerville Town Council gave in, the mayor proclaiming that the move was necessary "if for no other reason than to back up the government ... as a matter of principle." Patriotism once more became a major theme in the controversy over Windsor's cross-border economy and culture. Over the coming days, most of the other border cities also capitulated, citing similar reasons, leaving Windsor and Ford City alone in opposition to DST.[106]

Pressure on Windsor to adopt the new measure mounted over the coming week. Increasingly, the question became whether the citizens of Windsor were being "unpatriotic" by refusing to adopt DST. Resident T.D. Niven noted these feelings in a letter to the *Evening Record* on April 27: "I should not be surprised to hear that the man who ... permits his watch to run on [Eastern Standard Time] is regarded as a pro-German and fast qualifying for internment."[107]

Questioning their loyalty was too much for most border cities businesses and municipalities. Everywhere the question seemed to be whether or not it was unpatriotic for a city to refuse a government measure such as DST. But Niven vehemently defended the city's request for an exception to the rule, since, as so many Windsor residents had emphasized before, conditions in the border cities were exceptional. "Certain parts of this wide Dominion are subject to very unusual conditions," Niven proclaimed. "In this special class are Windsor and her sister municipalities. Our connection and intercourse with Detroit are so extensive, so vital and so constant that we simply cannot afford to use a different time standard."[108]

Nevertheless, patriotism remained a persuasive tool for the government. Feeling in Windsor was that, as the only municipality in the country not to adopt the change, the city had left itself open to attack from the likes of William Rochester. Indeed, the *Detroit Free Press* noted these emotions when it suggested that Windsor was "in bad" with the rest of the dominion, a black sheep that throughout the war had demanded its own way on matters involving provincial as well as federal legislation.[109] Critics of Windsor's intransigence in the DST matter blamed Mayor Tuson, who defended himself by asking "what am I to do if a majority of the people are against a change?"[110]

Ford of Canada General Manager Gordon McGregor's decision to adopt DST on April 27 was the last straw.[111] As the largest employer of labour in the border cities, Ford had considerable sway there.[112] Within two days, Windsor City Council and the Border Chamber of Commerce acquiesced to the government's demands for DST. The decision was by no means unanimous – manufacturers with a substantial number of Detroit men in their labour force, including the Kelsey Wheel Company, Canadian Bridge Company, and Seely Manufacturing Company, all protested the change. Each insisted that its opposition "was not a matter of patriotism but of business." However, despite their boisterous support for Windsor's special time (the *Evening Record* reporting that Mayor Tuson barely maintained control of the April 29 council meeting), the DST measure was adopted.[113]

In many ways, Windsor was not unlike other Canadian communities during the First World War. True, local citizens met the war with a mixture of excitement and uncertainty, the doubts inspired in part by the determined neutrality of their neighbours in Detroit. Whereas Torontonians greeted the conflict as an opportunity to demonstrate loyalty to the great British Empire, in Windsor the *Evening Record*'s editor expressed a deep fear that the war would rob the country of its best and brightest, suggesting that the Allies send their lunatics and criminals to the front instead.[114] But Windsor men joined the colours anyway, and they did so in numbers comparable to their compatriots in Toronto, Ottawa, Halifax, and Vancouver. Not until 1916 did battalions recruiting for service overseas fail to meet their manpower goals, and by then most other communities in Canada were facing the same problem.

But for every characteristic of life in wartime Windsor that seemed to reflect other communities in Ontario, there were just as many that set it apart. This was a region that repeatedly emphasized its uniqueness in the Canadian cultural and economic landscape. Before the war, the people of the border cities engaged in cross-border activity to an extent that blurred boundary lines. Men living in Detroit and Windsor often worked across the river. Women in Windsor did much of their shopping across the boundary, while social and sporting events in the Canadian border city often drew the attendance of Detroit people. Courting knew no boundaries, and cross-border marriages were common. Families were often a ferry ride away. Windsor-based athletic teams rarely met up with clubs from Ontario centres London or Chatham, but they regularly engaged in intense but friendly matches against Detroit competitors.

When war came, few Windsorites thought it necessary to adjust this vibrant border-crossing culture. Locals were willing to go overseas to fight, they were willing to part with their hard-earned wages to support the families of soldiers, but many were not willing to allow either the federal government or the provincial government to complicate matters at the ferry dock. Tighter border controls, through more thorough customs inspections, the banning of Detroit goods, or the imposition of a passport system, were seen as anathema to the region's border-crossing culture. And no wonder locals were so upset: while the rest of the country languished in recession in 1914, many businesses in the border cities were booming. Most credited this condition to the prewar era's relatively permeable border.

The war changed much in and about Canada, but for Windsor residents the challenge was to maintain the good times that predated it. Windsorites struggled throughout the conflict to uphold prewar conditions and lifestyles, most of which were defined by the city's proximity to and integration with Detroit. Those who challenged these traditions were denounced as outsiders who did not and could not understand the unique conditions in the Detroit River region. This kind of rhetoric, frequently used in Windsor's newspaper (by editors and residents alike), demonstrates the existence of a distinct borderland identity that set the people of this area apart from other Canadians. The people of Windsor were willing to do their part to protect Canada, but there were clearly limits to the sacrifices that they would make on the home front.

Perhaps this borderland identity was best demonstrated not by the lady searcher episode or even the Sunday newspaper debate but in 1917 during the early stages of amalgamation of the border cities (eventually completed in 1935). The question was what would a metropolitan area encompassing Windsor, Ford City, Walkerville, Sandwich, and Ojibway be called? In a May 1917 letter to the *Evening Record*, Windsor resident Robert Timms thought that South Detroit was the best choice. It had a history: when the French Canadians of Detroit departed for the opposite shore after announcement of the Jay Treaty in the late eighteenth century, this was the name that they allegedly gave to the new community. In the time since, South Detroit had been replaced by several other names, including Richmond, Sandwich Ferry, and finally Windsor in 1836.[115] But for Timms, South Detroit seemed to be the most appropriate: "It has always been my impression ... that the name South Detroit would have

FIGURE 12 Residents of Windsor greet thousands of American soldiers as they pass through in 1918 en route to the front. Many were lavished with gifts, from cigarettes to postcards. *Source:* Jonathan Vance.

been received in a kindlier spirit by the people of Detroit, and might have redounded to its advantage in a greater measure than its present purely English name."[116] In the months following, his proposal gained strength. Dr. Thaddeus Walker, president of the Border Chamber of Commerce, publicly agreed with the idea, arguing that the name was evocative of life along the border.[117] Shortly thereafter, Windsor resident George Bouteiller wrote to the *Evening Record* to voice his support for the name, though he suggested dropping the "South."[118] The road toward amalgamation was a long one and would not reach its end for nearly two decades, and eventually Windsor would become the region's all-encompassing name. But in May 1917, when the rest of the country was revelling in the Vimy Ridge victory, in Windsor the pre-eminence of national over transnational identities was not quite so clear.[119]

Part 2

St. Stephen, New Brunswick, and Calais, Maine

In the spring of 1813, the Americans attacked York, a small but growing community along the shores of Lake Ontario. They were met by a much smaller contingent of British soldiers who made a desperate gamble by blowing up the local fort's gunpowder magazine. The explosion cut a swath through the invaders, sending roughly 250 Americans to their knees. But there were simply too many attackers, and within hours York was in their hands. For six days, they looted homes, burned government buildings, and generally harassed a terrified populace. Eventually, they left smouldering York behind but returned just a few months later to reopen the wounds. In late July, American soldiers set fire to the town's barracks and several other buildings that had previously, perhaps miraculously, eluded the torch.[1]

In York, later Toronto, the bitterness brought on by the War of 1812 would linger for generations. But feelings were much different more than 1,000 kilometres to the east in the quiet lumbering communities of the St. Croix Valley, including St. Stephen and Milltown, New Brunswick, and Calais and Milltown, Maine. There people never saw such violence during a war that so clearly defined the development of an Anglocentric identity in Upper Canada (later Ontario). Located along the winding and relatively isolated St. Croix River, these towns remained at peace throughout the conflict; in fact, one local legend states that the good people of St. Stephen saw so little use for their gunpowder magazine that they gave the entire cache to their neighbours in Calais, who used it to make Fourth of July fireworks.[2]

By the outbreak of a new and very different kind of war in 1914, decades of transnational social, cultural, and economic integration had led to the emergence of a distinct border-crossing culture in the St. Croix Valley. This did not mean that locals dismissed their affiliation with the national community, but it did affect how they approached traditionally national events and how they reflected on government policies that directly or indirectly affected the region's border-crossing culture.

The first people to visit the St. Croix Valley – long before it was known as such – were the Passamaquoddy Aboriginal people, who engaged in a friendly trade network with the nearby Maliseet of the Saint John Valley and the Penobscot of present-day Maine.[3] According to historian Harold Davis, this was a quiet region where hunters and fishermen passed through rather than populated the environs. This was also the case when Europeans first arrived in 1604: that year the French under Pierre du Gua, Sieur de Monts, and Samuel de Champlain made a brazen and rather foolish attempt to establish a settlement on nearby St. Croix Island, where the St. Croix River meets the Bay of Fundy. When winter set in, wicked winds whipped across the island and froze the settlers' supplies in the storehouse. Inevitably, scurvy and starvation took many lives. Eventually, the crew withdrew to the Annapolis Basin across the great bay, where they established Port Royal in 1605.[4] With the exception of a few travelling French missionaries, it would be more than a century and a half before Europeans again spent substantial time in the quiet forests lining the majestic and peaceful St. Croix River.[5]

Following the Revolutionary War, however, this region proved to be a haven for Loyalists and Patriots alike. The founders of both St. Stephen and Calais hailed from various parts of New England, though many of St. Stephen's first settlers had sided with the Crown, Calais pioneers with the revolutionaries. But political ideology had little bearing on the relationship that emerged between those who settled at the head of the tidewater along the St. Croix River. In day-to-day life, residents of Calais and St. Stephen shared similar occupations, with farming and lumbering emerging as the primary concerns of Americans and Canadians alike.[6]

Over the next few decades, sawmills were built among, and more farms carved out of, the dense forest lining the meandering river.[7] Lumbering was the primary industry, and cut timber entered both the British and the American markets.[8] Initially, those settling on the British side of the line fared better, primarily because the British colonial government in Nova Scotia was willing to offer 100-acre land grants to Loyalists.[9] In contrast, in the late 1780s, Calais pioneers became entangled in land negotiations with wealthy merchants who bought up the surrounding townships. The legal wrangling that followed forced many Calais residents to pay high prices for the lands that they had held for years and probably delayed the development of the surrounding environs.[10]

From the beginning, relations between Loyalist residents of St. Stephen and Americans of Calais were amicable. The first store in the area, built in the late 1780s, was located on the Calais side, not far from where the Ferry Point Bridge connects the two communities today. Residents of both towns purchased goods from the store and paid in kind before the development of a recognized monetary system.[11] (Even when distinct currencies did emerge in the early nineteenth century, the banks and businesses of the St. Croix Valley accepted both Canadian and American currency. Such a tradition continued into the First World War era.[12]) Customs duty was a foreign idea to residents of Calais and

St. Stephen at this time, and lumberjacks from both sides of the St. Croix River cut timber without paying heed to the boundary. Not even rising tensions between Britain and the United States affected this perspective; locals ignored both governments' insistence that cross-border trade be terminated shortly before and during the War of 1812.[13] By 1820, there were more than forty sawmills operating along the river, twenty on each side. These mills often used the river to transport materials and were so tightly packed together that it was often hard to tell if the timber was located in British or American territory.[14]

The War of 1812 had little impact on the quiet lumbering communities of St. Stephen and Calais. This was the result of regional factors; although New Englanders were upset with Britain's policy of naval impressment, many were not prepared to go to war over the issue.[15] The continuation of a vibrant cross-border economy – even when the British and American governments discouraged such activity – was a key factor in shaping northeastern attitudes toward the international frontier. Beyond economics, the people of this region shared similar ethnicities: most were English-speaking Protestants descended from New England stock. So opposed to war were New Englanders that, following setbacks for the American army at Detroit and Queenston Heights in 1812, many states in this region threatened President James Madison with secession from the union.[16]

Along the St. Croix River, amity was maintained thanks to the diplomatic work of locals. Because the origins of the war had little to do with residents of the northeast, there was minimal interest in fighting among residents of New Brunswick (which became a British colony in 1784) or Maine (which became a US state in 1820). Residents of nearby St. Andrews, New Brunswick, and Eastport, Maine, met and agreed that no fighting would occur across the international boundary.[17] Farther up the river at Calais and St. Stephen, Reverend Duncan McColl preached peace in sermons to inhabitants of both communities, and by all accounts his efforts appear to have been successful in maintaining harmony.[18]

Although the War of 1812, for the most part, more directly impacted Americans and Canadians in other parts of the continent, the "Aroostook War" threatened to embroil this long-peaceful region in a new conflict in 1839. That year Maine authorities were alerted to the lumbering operations of approximately 350 New Brunswick men in the Aroostook Valley, a contested border zone roughly 250 kilometres from St. Stephen and Calais.[19] Eventually, both Maine and New Brunswick dispatched troops to the region, and for a time it looked as though the northeast would have its War of 1812 after all. Luckily, at the last moment, British and American officials reached a truce, and both sides committed to determining finally the exact location of the international boundary.[20] In the spring of 1842, Britain's representative in the matter, Lord Ashburton, left England for Washington. His counterpart was Secretary of State Daniel Webster. They met in June, concessions were made, and an agreement was arranged by early August. In the end, the Americans made out better than the British, acquiring 58 percent of the disputed territory.[21]

Relations between Calais and St. Stephen were not affected by the Aroostook War, primarily because the St. Croix River had long been established as the international boundary in this part of the New Brunswick–Maine frontier. In the St. Croix Valley, the conflict was popularly known as the "Bloodless Aroostook War," its only noticeable impact being Maine's decision to temporarily increase the number of militiamen stationed at Calais.[22]

Peace reigned in the St. Croix Valley until the mid-1860s, when Irish American nationalists known as the Fenians targeted British North America in an attempt to trade Canadian sovereignty for Irish independence. At one point, the rebels gathered there, planning to invade New Brunswick from American territory. However, the Fenians stationed in the northeast had less intestinal fortitude than their colleagues forming along the Niagara frontier.[23] Using Eastport, Maine, as a launching point, in mid-April the Fenians briefly landed on Indian Island in British territory. They charged the island's customs house and seized its Union Jack before triumphantly returning to Eastport.[24] In response, the British sent several naval vessels to the area in a demonstration of force that the Fenians had no hope of matching; their elation defused, the frustrated Irish dispersed and abandoned the international frontier for good.[25]

Early on, navigation between Calais and St. Stephen was limited to travel by boat during the summer and by foot across the frozen river in the winter. Because of the relative narrowness and slow current of the St. Croix, such passages were not particularly difficult, though eventually locals pressed for the construction of bridges across the waterway. The first was built in 1804 at Upper Mills, New Brunswick, and Baring, Maine, roughly eight kilometres from St. Stephen and Calais. As the populations of these communities increased, demands for a new bridge closer to home grew. Finally, in 1825, a bridge was constructed and linked the nearby Milltowns of New Brunswick and Maine, though because it was owned by private citizens crossing it was not free.[26] The same situation affected travel across the Ferry Point Bridge, linking downtown St. Stephen and Calais directly. This structure was completed in 1827, and for years the fee for crossing was one cent per pedestrian or three cents per carriage. In February 1894, the New Brunswick government and City of Calais jointly purchased the Ferry Point Bridge outright and waived the crossing fee. Locals on both sides of the river celebrated the event by blowing whistles, tolling church bells, lighting massive bonfires, and closing schools and businesses for the day.[27]

These bridges facilitated the advancement of an international economy along the St. Croix River between Calais and St. Stephen as well as the adjoining Milltowns. In the mid-nineteenth century, expansion of the local lumbering industry led to the development of equally successful shipbuilding operations along the boundary waterway. Although a number of shipbuilding firms were established at this time, few were as successful as that run by the Short family, which constructed vessels for the American and British markets in facilities on both sides of the river.[28] Between 1861 and 1878, the Shorts constructed thirty-five ships, twenty in St. Stephen and fifteen in Calais. Those built on the Canadian side were sold to Britain, whereas those completed on the American side made their way into the US market.[29] Technically, the Calais branch of the firm was known as Short Brothers, whereas the St. Stephen wing went by J. and C. Short. A number of Short siblings were involved in the family's operations at this time, and their residencies reflected the international character of their profession. Three of the brothers – Daniel, James, and Cornelius – lived in Calais, while John and Charles lived in St. Stephen.[30]

For generations, the basis of a border-crossing culture was the St. Croix River lumbering industry. Ironically, it gained momentum in the late eighteenth century precisely because the boundary was so permeable; both American and British residents profited from selling their lumber in the British market in the wake of the Revolutionary War. The people of the St. Croix Valley effectively exploited the boundary for their own benefit, using its liminality to their economic advantage. As time progressed and Britain and the United States clashed once again in the War of 1812, the international character of the St. Croix Valley only became more visible as the mighty lumbering industry grew to include a number of vibrant shipbuilding operations, like that run by the Short brothers.

But the good times would not last. Just as these communities shared the lumbering and shipbuilding boom of the post–Revolutionary War period, so too would they share the unhappy result of those industries' steady decline in the late nineteenth century. In this regard, St. Stephen and Calais shared the fate of many other communities in New Brunswick and Maine; by the 1870s, it was becoming apparent that the northeast's dependence on a select few industries – fishing, farming, and especially lumbering – would become a problem as the North American economy rapidly industrialized.[31]

Until the 1840s, New Brunswick's economy had depended largely on exchange with Britain: into the British market went New Brunswick timber and wooden vessels in exchange for British manufactured goods, such as china,

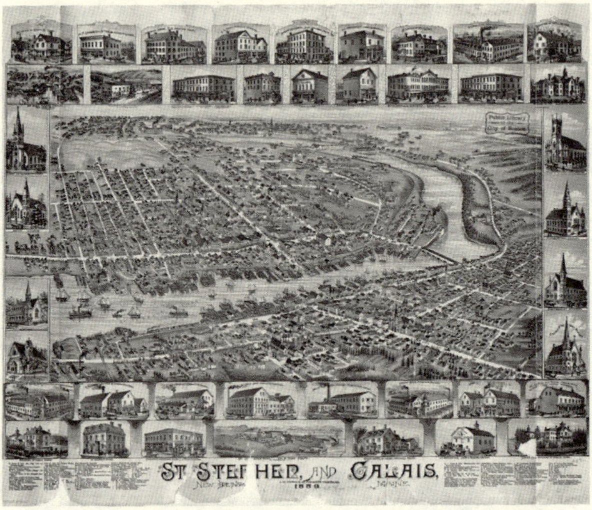

FIGURE 13 St. Stephen and Calais, still booming places in 1889, when this map was produced. *Source:* "St. Stephen, New Brunswick and Calais, Maine: 1889," L.W. McAnn, Boston Public Library, https://www.digitalcommonwealth.org/search/commonwealth:wd376126c.

silver, furniture, and textiles. In the early nineteenth century, between two-thirds and three-quarters of New Brunswick's exports went to Britain and other colonies within the empire.[32] That changed considerably with Britain's decision to dismantle preferential trade with its colonies in favour of free trade.[33] For a time, disaster appeared to be on the horizon for New Brunswick's economy with the loss of this guaranteed market. The solution for New Brunswick – indeed for all of British North America in the 1850s – was reciprocity with the United States. Between 1854 and 1866, the United States became an important trading partner for New Brunswick, with roughly one-third of all exports going south of the border.[34]

Generally speaking, the period between 1850 and 1880 marked a high point for the economies of New Brunswick and Maine. Timber cut and ships built in the region entered both British and American markets. It was a "wood-wind-sail" economy that depended heavily on exports far more than other parts of the continent, particularly the comparably self-sufficient United Province of Canada.[35] In 1861, 76.4 percent of all New Brunswick exports were forest products.[36] Unfortunately, this made the province extremely vulnerable to fluctuations in world markets. The American abrogation of the reciprocity agreement in 1866 reduced the demand for lumber and wooden sailing vessels south of the boundary, while demand for such goods in Britain remained low since it continued to pursue free trade.

Complicating this dependence on international trade was reliance on a single export commodity, timber and related products, which in the late nineteenth century saw demand reduced dramatically by the advent of steel steamships. Even though New Brunswick's dependence on forestry did not change in the period that followed, the market for such goods did. In the 1880s, the demand for New Brunswick timber in the British market declined substantially as steam and steel ships – faster, safer, and capable of carrying larger cargoes – appeared on world trade routes.[37]

Making this transition more difficult was the greater appeal of central and western Canada as sites of agricultural development in the late nineteenth century. Compared with central Canada, the American Midwest, and the western plains and prairies, both Maine and New Brunswick featured less arable land and shorter growing seasons.[38] The result was population growth that remained far behind the rest of North America.[39] This only compounded the problem of the economic stagnation in the Maritimes in the late nineteenth century because the lack of nearby urban markets kept agricultural incomes low.[40] Furthermore, population growth in central Canada and the American Midwest provided the capital required to expand the wider region's nascent transportation networks. Put simply, by the outbreak of war in 1914, it was much easier and much cheaper to ship goods into the rapidly developing west from central Canada and the American Midwest than the increasingly isolated northeast.[41] In New Brunswick, these factors reduced the province's influence on the federal government, further limiting the chances for recovery.[42]

In St. Stephen and Calais, decline of the shipbuilding industry had lasting economic as well as cultural impacts on local residents. In the mid-nineteenth century, when ships and lumber packed the St. Croix River between the towns, hopes for local development were high. People arrived in search of work at either the shipyards or the lumber camps a few miles into the surrounding forest. In exchange for St. Croix lumber, ships carrying West Indies fruit, British china and beer, German woolen textiles, and French wine docked at both St. Stephen and Calais. By 1860, this vibrant economic activity supported a local population of about 13,500, with roughly 7,500 living on the Canadian side (including St. Stephen and Milltown, New Brunswick) and another 6,000 on the American side (including Calais and Milltown, Maine). At the time, it appeared that the lumber boom would see expansion of the wider region in the ensuing years, and in 1875 local reverend and historian Isaac Knowlton predicted that together the two American and two Canadian border communities would one day become the singular "Queen City of the East."[43]

But by the beginning of a new century, the total number of people living along the St. Croix River had not increased substantially since the American Civil War. Many of the reasons for economic decay in the Maritimes at this time apply to St. Stephen and Calais, though a few factors were specific to the St. Croix Valley region. First, termination of the reciprocity agreement in 1866 had an adverse effect on the local economy.[44] Second, extensive lumber cutting in the region since the Revolutionary War drastically reduced the number of tall trees, meaning that, even if wooden shipbuilding had remained active in the Maritimes after 1900, it is unlikely that the St. Croix Valley would have factored prominently in it.[45] Third, extensive dumping of sawdust by local mills in the late nineteenth century resulted in mounting deposits along the bottom of the St. Croix River, preventing large trading vessels from easily reaching St. Stephen and Calais by the 1890s. Worse still, the dumping meant disaster for local fishermen, who eventually noticed that the pollution reduced the number of salmon headed upriver.[46] Finally, in 1905, a new pulp mill and dam completed at Woodland, Maine, further reduced the depth of the river as it reached St. Stephen and Calais, making shipbuilding virtually impossible.[47] During the centennial celebration of Calais in 1909, visitors remarked at how the sweet smell of pine lingered, even if the sight of grand sailing vessels launched into the river had become little more than a distant memory.[48] With fewer and fewer trading ships coming to the region, even the local lumbering industry reached its conclusion at this time, with most sawmills terminating production by the end of the First World War.[49]

Although in no way could they replace the shipbuilding and lumbering industries, a number of new and profitable businesses did emerge in the St. Croix Valley during the late nineteenth century. These industries, though considerably different in terms of resources used and markets targeted, were, like their predecessors, dependent on the permeability of the international boundary in this section of the northeast. Some were more successful than others, but all ignored citizenship when hiring employees.

One of the first transnational industries to emerge in the St. Croix Valley in the late nineteenth century was axe making, after the Massachusetts-owned Douglas Axe Manufacturing Company established a plant in St. Stephen in 1866. For nearly twenty years, the firm thrived in the region, primarily because it could sell its axes into either the British market or the American market and avoid having to pay duties on raw goods shipped from the United States for manufacturing in St. Stephen. However, the Canadian government's introduction of the National Policy in 1879 (which forced firms to pay heavy tariffs on products shipped across the boundary into Canada) had a hugely negative impact on the economic viability of the St. Stephen plant, and the Massachusetts owners sold the operation to a Saint John businessman in 1885.[50]

Although the National Policy reduced the number of raw goods crossing the border in the 1880s and afterward, there appears to have been no decline in the number of people who daily moved back and forth across the St. Croix River to work. Perhaps the best example of this cross-border traffic was seen after establishment of the Ganong chocolate company in 1873. Throughout the late nineteenth century and during the First World War, the St. Stephen–based Ganong plant employed hundreds of Calais residents.

James and Gilbert Ganong represented the driving force behind a candy empire that would flourish in the late nineteenth century. Born to a farmer in King's County, New Brunswick, in 1841 and 1851, respectively, James and Gilbert were brought up in an intensely devout Baptist family. When they set out to build careers for themselves, neither James nor Gilbert was particularly interested in farming or confectionary. After a brief stint as a jockey, James took a job as a travelling salesman.[51] Gilbert, in contrast, became a teacher with the hope of eventually entering medical school. Instead, in 1873 James convinced his younger brother to invest in a wholesale grocery business in St. Stephen.[52]

The business struggled early on, largely because people in St. Stephen and Calais were suspicious of outsiders like the Ganongs. Finding good help was also tough – luring men away from the profitable lumber camps and shipbuilding yards to help in a grocery store was nearly impossible.[53] But the Ganongs' biggest problem was the fact that, in the late nineteenth century, many men in the St. Croix Valley were paid in goods rather than in wages and received most of their supplies from a company store.[54] That left little cash to spend on the Ganongs' groceries, and since no one really knew the brothers there was little incentive to visit their establishment. There was one ray of sunshine, however, in an otherwise cloudy first few years along the St. Croix River: people gobbled up the candy made by the Ganongs, which they produced by combining the molasses, coconut, and sugar shipped to the region in the hulls of West Indies trading vessels.

Eventually, the candy proved to be just what the Ganongs needed to set themselves apart from other grocers in St. Stephen and Calais. Not only did the revenue from confectionary help their grocery store to survive, but also it gave the brothers the financial capital necessary to establish the St. Stephen–based St. Croix Soap Manufacturing Company in 1879. Five years later James and Gilbert dissolved their partnership, with James focusing on soap, Gilbert on candy.[55] The latter raised the stakes further by building a three-storey factory facing the St. Croix River in 1886.[56] To fill the plant with labourers, Gilbert looked beyond St. Stephen to Calais, hiring a number of Americans.[57]

Both Ganong enterprises were extremely successful in the years that followed. Over at the St. Croix Soap Manufacturing Company, James blended caustic soda, grease, and fat shipped from Australia and New Zealand to produce a highly effective laundry detergent.[58] Called Surprise Soap, the product proved to be so popular that James was able to make four additions to his company's Depot Street facility in the 1880s.[59] Business continued to boom thereafter despite his death from pneumonia in 1888.[60] Meanwhile, the 1891 census revealed that Ganong candies accounted for 7 percent of all confectionary produced in Canada. Profits were large enough that Gilbert was able to afford two rebuilding ventures after fires destroyed his plant in 1888 and again in 1903.[61] By this point, the total workforce had reached 200, and gross annual sales were $330,000.[62]

From the beginning, the Ganong operations were transnational. As they slowly expanded their confectionary enterprise in the mid-1870s, the Ganongs began both storing and selling candy across the border in Calais.[63] When they decided to use their candy capital to enter the soap market in 1879, additional funding came from Calais businessman James Picard.[64] The Ganongs' first candy producer was a Calais confectioner named J.Q. Gould; the Ganongs provided him with the necessary supplies, and he made the treats that became so popular among locals.[65] By the end of the First World War, Arthur Ganong (son of James) had 500 employees from both sides of the river, making his firm one of the largest candy businesses in the dominion.[66]

The Ganong company was not the only one in the St. Croix Valley that hired American labourers or depended on American capital for its survival. The St. Croix Cotton Mill was established in 1882 through the organizing efforts of a joint committee consisting of businessmen from both sides of the river and funding from a Rhode Island capitalist.[67] When the Providence-based investor requested that the organizing committee raise $30,000 to help with start-up costs, all four communities – Calais, St. Stephen, and the Milltowns – jumped into action. With the help of contributions from each town, the $30,000 was raised, and construction of the cotton mill began in June 1881.[68] The participation of Calais and Milltown, Maine, in paying for construction costs was contingent on the expectation that American residents of the St. Croix Valley would be employed in the mill once it was complete. They were not disappointed – by 1887, there were 650 workers at the St. Croix Cotton Mill, many of whom were American.[69] Although the plant suffered a number of financial setbacks and labour crises in the 1890s and early 1900s, during the First World War business boomed.[70]

Although the cross-border traffic of workers between Calais and St. Stephen in the late nineteenth century generally favoured Canadian plants and American labourers, a number of successful businesses operated on the US side of the river and employed New Brunswick residents. In 1893, the Maine and New Brunswick Granite Company was established in Calais by St. Stephen and Calais businessmen. The factory employed 200 men to polish granite mined from St. George, New Brunswick; the refined material was then used for various construction projects, notably New York City's Museum of Natural History in 1894.[71] The shoe factory in Calais also hired St. Stephen residents, who crossed the border on a daily basis.[72] Down the river at Eastport, Maine (forty kilometres from Calais), many St. Stephen residents worked at the local sardine canneries, often on a seasonal basis.[73]

Throughout the nineteenth century and in the early twentieth century, the governments of the United States and Canada allowed the frequent cross-border movement of workers among Calais, St. Stephen, and the surrounding communities. Historian Harold Davis notes that there was a constant fear in the late 1880s that the US government would investigate this activity and force St. Stephen and Calais business owners to respect the American alien labour laws.[74] Luckily, federal officials advised local collectors to treat the matter moderately, and the result was no apparent pressure on Canadian or American firms to hire from within their own borders exclusively.[75]

The St. Croix Valley's economic integration translated into deep social and cultural connections among St. Stephen, Calais, and the Milltowns. Local men joined fraternal organizations that not only welcomed members regardless of their citizenship but also attempted to maintain good relations between residents of St. Stephen and Calais. For example, the Orphan's Friend Lodge, established in 1809, held meetings on both sides of the river during the War of 1812 in an attempt to maintain harmony along the border.[76] They were greatly aided in this endeavour by Reverend Duncan McColl, who preached peace throughout the area. In the ensuing years, the construction of new bridges facilitated greater social integration. Many local merchants imported goods across the border and rarely faced heavy customs duties; in fact, it is said that customs officers stationed there in the late nineteenth century and early 1900s held unlimited credit at local stores as a kickback for overlooking the region's rampant smuggling operations.[77] Although their textbooks and curricula varied – with the emphasis in New Brunswick and Maine institutions being British and American society, respectively – St. Stephen residents often attended Calais schools and vice versa.[78] In the late nineteenth century, the communities regularly engaged in athletic activities with one another, and national events and holidays – such as Queen Victoria's Diamond Jubilee in June

FIGURE 14 St. Stephen's Water Street in 1906. Known as Milltown Boulevard today, the street runs parallel to the St. Croix River. Before and during the First World War, it was the site of many parades, some of which ran seamlessly across the international boundary and into downtown Calais. *Source:* Provincial Archives of New Brunswick, Isaac Erb Fonds, P11–105.

1897 or the Fourth of July – became international celebrations.[79] Calais and St. Stephen even shared the same city directory (published by E.H. McAllister and Sons in Calais) in the late nineteenth century and just prior to the First World War.[80] All of this interaction fostered plenty of romances between men and women from the adjacent communities; Calais marriage records show that nearly one in ten marriages in the 1890s involved a resident of Calais marrying a person from St. Stephen or Milltown, New Brunswick. During the decade encompassing the First World War (1910–19), approximately 17 percent of all marriages recorded in Calais were of the transnational variety.[81]

When they built a home for themselves, chances were that these couples depended on a foreign company for at least one of their basic utilities. In the mid-nineteenth century, a central water system was established by the Calais Water Company. However, pollution by a local pulp and paper mill forced area residents to look for an alternative water source, which they found at Maxwell's Crossing not far from St. Stephen. The spring water was pumped to all of the surrounding communities, including Calais and Milltown, Maine.[82] In the twilight years of the nineteenth century, homes in the St. Croix Valley were powered by electricity distributed by the St. Croix Gas and Light Company of Calais.[83]

In an emergency, St. Stephen and Calais residents could contact one another through a shared telephone exchange, first established in 1894. (Unfortunately, the service was wracked with problems, and it remained easier to simply walk across one of the three adjoining bridges in order to chat with a friend or family member.[84]) In the case of a fire, St. Croix Valley residents could summon help from any or all of the surrounding fire departments, automatically alerted when a blaze occurred. If it was a particularly serious fire, then people would seek safety across the river, the bridges temporarily waiving their tolls.[85] If someone was hurt in such a blaze (or any other kind of accident, for that matter), then chances were that he or she would be cared for at St. Stephen's Chipman Memorial Hospital. Established in 1902, it was considered the region's best health-care facility and attracted both patients and medical professionals from Calais.[86]

The daily movement of people across the dividing St. Croix River for work and pleasure remained a prominent part of local culture during the period leading up to the First World War. In a transnational border region where the vast majority of Canadians and Americans were born in the state and province in which they lived – and where immigration from Europe was virtually nil – the focus of St. Croix Valley residents was on this permeable section of the Canada–US boundary.[87]

But the war would place new pressures on this international community. First, the United States would remain neutral for the first three years of the war, while Canada diligently sent its young men to face the enemy in late 1914. This led many St. Stephen boys to join the colours while Calais residents looked on with a mixture of skepticism and fascination. As the next chapter demonstrates, sometimes this combination manifested itself in criticisms of the war and Canada's participation in it.[88] But the residents of Calais ultimately threw their support behind the Allies because of their deep social connections to St. Stephen and Milltown, New Brunswick.

3

The "Ties that Bind"

Relations between St. Stephen and Calais

As spring turned to summer along the St. Croix River in 1914, the focus of locals was not on troubles abroad in Europe but on planning a grand celebration of 100 years of peace among Canada, Britain, and the United States. Since 1911, representatives from all three countries had been working together to commemorate the occasion with a series of events along the Canada–US border. Known as the Anglo-American Peace Centenary, the celebration involved the construction and erection of monuments across the three countries. But there were also plans for what St. Stephen's newspaper, the *Saint Croix Courier,* described as "educational propaganda" – teaching local schoolchildren about the border's history and mostly harmonious Canadian-American relations. "The most important feature of the celebration will be its educational side," the *Courier* noted. "The peace of the next hundred years will depend upon the children in our schools to-day."[1]

As a major border-crossing point in the northeast, the Ferry Point Bridge linking Calais and St. Stephen appeared to be the best site for a monument celebrating a century of peace between the United States and Canada. St. Stephen's newspaper hoped that the memorial would be something grand. "Ferry Point bridge is the artery through which flows the life of the two communities during the passing years, and a grand arch spanning the bridge and resting on piers at either side would be an impressive and enduring reminder of the event celebrated," the *Courier* noted.[2] The newspaper embraced the idea of making Ferry Point the site of a major peace memorial because, after all, relations between the people of Calais and St. Stephen had remained harmonious even as war afflicted other parts of the continent in 1812.[3]

This attachment to a regional and, in the case of the St. Croix Valley, transnational identity was visible as residents of St. Stephen, Calais, and the Milltowns turned their attention to celebrating Dominion Day and the Fourth of July in 1914. Although both were officially national holidays, in St. Stephen and Calais they were equally celebrated by Canadians and Americans.[4] On Dominion Day, residents of Calais and St. Stephen lined up in the latter town for a parade that slowly made its way through all of the neighbouring communities. Leading the revellers across the St. Croix River was the Calais City Band, followed by local mayors, councillors, and visiting dignitaries. Residents of both

FIGURE 15 Horse racing was wildly popular in the St. Croix Valley before and during the First World War. Events like this one, held in Calais in 1912, drew attendees from both sides of the international boundary. *Source:* St. Croix Historical Society.

communities built floats for the parade, which wound up in St. Stephen in the afternoon and was followed by foot races, horse races, and a baseball game between Milltown, Maine, and St. Stephen.[5] Several days later similar events – including baseball games between St. Stephen and Milltown, Maine, and Calais and Milltown, New Brunswick – occurred in Calais for that community's Fourth of July celebration.[6]

News involving these communities dominated the pages of the local newspaper, the fiercely pro-Conservative *Saint Croix Courier.*[7] Rarely did events from outside the immediate region – such as the assassination of Austrian Archduke Franz Ferdinand in June 1914 – arouse much attention. That week it was the death of a prominent local politician and businessman, George A. Murchie, that had a clear impact on residents of the St. Croix Valley. Born in St. Stephen in 1849, Murchie moved as a young man across the river to Calais, where he became an alderman and was then elected mayor in 1892. During his four-year mayoral tenure, Murchie fought hard for the purchase by Calais of the Ferry Point Bridge, which put an end to toll payments by locals.[8] After his term as mayor, Murchie went on to serve in the state senate. He also figured prominently in the regional lumber industry, owning and overseeing operations in both New Brunswick and Maine.[9] For these reasons, his death was felt throughout the St. Croix Valley, and coverage of his passing dominated the Calais newspaper, the *Advertiser,* on July 1. In contrast, Archduke Ferdinand's assassination was relegated to a small section in the bottom right corner of the newspaper's first page.[10] In St. Stephen, the *Courier* was even more apathetic about events in the Balkans, wedging its article on Ferdinand's assassination between a page 7 story on dandruff prevention and another relating the health benefits of eating eggs.[11]

It would be more than a month before either of these publications speculated that Europe's political troubles – partly resulting from the archduke's death – would lead to war between the world's greatest imperial powers.[12] Even when Britain finally declared war on August 4, bringing Canada into the fray, the bulk of the *Courier*'s content remained focused on local events, including a highly anticipated baseball game between Calais and St. Stephen and the Charlotte County Sunday School Convention.[13] News of Canada's contribution to the fighting, including an estimated 20,000 troops to be sent overseas, was relegated to page 3.[14]

Although the *Courier*'s editor threw his support behind Conservative Party Prime Minister Robert Borden and, unlike Windsor's *Evening Record*, immediately expressed support for the notion of protecting the mother country in its time of need, it appears that the vast majority of Canadians living in the St. Croix Valley had only a marginal interest in the war overseas.[15] Aside from Reverend E.B. Wyllie's sermon "War" in the local Presbyterian church, there is little evidence to suggest that the conflict was a popular topic of discussion in the days following August 4. Members of the local Roman Catholic and Methodist churches went ahead with plans to picnic at nearby Oak Bay, New Brunswick; the ball game between Milltown, Maine, and Milltown, New Brunswick, was played out as scheduled; and the Calais City Band crossed the boundary to play a concert at St. Andrews.[16] And unlike Windsor residents, the people of St. Stephen do not appear to have rushed into the streets to celebrate the declaration of war, nor did they bombard local recruiting offices – in those first two weeks, enlistments were slow but steady, with thirty-two men from St. Stephen and seven from Milltown joining the cause.[17]

Canadians in the St. Croix Valley were also slow to contribute financially to the war effort. At an early meeting to discuss raising funds for the newly formed Canadian Patriotic Fund, which would provide soldiers' dependants with financial support while breadwinners were fighting overseas, organizers lamented that residents of St. Stephen appeared to care little about defending the British Empire in its time of need.[18] Reverend Wyllie emphasized that Canadians had a duty to defend their country and their empire but bemoaned the fact that, in his opinion, residents of the St. Croix Valley had failed to take the matter as seriously as they should. "It is the duty of the young men to go to the front," the *Courier* reported Wyllie as saying. "They should all give up their pleasures and be out drilling. We may not have to shoulder guns but we should be ready. Our first duty is to the flag and if it is worth living under, it is worth fighting for."[19]

Others criticized the St. Stephen Town Council for failing to set an example by providing a satisfactory contribution to patriotic organizations. Whereas other municipalities in Charlotte County had already begun such fundraising by September, in St. Stephen neither the mayor nor his councillors had organized a committee capable of collecting financial contributions. Business leader Gilbert Ganong chastised the local council for failing to establish such a fund. "This town and county should raise $5,000 to $10,000 for this fund, on the basis of its assessed valuation," Ganong said. "It is time the town was taking some action instead of waiting until the war is over."[20] The *Courier*'s editor supported this criticism of the local council, noting that, "while this community is rich in many things, it is poor in leadership."[21] Although Mayor of St. Stephen William Dinsmore reacted to this pressure by establishing a local account for contributions to be forwarded to the national CPF, his council contributed just $1,000 in October 1914 – far short of the donation earlier proposed by Ganong.[22]

It is not clear why some residents of St. Stephen were slow to get behind the war effort. Their reluctance might have been the result of the region's lack of immigration from Britain – with most of Canada's early recruits hailing from the British Isles, an almost total absence of St. Croix Valley residents born and bred in England, Wales, Ireland, or Scotland likely affected how they saw the conflict.[23] However, St. Stephen's slow response to the war might also have been the result of its relationship with its American neighbour, Calais. Across the St. Croix River, the *Calais Advertiser* wholeheartedly adopted President Woodrow Wilson's policy of neutrality, a position that led the *Advertiser* to criticize not only the war but also those who embraced it.

Like the *Saint Croix Courier*, the *Calais Advertiser* did not immediately suspect that the assassination of Ferdinand would lead to a global conflict. A month later it deduced that the disagreement between Serbia and Austria-Hungary could balloon into war but expected that the fighting would be limited to the Balkans. A few days later all of that had changed; with Germany, Russia, France, and Britain involved, the *Advertiser* speculated that the war would become a "world-changing" event. "You will have to learn your geography over as soon as its treaty of peace is signed," the newspaper insisted. "If England loses, India and her colonial empire goes. Russia would be relegated to a third rate power. France would be hopelessly crippled in the race of nations."[24]

As the war moved into high gear by late August 1914, the *Advertiser* provided its readers with a steady diet of news from the front. As in many American newspapers, including the *Detroit News, Detroit Free Press,* and *Blaine Journal,* these stories were distinctly neutral in tone.[25] The *Advertiser* also provided some startling criticisms of the war, suggesting that it would cost Canada $90 million to keep a force of 50,000 men under arms and predicting that all of the belligerents together could expect to spend roughly $20 billion on the conflict.[26]

Like newspapers in Detroit, the *Advertiser* also offered a less optimistic forecast of how long the war would last. Although many Canadians hoped that the conflict would be over by Christmas 1914, the *Advertiser* believed that it would continue well into the following year.[27] When such a prediction proved to be accurate, the *Advertiser* raised its criticism to ridicule not only the war's economic cost but also its human toll. "Thousands of soldiers have received iron crosses," the *Advertiser* noted in April 1915, "but hundreds of thousands have had to be content with crosses made of wood."[28]

Early on, the attachment of Calais to the official US policy of neutrality does not appear to have aroused anger in St. Stephen, where the first period of the war had only a limited impact on the Canadian border community. Casualties for the nation's first contingent – which did not reach the front lines until February – were relatively light until late spring 1915.[29]

But Canada's participation in the Second Battle of Ypres in April changed how St. Stephen residents perceived the conflict, their role in it, and their opinion of US neutrality. For the first time, the Canadian Expeditionary Force encountered stiff resistance from the Germans, as revealed in letters home by St. Stephen soldiers. "I suppose you have read all about the big battle," wrote Private Harry Bonnell in a letter to his mother later published in the *Saint Croix Courier*. "It was long and very nerve-breaking, the shelling was terrific, the asphyxiating gas terrible, and I thought my days were numbered ... If we ever get a chance at the Germans again we will hand them some hot dope to pay for our men who are lost."[30] Although word of the first St. Stephen soldier's death in battle would not reach the community until June, events at Ypres changed the public's perception of the conflict and led to friction between residents of the Canadian border community and the people of Calais.[31]

New tensions were revealed in May 1915 when the *Advertiser* aroused anger in St. Stephen after it suggested that recruits departing from the Canadian town for training in Saint John were undersized and underaged for the physical demands of warfare. "We had always thought [of] the British soldier as a big stalwart fighting machine, but when we saw the volunteers who left St. Stephen ... we couldn't help thinking why don't the big fellows enlist?" The *Advertiser* correspondent then added that "none of these seems to have enlisted, to judge by the size of the kids just departed."[32] When the comment spread through St. Stephen, the *Courier* responded by passionately defending its local recruits. "There are not many of their critics who would stand much show

FIGURE 16 The 55th Battalion departing from Charlotte County for the front in 1915. The *Calais Advertiser* aroused the anger of St. Stephen residents when it referred to the men who enlisted as "kids" and asked "why don't the big fellows enlist?" *Source:* Jonathan Vance.

with them in any trial of physical endurance," the *Courier* shot back, adding, "don't worry about those boys or the others serving under the colors, they are made of the right kind of stuff and will give good accounts of themselves."[33]

For months, the *Advertiser*'s remark stirred animosity. With the *Saint Croix Courier* circulated among the men in the trenches and training overseas, even St. Stephen soldiers stationed in England and France learned of the controversial comment. One St. Stephen soldier, Sergeant Christopher McKay, decided to weigh in on the subject in late June from Shornecliffe, England, his letter being published in the *Courier* on July 15. Clearly bothered by the *Advertiser*'s "kids" quip, McKay took aim at the Calais newspaper:

> Say, if that correspondent of the Advertiser only knew what the world thinks of the stand that the United States is taking he would not say a word about the so called "kids" of the 55th battalion. They may be kids but when they are called to do a man's work it shows that they are not afraid of the job.

McKay then focused on US neutrality, which he thought was far more shameful than the recruiting of a few (allegedly) undersized or underaged Canadians: "I have talked with a number of Americans, one of whom served seventeen years in the United States army, and they are all disgusted with their own country."[34]

Together McKay's letter and the *Courier*'s editorials (presumably accompanied by some testy words shared in private conversations) prompted the *Advertiser* to offer this explanation in late July 1915: "The fact is we used the term 'Kids' more in a spirit of admiration than of derision, just as some of the greatest pugilists have been called kid this and [kid] that." The *Advertiser* also noted that the people of St. Stephen had become "so touchy" about "anything pertaining to Canada," to the point that "one must guard one's words."[35]

Indeed, by the summer of 1915, residents of St. Stephen had become quite sensitive about their role in the ongoing international conflict. The war had not ended in late 1914, as many had expected, and as it became clear that the hostilities would not soon end pressure on locals to take the conflict more seriously grew. As spring turned to summer in 1915, both the *Courier* and Reverend Wyllie pressed men to enlist in separate forums – the newspaper in its editorials, Wyllie in sermons throughout Charlotte County.[36] Finally, in June, it appeared that the pressure was starting to have an impact on the once intransigent young men. After announcing the enlistment of thirteen new recruits, the *Courier* noted that it expected that "the number will be considerably augmented in a few days, as the young men and the mothers are beginning to more fully understand the stress that is upon the nation and the need of men."[37] In the same issue, the *Courier* ratcheted up its pressure by taking aim at St. Stephen women: "Is your 'Best Boy' wearing Khaki? If not, don't *you think* he should be?"[38]

Two weeks later the true cost of the war hit home when St. Stephen received word of its first man killed in action. Chester McLaughlin, just nineteen years old when he enlisted in late 1914, had followed his father and uncle into the CEF. "Private McLaughlin has paid the full price of his devotion to King and country," the *Courier* solemnly noted on June 17, 1915. "He saw his duty and he did it nobly and in his death he has done honor to his family and to his town. The liberties that we hold dear are that much more secured to us by the sacrifice that he has made."[39]

It was also during the summer of 1915 that the *Saint Croix Courier* began publishing letters from St. Stephen recruits stationed overseas. Starting with Private Bonnell's note in May, the *Courier* published several letters during the war's remaining years. In most cases, the letters reassured friends and family back home that their authors were alive and well. However, in some cases, these soldiers offered their opinions of events back home, including young men not yet in uniform.

After receiving a letter outlining recent bowling games played in the St. Croix Valley, Sergeant Christopher McKay, training on Salisbury Plain in January 1915, wrote that

> now I would sure like to come in and roll a few strings, but at present I have something to do that is needed more than bowling. Some day I will come and show you all up in hitting the pins, but just leave it to us to make strikes and spurs in the little game we are playing now, because I believe that the boys here all mean business and they will give a fine account of themselves before they get home.[40]

Writing from Belgium in August 1915, Private Archie Connolly had little patience for young men who refused to enlist. "Every man in Canada, who should come here and doesn't do so, is, in my estimation, purely and simply a coward," Connolly wrote.[41] Lance Corporal Fred Clark was equally critical of the men who stayed at home: "Just tell the boys around there to forget the movie shows and ball games and put on a nice new khaki suit and they will get a free ticket to England and France where they will get lots to eat of the best English beef, potatoes, soup, puddings, tea and coffee."[42]

Combined pressure from local preachers, newspaper editors, and soldiers already abroad had an indirect impact on the border-crossing culture of the St. Croix Valley. Activities and events that had been shared for generations among the American and Canadian communities of this region underwent significant changes as residents of St. Stephen and Milltown, New Brunswick, shifted their focus from peacetime pastimes such as baseball and holiday parades to winning the war. In July 1915, Dominion Day festivities were almost cancelled in St. Stephen after several members of council suggested that it would be in poor taste to hold a full day of events while some of the community's young men were fighting a life-and-death struggle in the trenches overseas.[43] Only when Mayor Parker Grimmer insisted that the day's events feature a baseball game, horse racing, and band concerts did the celebration include more than just patriotic addresses by prominent members of the local community.[44]

Three weeks later this kind of pressure led to outright cancellation of the St. Croix Baseball League, which for several years had featured clubs from the four St. Croix Valley communities: St. Stephen, Calais, and the Milltowns.[45] From that point forward, young men of military age were not quite told that they could not play baseball (exhibition games among all four towns continued to be played regularly), but there was no effort to raise the funds necessary for league play. The following spring, when Milltown, Maine, ball players attempted to revive the league, they were met with disappointment for reasons summed up by the *Saint Croix Courier:* "On this side [of] the line it is not likely that much will be heard of senior baseball 'till the boys come home. Then St. Stephen will be heard from with a big noise."[46] For the remainder of the war, the only organized baseball league in the St. Croix Valley featured teenaged boys too young to enlist.[47]

Intensification of the war also brought out somewhat dormant attachments to the British Empire in St. Stephen and Milltown, New Brunswick, communities that, prior to the war, had demonstrated only mild interest in their imperial connection. This had been something of a tradition; according to the *Saint Croix Courier*, in May 1886 there was "no great demonstration" of the queen's birthday, with the celebration amounting to little more than a short concert by a local band.[48] By 1914, things had hardly changed, the *Courier* noting that the day had passed "with no particular observance in the border towns."[49] This was again the situation in May 1915, with most locals leaving town rather than staying to remember their dead queen.[50]

But there was a dramatic change in local attitudes toward the holiday in May 1916. Along with a day commemorating the second anniversary of the war, Victoria Day was the year's biggest celebration, with troops visiting St. Stephen from New Brunswick centres Fredericton, St. Andrews, and Woodstock.[51] Some of these soldiers attended the day's exercises at the local schools, giving each program "a touch of reality," according to the *Courier*.[52] It was an affair "all for the soldier boys," the *Courier* noted, with the holiday's main event being a concert and ball organized to raise money for the local Red Cross.[53]

Revival of the British connection was not visible only on holidays, however; instead, for locals, defending the empire became a way to justify making great sacrifices in the ongoing struggle. When St. Stephen resident Augustus Cameron learned of the death of his son Morton at the front, he told the *Courier* that he remained confident that the Allies would win the war "in the old British form."[54] At a dinner held by the St. Stephen Retail Merchants Association in June, members toasted the king, pledging their devotion "not only ... to the person of the sovereign, but to the principles for which he stands."[55] In a December retrospective on the challenging year, the *Courier* made known its feelings, in a characteristically sentimental editorial, about defending the empire: "What a favoured land we live in ... Generation after generation have grown up within her confines and … known naught of the rude alarms of war because Britain's might protected her."[56] There were also several clubs in St. Stephen and Milltown that celebrated the British connection at this time, in particular the Women's Canadian Club, the St. Andrews Society, and the Over-Seas Club (organized in 1915 to "promote the unity of British subjects the world over," with membership limited to subjects of the empire).[57]

The emergence of a pro-British identity in St. Stephen by mid-1915 was accompanied by a growing interest in the military. The community's budding martial spirit was on display in early August during a commemoration of the second anniversary of the war. Only enlisted soldiers were invited to participate in the day's festivities, which included a parade led by members of Fredericton's

236th Kiltie Battalion, Woodstock's 65th Battery, and St. Andrews's 4th Pioneer Battalion. In the afternoon, troops from these units engaged in a baseball game at St. Stephen's diamond, followed by a series of horse races at the local trotting park. But it was the martial events that caught the attention of locals. Local and visiting troops participated in a boots and puttees race, a bayonet exercise, a skirmish demonstration, and a tent-pitching contest. As the athletic events wound down in the late afternoon, donations of cash for the soldiers were collected while the women of St. Stephen's Red Cross Society prepared a meal for the troops in the evening.[58]

Calais and Milltown, Maine, residents probably attended these events in St. Stephen – they received ample attention in the *Calais Advertiser* – but unlike in previous years they were not a central part of them.[59] By the summer of 1916, US neutrality was the subject of regular derision in the pages of the *Saint Croix Courier* and likely ruffled a few feathers on the American side of the line. Criticism started with the sinking of the *RMS Lusitania* in May 1915, when the *Courier*'s editor expressed disappointment with President Wilson's decision to maintain his nation's neutrality. After Wilson was reported to have spent the days following the ship's torpedoing by a German U-boat motoring and golfing, the *Courier* suggested that the US commander-in-chief was out of touch with American sentiment on the war.[60] Across the St. Croix River in Calais, the *Advertiser* offered no editorial on the subject of the *Lusitania* and over the next several months affirmed its commitment to neutrality by suggesting that, if America were to join the war, it would lead to economic ruin.[61]

Ultimately, however, neither the debate over American neutrality nor the emergence of an imperial identity in St. Stephen and Milltown, New Brunswick, led to the eradication of a transnational identity in the St. Croix Valley. True, the war's length coupled with rising casualties resulted in an adjustment of traditional events and activities that for years had been key parts of this region's border-crossing culture, but for the most part the communities adapted to these changes. The *Courier*'s attacks on US neutrality and the *Advertiser*'s "kids" comment represented exceptions to the rule – the people of Calais appear to have been very sensitive to the situation affecting the people of St. Stephen and Milltown, from the beginning of the conflict in August 1914 to the Americans' own declaration of war in April 1917 and beyond.

On a number of occasions following the British declaration of war, the *Advertiser* and residents of Calais also threw substantial moral support behind Canadian friends and family across the St. Croix River in St. Stephen and Milltown. Shortly after the war began, an inebriated German found screaming "hail the emperor!" in downtown Calais had his face lit up by a barrage of tomatoes.[62] The Calais City Band provided music for patriotic fundraising

FIGURE 17 The 55th Battalion entraining at the St. Stephen railway station in May 1915. Several thousand residents of Calais – visible in the background to the left – attended the send-off. *Source:* Provincial Archives of New Brunswick, Charlotte County Historical Society Collection, P128–69.

concerts and recruiting drives during the war's early stages in the fall of 1914, and the *Calais Advertiser* saw this as evidence that the people of the American border town were behind St. Stephen and Milltown.[63]

Calais residents also showed their support for the Allies by contributing money to various Canadian patriotic fundraising campaigns during the early stages of the war, including a drive to raise $100 for the purchase of two beds to be used in the Duchess of Connaught Hospital in France. The St. Stephen Red Cross Society reached its goal with great help from the people of Calais, including one American woman who contributed fifty dollars.[64] In November 1914, members of the Calais Tennis Association held a bridge party to raise money for the Belgian Relief Fund, established to purchase food and other supplies for occupied Belgium.[65] A month later the Calais Baptist Church contributed $106 to the same fund.[66]

Calais residents also made substantial contributions to the CPF after St. Stephen organized a local branch in October 1914. In a letter to the *Courier* outlining why he decided to contribute to the CPF, a Harvard University professor and former Calais resident said that he wanted his donation to be used "for hospital relief or whatever will give most aid to my friends and neighbors of St. Stephen in the field ... or families left at home."[67] Calais women also contributed to the Allied war effort during the period of American neutrality, with some joining St. Stephen's Women's Canadian Club, which throughout the period of fighting collected items desired by the soldiers overseas, including socks, handkerchiefs, tobacco, Ganong candy, pencils, and paper.[68] Finally, prior to the US entry into the war, Calais residents attended soldier send-offs to wave goodbye to their Canadian friends and family members heading off to fight the Germans. When members of New Brunswick's 55th Battalion departed from St. Stephen in May 1915, an estimated 4,000 locals attended the event, which reportedly included "a large contingent from Calais."[69]

The fact that a substantial number of Maine residents had joined the Canadian Expeditionary Force during the period of US neutrality contributed to the interest of residents of Calais in the events overseas.[70] Although the Calais newspaper continued to support American neutrality until President Wilson's decision to declare war in 1917, it condoned the movement of Maine men across the border to New Brunswick in order to join the Canadian army and specifically the American Legion.[71] After reminding its readers of the role played by Canadians in helping the Union Army win the American Civil War, the *Advertiser* suggested that those who joined the American Legion were not "mercenaries, nor soldiers of fortune," but "knights errant, offering their lives, without hope of distinction or emolument, for a cause which they believe to be the cause of America as well as of Great Britain, and in a supernational sense the cause of humanity and righteousness."[72] Beyond approving of American enlistment in the Canadian army, the *Advertiser* advertised patriotic fundraising events in St. Stephen and reported on the events affecting St. Croix Valley Canadians stationed overseas.[73] The *Advertiser* also followed recruiting in Charlotte County and periodically listed St. Stephen and Milltown, New Brunswick, men killed, missing, or wounded in action.[74]

Aside from termination of the St. Croix Baseball League, the American and Canadian communities of this region remained socially integrated as the war progressed. Transnational organizations such as the Oddfellows and Ladies Friendship Club, which included members from both sides of the boundary, continued to operate.[75] A religious integration reminiscent of Reverend Duncan McColl's early-nineteenth-century cross-border preaching endured, evidenced by the April 1916 exchange of pulpits by Dr. Ramsdell of Calais and Dr. Goucher of St. Stephen.[76] Blazes such as the October 1916 wood shop fire in St. Stephen or the May 1918 brush fire in Milltown, New Brunswick, continued to prompt a response from the fire departments of St. Stephen, Calais, and the Milltowns.[77] St. Stephen's Chipman Memorial Hospital remained the health-care facility of choice for all residents of the St. Croix Valley throughout the Great War era.[78] Even in death there were connections among these communities, as demonstrated by the funeral service for John G. Murchie, born in Milltown, New Brunswick, who spent time as the director of both the St. Stephen Bank and the Calais Tugboat Company. Passing away in January 1916, Murchie was buried in St. Stephen Cemetery, with Calais businesses closing so that locals could attend the funeral.[79]

Towns in the St. Croix Valley also remained economically entwined during the war years. When the retail trade lagged during the summer months, store owners in St. Stephen and Calais coordinated Thursday-afternoon closures so that neither community would have an unfair advantage.[80] The same retailers also accepted foreign currency at face value in 1916 – even though the Canadian dollar was worth less.[81] Finally, both Calais and St. Stephen businesses continued to advertise in the *Saint Croix Courier* and *Calais Advertiser,* just as they had done prior to the war.[82] In comparison, in White Rock, British Columbia, and Blaine, Washington, cross-border tensions led to a termination of this kind of advertising as the war progressed.

Even the divisive issue of neutrality faded into the background as the war progressed. In 1916, Americans faced a difficult choice: return Wilson and the Democrats to office or elect presidential candidate Charles Evan Hughes, whose main platform included a foreign policy shift toward "military preparedness." To many Americans, the decision was this: vote for Wilson and neutrality or vote for Hughes and war. As the campaign heated up that summer, several Democrats visited Calais. To their surprise, trumpeting Wilson's ability to maintain American neutrality failed to receive approval among their audiences. "One of the speakers enlarged on the fact that President Wilson had kept the United States 'out of the war,'" the *Courier* reported. "But it was noticeable to people from this side of the river who were in attendance that his glorification of this achievement was received in silence by his audience."[83] In the end, the people of Calais voted Republican.[84]

Perhaps, then, it is easy to understand why residents of St. Stephen and Milltown, New Brunswick, were so pleased to hear of the US entry into the increasingly desperate conflict in April 1917. When hosting the Maine convention of the Independent Order of Oddfellows – a fraternal organization designed to provide members with a social outlet as well as sickness and life insurance – on April 6, 1917, the Calais chapter invited Oddfellows from St. Stephen to participate.[85] While waiting for their dinner show to begin, both Maine and St. Stephen members broke into song, belting out "God Save the King," before offering "three lusty cheers for the Red, White and Blue."[86] Shortly thereafter, St. Stephen residents of all ages were invited to a children's festival at St. Croix Opera House in Calais, where young ones from both communities put on a show to raise money for patriotic purposes. The program included a solo dance by Elizabeth Miner (daughter of Mayor of Calais W.N. Miner), a recitation by St. Stephen's Barbara Vessie, and a procession of Allied flags, carried by the local Boy Scouts.[87] It was a fundraising effort, according to the *Saint Croix Courier,* designed to involve "children from both sides of the river, since the fund is to be sent from the children of the St. Croix Valley."[88]

The *Saint Croix Courier,* which had criticized for two years President Wilson's policy of neutrality, could hardly contain its pleasure in discussing the economic and military potential of the United States in April 1917. "Both branches of the US Congress approved of the principle of the measure giving the Government power to borrow $7,000,000,000 for carrying on the war against the Teutonic allies," the *Courier* noted. "Not even Great Britain has made such a single grant for the common cause. If the rest of the services required are conducted on a like scale and with like speed, the newest entrant into the great struggle will indeed be a factor of force in the final days."[89]

As the United States mobilized its armed forces during the summer of 1917, the *Courier* reflected on what fighting for a common cause would mean to Canadians, Americans, and residents of the St. Croix Valley. Referring to the US entry into the war as an occasion to celebrate "a renewal and a strengthening of the 'ties that bind,'" St. Stephen's newspaper suggested that "the longer the strife against a common foe the stronger will be cemented the tie between two peoples who have shown their worth, separated brethren for a century and a half but now in sentiment happily united to a common cause."[90]

After several years of supporting American neutrality, the *Calais Advertiser* similarly looked forward to a "new era" of Canadian-American relations in which a "commingling of spirit" would aid the "two great nations" in their fight for democracy.[91] The *Advertiser* changed its perception of the war considerably in 1917; gone were estimates of its economic or human cost to the belligerents noted earlier in the conflict.[92] Also gone were reports of military victories by the Germans, referred to for the first time in early 1917 by the *Advertiser* as "Teutons," the derogatory term used frequently in the Allied media to describe the enemy. The conflict itself was described as the "War of Teutonic Aggression" by the Calais newspaper in February 1917, a marked change for a periodical that had embraced neutrality throughout the war's first two and a half years.[93] In its place was a glorification of Allied military accomplishments: in one April 1917 story, the *Advertiser* described a British offensive as "crunching the German defences in its jaws."[94] Later that year the *Advertiser* portrayed a Canadian cavalry charge in heroic terms: "Canada was splendidly represented in the great British advance of Nov. 20 ... Charging straight for the battery sabring [sic] everything as they came, the officers and men raced to the guns. In line of troop columns they advanced, coming on so quickly that the enemy had no time to man two of the guns."[95]

As America mobilized in 1917 and Calais residents prepared to make the kinds of sacrifices made by their Canadian neighbours for years, members of the two communities came together on a number of occasions to celebrate this renewal of the social, economic, and cultural ties that bound them together. Some of these shared events were merely continuations of past traditions; for example, at St. Stephen's Victoria Day festivities in May 1917, the keynote speaker before a gathering of schoolchildren in the local curling rink was an associate justice of Maine's Supreme Judicial Court, George M. Hanson, a former mayor of Calais.[96] As in years past, the Dominion Day and Fourth of July celebrations that year featured Canadian and American participants, and both observances were well attended by residents of the St. Croix Valley.[97]

But there were also a number of shared events that celebrated not only the border-crossing culture of the St. Croix Valley but also the region's common goal of defeating imperial Germany. With local senior baseball defunct in 1917, organizers of the Charlotte County Exhibition used a reproduction of the European trench system as its main attraction for the September event. Designed by members of the local Great War Veterans Association, the trenches – complete with barbed wire and machine gun nests (and operational machine guns) – were constructed at St. Stephen's fairgrounds.[98]

The event was well attended by residents of Maine, who anxiously waited to see what impact the American doughboys would have on the fighting overseas. Many, having taken the Maine Central Railway (which offered reduced fairs for the event), stayed in Calais and St. Stephen hotels, though some were forced to wander the streets all night as vacancies quickly ran out.[99] And though people came from all over New Brunswick and the neighbouring American state to see horse races and the usual agricultural displays, it was the trench warfare reproduction that drew the most attention. "The trenches built by the returned soldiers are thronged all day and evening and the realistic reproduction of the life that the boys are living on the Western Front in France is greatly enjoyed," the *Courier* noted, adding that "we can only say to our readers, see it all, early, and often."[100]

When St. Stephen hosted the Charlotte County Exhibition in September 1917, few American doughboys had reached the front lines. But by the following spring, the United States had several hundred thousand troops stationed along the Western Front and were about to experience one of the most frightening offensives launched by Germany since the beginning of the war.[101] Between 200 and 250 Calais and area recruits in the American Expeditionary

Force were stationed in France at the time, with an indefinite number (perhaps a few dozen) also serving in the CEF.[102]

Thus, by the spring of 1918, Americans and Canadians from the St. Croix Valley were fighting and dying together in the trenches of Europe. Communities that had shared festivals and sports for generations were now sharing in the sacrifices of a brutal and merciless war. It was a realization that would have a huge impact on the towns lining the St. Croix River. "It is a time when we should 'get together' and become as one people," the *Saint Croix Courier* proclaimed to its American and Canadian readers, adding that "most of all should we, on both sides of the little river, hold sacred above reproach the conduct of the real men among us who have gone and who are going to fight our battles and to preserve for us all that we have regarded as our birthright from our infancy."[103]

These "real men" had been the focus of the Charlotte County Exhibition in September 1917, and they would continue to be the focus of transnational events of this kind in 1918. After members of St. Stephen's Great War Veterans Association appeared before Calais City Council to formally request that members of the latter organization attend the Canadian border community's Victoria Day celebration, the mayor and aldermen of Calais – along with the Calais Boy Scouts, Calais City Band, and members of the American border town's fire and police departments – joined New Brunswick soldiers, fire fighters, Boy Scouts, and other dignitaries in the day's parade, which wound through both St. Stephen and Calais.[104] Also joining the procession that year were members of the Calais branch of the Grand Army of the Republic, the first recorded instance of their participation in Victoria Day festivities in the St. Croix Valley during the Great War era.[105] With the procession passing through both St. Stephen and Calais and receiving the waves and cheers of thousands of bystanders, the *Courier* referred to the event as "a happy manifestation of the bonds of sympathy that unite the allies."[106]

A few days later, at the Memorial Day exercises in Calais, returned Canadian soldiers were invited to parade with local members of the Grand Army of the Republic. Until then, Memorial Day exercises had been limited to US veterans; however, this changed as Canadians and Americans faced a common foe in the trenches of France.[107] Marching alongside GAR members, the Calais Boy Scouts, the Calais Academy junior cadets, and the Calais City Band were eight Canadian soldiers returned from France and members of the St. Stephen branch of the Independent Order of Oddfellows. As was the tradition, the procession made its way through downtown Calais before stopping at Ferry Point Bridge, where flowers were strewn across the St. Croix River. Also new to the program was a recitation of the poem "An Englishman's Tribute upon the Entry of America into the War" by Miss Marion Cobb, a student at Calais Academy.[108]

The American entry into the war marked a turning point in the conflict. By the fall of 1918, both sides were exhausted, but with American men and materiel reaching the Allied lines in ever-increasing proportions the Germans were forced to admit defeat in November.[109] In the St. Croix Valley, rumours of an impending armistice began circulating on November 10. St. Stephen residents constantly flowed into and out of the Western Union office in search of telegrams bringing news of peace. The local telephone exchange was overwhelmed by gossiping men and women.[110] Finally, at four in the morning on November 11, official word came: an armistice had been signed, and the war was over. Almost immediately people in St. Stephen and Calais were awakened from their slumber by the sounds of bells chiming and whistles blowing. By 4:30 a.m., hundreds of sleepy-eyed men, women, and children poured into the streets to learn what the fuss was about. On the sidewalk in front of Thomas McCurdy's St. Stephen barbershop, dozens gathered to hear Baptist, Methodist, Presbyterian, and Roman Catholic preachers conduct services under the shining stars. No matter their faith, all appreciated the sentiment of Baptist Reverend Dr. Goucher, who proclaimed before the gathering that "the message of peace which is being flashed over a war weary world at this hour … is the greatest news … which has come to man since the morning the angel choir sang its song of 'peace and good will to men' when the Prince of Peace was born."[111]

In St. Stephen, Calais, and the Milltowns, locals spent the morning merrily cheering, chatting, and hanging American and Canadian flags in preparation for an afternoon parade. Beginning at 2:30 p.m., the procession – described as "the most impressive that has ever been seen in the border towns" – formed in St. Stephen and from there slowly made its way west to Milltown, where the automobiles, horse-drawn floats, and flag-waving pedestrians turned and crossed the upper bridge to Milltown, Maine, before proceeding back east to Calais.[112] Commanding the most attention and applause along the route were veterans returned from Europe and Calais members of the Grand Army of the Republic, who waved proudly to the crowd. It was such a long procession that, by the time its leaders reached Calais, they could look across the river to St. Stephen and see the tail end just beginning its long and happy march. Later that evening thousands of St. Croix Valley residents gathered in front of St. Stephen's Queen Hotel for speeches by local political and religious leaders. Afterward, all gathered at the foot of the river for a colourful fireworks display that lit up the serene St. Croix River.[113]

As was the case along the Detroit River, in the St. Croix Valley the war's end brought Americans and Canadians together to celebrate the Allied victory. But initially the war presented significant challenges to Canadian-American relations in the St. Croix Valley, particularly when the people of Maine remained committed to their federal government's official policy of neutrality. The war aroused the kind of national pride not typically seen in this region: in St. Stephen and Milltown, it renewed interest in the British connection, whereas across the river US neutrality led the *Calais Advertiser* to make frequent criticisms of the war and, in one rather notorious case, of the men volunteering for the Canadian Expeditionary Force. These differences all contributed to the emergence of nationalism and patriotism, on both sides of the dividing St. Croix River, rarely seen prior to the war.

But such slings and arrows were not enough to poison positive relations between the Americans and Canadians living in this unique borderland. Although the Calais newspaper periodically offered criticisms of the Allied war effort from late 1914 until early 1917, the people of Calais showed their support for their Canadian "cousins" by contributing to patriotic fundraising campaigns and even joining the CEF. When the Americans finally did declare war on Germany in 1917, it was as if those minor squabbles over US neutrality and the size of St. Stephen's recruits had never existed. American entry into the war renewed and perhaps even enhanced the relationship between these communities.

As the next chapter shows, it might also have made the people of St. Stephen less accommodating when the federal government attempted to increase border security during the war, making the movement of people and goods across the international boundary more challenging than ever before.

4
"A Very Convenient Arrangement"
Administering the St. Stephen–Calais Border

PRIOR TO THE First World War, St. Stephen was considered a peaceful section of the international boundary. Local customs officers reported seeing few "undesirables" – men and women with criminal histories or mental, physical, or financial deficiencies – making their way into the country from the United States. Few people of Asian heritage had ever seen St. Stephen – in fact, according to the census of 1911, not a single person of East Indian, Japanese, or Chinese descent lived within town limits.[1] Given that more than 90 percent of Charlotte County residents reported being born in New Brunswick, it is unlikely that many would ever have carried on a conversation with someone of Asian descent. In effect, for the people of St. Stephen, the "Chinese Question" was out of sight and out of mind, a fact that would have made attitudes toward the border much different there than in White Rock, British Columbia, where more than 1,000 people of Chinese and Japanese descent lived in the surrounding census district of Delta.[2]

Given the absence of undesirable traffic, it was determined that, rather than appoint a full-time inspector to patrol the region's three bridges (Ferry Point, Union, and Milltown), federal immigration authorities would train a local customs officer to prevent undesirables from entering the country.[3] In October 1908, Ottawa decided to pay one of the four customs officers operating in the St. Stephen and Milltown, New Brunswick, area, S.N. Hyslip, an additional $100 per year to perform both jobs.[4] Not until May 1912 did the department finally appoint a single, full-time immigration inspector at St. Stephen.[5]

Such actions reflected the relatively relaxed attitude of the federal government toward cross-border traffic in the Maritimes and New England.[6] The St. Croix Valley did not represent a problem area for Ottawa officials in 1914, evidenced by their decision that spring to abstain from appointing an agent to Milltown, believing that a single immigration inspector in St. Stephen was enough to cover the wider region.[7]

The war, however, introduced new challenges for immigration inspectors manning the Canada–US border. Not only were agents expected to weed out traditional undesirables, but also they were told to prevent Germans, Austro-Hungarians, and other enemy aliens from crossing the border. Pressure on local immigration agents to prevent these enemy aliens from doing so increased

FIGURE 18 The first bridge connecting the downtown areas of St. Stephen and Calais was completed in 1827. People on both sides of the border celebrated with fireworks and bonfires when bridge tolls were eliminated in 1894 – roughly a decade before this photograph was taken. *Source:* Provincial Archives of New Brunswick, Isaac Erb Fonds, P11–86.

following the attempted bombing of an international railway bridge running between Vanceboro, Maine, and St. Croix, New Brunswick – a short distance from Calais and St. Stephen. Agents were also told to keep Canadian soldiers from visiting the United States, and when recruiting stalled later in the war agents were pressured to prevent all men of military age from crossing the boundary without proper documentation.

The war introduced other changes to the border. In 1916, the federal government began discussing the introduction of a daylight saving time scheme that in theory would increase productivity and save fuel. It was believed that it would increase the number of sunlight hours during which people were awake, reducing the number of candles burned and amount of coal used while getting the most out of workers.[8] Historians have examined how this measure aroused controversy between rural and urban residents (the former preferring to stick with nature's time), but it also received considerable criticism in border communities such as St. Stephen and Milltown, where the change to DST affected the area's border-crossing culture.

As the following chapter demonstrates, government measures directly or indirectly affecting the border were not always popular in St. Stephen and

Milltown – even if the intention was to protect Canadian citizens from enemy aliens, prevent soldier desertion, and increase the nation's productivity. Changes that threatened the permeability of the Canada–US border were seen as anathema to the St. Croix Valley's border-crossing culture, which, above all else, included a relatively lax attitude toward the movement of people and goods from one side of the river to the other.

Initially, the war had little effect on the administration of the border separating St. Stephen from Calais. As the previous chapter showed, cross-border social activity continued unabated.[9] The movement of workers across the border was also unaffected by the war during its first full year. In his late-1914 correspondence with Canadian Superintendent of Immigration W.D. Scott, St. Stephen business mogul Gilbert Ganong referred to a "large floating population" across the St. Croix River, specifically between his town and Woodland, Maine, home to a large pulp and paper mill.[10] The attitude of Canadian as well as American immigration inspectors stationed in the St. Croix Valley toward this kind of traffic was considerably relaxed from 1914 to 1916, as it had been prior to the emergence of immigration bureaucracies in the early twentieth century.[11]

For residents of the St. Croix Valley, then, life along the international boundary stayed mostly the same through the war's first twelve months. For the vast majority of people living in this region, the act of crossing the border remained just as simple as it had been before August 1914 – a surprising fact given that there were several significant threats to local security during that time.

Shortly after war was declared, two German reservists attempting to make their way back to Europe via the United States were arrested by immigration officials at McAdam Junction, not far from the international boundary and roughly fifty kilometres from St. Stephen.[12] A month later a suspicious-looking Austrian walking the streets of St. Stephen on a Sunday afternoon was found by the local immigration inspector, C. Herbert Maxwell. The enemy alien was locked up overnight before being escorted by three armed guards to the Canadian Pacific Railway station, from which he was sent to a military prison in Saint John.[13] None of the Germans apprehended appears to have posed a legitimate threat to the security of locals, and as a result neither episode warranted much comment from local newspapers.

There were rumours, however, of more sinister plots, including reports that Germans were planning to invade Canada from the United States. In late August 1914, the *Calais Advertiser* documented an alleged scheme by Germans to blow up the Milltown Cotton Mill or perhaps a critical section of a nearby rail track. The newspaper hardly bought into the supposed plot, however, noting that "the story is without the slightest foundation."[14] In St. Stephen, the *Courier* never bothered to report the rumour.

A few days later Governor of Maine William T. Haines learned of a rumoured scheme by German subjects to invade Canada through the forests of Vermont, Maine, or both. Haines dismissed the rumour, as did the *Bangor Daily Commercial*, which (as reprinted in the *Courier*) noted that "it is considered extremely unlikely that anything in the nature of a raid on Canada by armed Germans would be attempted from northern Maine or Vermont."[15] Both Haines and the *Daily Commercial* doubted that such an attack would occur because New Brunswick was not a major training area for the Canadian military, and few soldiers travelled along the province's rail lines between Canada's primary training ground, Valcartier, Quebec, and its main naval port, Halifax, Nova Scotia. Given these circumstances, it made little sense to target the province, and the *Daily Commercial* suggested that any such attack would be "valueless" for the Germans.[16] However, the *Daily Commercial* did suggest that German reservists stationed in the United States might attack New Brunswick's transportation lines in an attempt to degrade (however minutely) the Allied war effort by preventing the easy movement of supplies.[17]

This proved to be an accurate prediction. In February 1915, a German reservist attempted to demolish the international railway bridge at Vanceboro, Maine, only fifty kilometres from Calais.[18] Leaving New York City, the reservist – a man by the name of Werner Van Horn – arrived in Vanceboro on January 30. That night he met with another man who supplied him with a dynamite satchel, which Van Horn later suspended from one end of the bridge.[19] On the morning of February 2, Van Horn detonated the charge, resulting in a massive explosion that rocked the surrounding community, shattering windows and startling local townsfolk. Rushing to the site of the blast, locals found the bridge and track in rough shape but by no means impassable. Tests showed that the structure could still withstand locomotives, and within a few hours trains from Saint John headed west were able to continue on to their destinations.[20]

Van Horn was immediately arrested at a nearby hotel by astounded local authorities who, only the day before, had ridiculed a Canadian man for raising concerns about suspicious activity at the boundary.[21] Because Van Horn claimed that he had never set foot in Canada, attempts by Ottawa to have him extradited initially failed. Instead, Van Horn – who was indicted on and subsequently pleaded guilty to a charge of transporting explosives from New York City to Vanceboro – was sent to an Atlanta jail.[22] Eventually, Canadian authorities learned that he had been paid the sum of $700 by Franz von Papen, the German ambassador to the United States (and later in life an ally of the Nazi leadership), to carry out the attack.[23] However, Van Horn remained in Atlanta until December 1919, when he was finally shipped across the boundary to New

Brunswick, where he was tried, convicted, and sentenced to time at Dorchester Penitentiary. In 1921, he was allowed to return to Germany.[24]

In the St. Croix Valley, the Vanceboro bombing had a noticeable impact on attitudes toward the border in the spring of 1915. Locals became far more attuned to activity along the border and watched keenly for suspicious behaviour or the presence of enemy aliens. After Milltown residents reported seeing a suspicious figure making notes near the bridge spanning the St. Croix River adjacent to the cotton mill, railway authorities on both sides of the border temporarily stationed more guards at either end of the overpass.[25] Shortly thereafter, a German who entered a Milltown, New Brunswick, barbershop received an amateur interrogation along with a shave.[26] Even more startling was the escape of several German prisoners from Halifax's Citadel prison. Making their way across New Brunswick and into the United States at Vanceboro only two weeks after the Van Horn bombing, they were eventually apprehended in the Maine town of Marion, a short distance from Calais.[27] The *Advertiser* noted the increased tensions at the border: "We heard a man say the other day ... that all one had to do to get the Canadians going was to disguise oneself a little, walk around the [Milltown] Cotton Mill or railroad bridge, and make a few marks in a note book and walk away."[28]

Although the *Advertiser* poked fun at the situation, the Canadian government took these threats seriously. Immediately following the Van Horn incident, Ottawa reached out to Washington with a request that the latter increase the number of guards stationed at critical border-crossing locations. Secretary of State William Jennings Bryan, unfortunately for Canadian officials, was more concerned with maintaining American neutrality and believed that stepping up border security would threaten this official position.[29] With the American government refusing to help, the Canadian immigration department's superintendent, W.D. Scott, encouraged agents stationed at the border to be especially alert in the months that followed. In a memo to inspectors on February 6, 1915, Scott warned that "it is possible that similar attempts may be made at other Border Points," and officers were "hereby advised to exercise vigilance in handling all suspicious strangers and also to detain for investigation where that action seems necessary."[30]

Locally, however, the influence of the bombing on cross-border activity and attitudes appears to have been minimal. Most people in Calais gave up on monitoring potential enemy aliens shortly after the attack because so many foreigners regularly passed through the community en route to nearby Woodland, where the pulp and paper mill attracted men of various European backgrounds.[31] Indeed, throughout Maine, locals appear to have considered the bombing an anomaly and not evidence that German agents were getting ready to launch regular raids on their communities or those across the border in Canada.[32]

In St. Stephen, the editor of the *Saint Croix Courier* rarely commented on the event in the pages of the local newspaper. Only one editorial touched on the topic in the weeks that followed the explosion, and in it the editor simply lamented that Van Horn was unlikely to be immediately extradited to Canada.[33] There was also no effort by St. Stephen residents to organize a home guard capable of monitoring the border and reporting on suspicious activity, like that seen near the Milltown Cotton Mill.[34] In Milltown, there were discussions on organizing such a force in April 1916 at a meeting of council; however, presumably because of a lack of interest or an absence of able-bodied men, the force never materialized.[35] Later there were attempts to have the militia department send men to patrol the boundary at Milltown, but there is no evidence that the federal government responded favourably to this call, and the matter was allowed to drop.[36]

Overall, the Vanceboro bombing, rumours of German invasions, and the apprehension of Germans or Austrians at the international boundary failed to convince St. Stephen residents that their section of the border required additional security. In 1917, town councillors even considered reducing the number of policemen patrolling the community at night from two to one.[37] There was also no public outcry when, on the night that part of the Ferry Point Bridge collapsed into the St. Croix River in August 1916, no immigration or customs agent was stationed close enough to hear or see the event occur.[38] It is safe to assume that, if part of the bridge could crumble without a customs or immigration officer knowing it, an enemy alien could cross it; it is likewise safe to assume that the apparent lack of frustration with this fact in the community in the days that followed indicates that few locals were worried that such a movement of Germans or Austrians was occurring.

People living along this part of the border did not suffer from a great fear of enemy invasion, nor did they face overbearing customs and immigration agents when trying to cross the boundary. Locals crossed the border frequently without contacting those officials stationed at the pedestrian and automobile bridges; for example, employees of the Milltown Cotton Mill living in Calais or Milltown, Maine, often used the unpatrolled Canadian Pacific Railway bridge to get to and from work.[39] In the winter, when the St. Croix River froze over, residents of the surrounding area made the trip between American and Canadian shorelines by walking across the ice.[40]

Until the late stages of the war, this was hardly a problem for local customs and immigration officials, who, for the most part, were integral members of the local community and appreciated the border-crossing culture of the

St. Croix Valley.[41] When customs collector Thomas McGeachy died in July 1918, the *Saint Croix Courier* ran an extensive biography that told of a man who had spent nearly his entire life along this section of the international boundary.[42] Immigration inspectors stationed in St. Stephen during the war were also locals; for instance, Inspector-in-Charge C. Herbert Maxwell was born to St. Stephen's Robert Maxwell in the early 1880s and died in the Canadian border community in 1947.[43]

Both customs and immigration inspectors stationed at St. Stephen during the war faced a number of new challenges after August 1914. Indeed, nearly every year of the conflict brought new demands on the few men stationed at this border crossing. First, in the fall of 1914, immigration inspectors (and customs officers performing dual roles) were told to prevent the passage across the boundary not only of enemy aliens but also of recruits in the CEF. In December 1914, the *Courier* reported that such measures were unpopular among St. Stephen recruits, who found it "a little curious to have to remain away from Calais."[44] Although the rule remained in place, several weeks later the American consul in St. Stephen and the immigration inspector at Calais successfully lobbied to enable St. Stephen recruits to visit the US border town over the holidays. It was "a favor that was much appreciated," the *Courier* reported.[45]

Customs and immigration inspectors were also responsible for preventing enemy aliens from moving back and forth across the boundary – a tough job when there were so few officers posted to Milltown and St. Stephen during the war. Nevertheless, the customs and in particular immigration agents stationed at these points did their best to prevent such cross-border movement, and in a few cases they were successful in picking out and apprehending their targets. For example, in a February 1917 letter by Superintendent of Immigration W.D. Scott, St. Stephen Inspector-in-Charge C. Herbert Maxwell was commended for catching US-bound Germans who had escaped from an Amherst, Nova Scotia, internment camp.[46] Having split up before making their attempt to cross the boundary, only those unlucky fugitives who chose Maxwell's section of the line were apprehended.

This accomplishment can only be appreciated if one notes how busy this border was during the war years. Even though Canadian immigration authorities stationed far fewer inspectors in this border region than at Windsor, the St. Stephen and Calais crossing received its fair share of travellers. The *Calais Advertiser* estimated that more than 3,300 people made their way over the Ferry Point Bridge connecting the downtown areas of St. Stephen and Calais on August 9, 1916. Although most crossed by foot, some were packed into the 411 horse teams or 311 automobiles that made the journey, with another 552 individuals crossing by electric streetcar. Although only 187 people were recorded crossing at the Union Bridge and another 517 at the Milltown Bridge, together the bridges of this region saw roughly 4,000 individuals pass in a single day, presenting an enormous challenge to the four full- and part-time immigration inspectors tasked with preventing the passage of soldiers and enemy aliens in addition to other undesirable classes of immigrant.[47]

Perhaps the greatest challenge for local immigration agents came in May 1917, when the Canadian government began demanding that all men of military age, even those not in uniform, acquire a passport before being permitted to cross the international boundary. In Windsor, the legislation, invoked overnight by Order-in-Council PC 1433, had an immediate impact on the lives of local day labourers attempting to make their way to Detroit shops and factories the following morning. In the bustling Ontario border city, where thousands daily made the trip to Detroit and back, all men were immediately forced to show identification. However, in St. Stephen, the legislation was not enforced in the same manner. According to the *Calais Advertiser*, men known to the immigration officials were allowed to pass without the documentation, and only those not recognized by Maxwell and his fellow inspectors were stopped and asked for identification. Still, the *Advertiser* suspected that such legislation could present a problem to the rural residents of Charlotte County in the habit of visiting Calais but not known to the local immigration authorities. "This may result in a suspension of social and business visits on the part of these people until such time as requisite documents are obtained," the *Advertiser* predicted.[48] Across the river in St. Stephen, the *Courier* noted that the new rules were seen as an "inconvenience" but that locals accustomed to going back and forth were "accepting them with resignation."[49]

No doubt the furor seen in Windsor was avoided because immigration agents stationed at St. Stephen and Milltown were willing to bend the rules for local men of military age who could be trusted to return from Calais or Milltown, Maine, after a brief visit. With most immigration and customs officers originally from St. Stephen and the surrounding area, they appreciated the importance of permeability of the border and made attempts to find a satisfactory middle ground between somewhat draconian federal policies and the interests of local residents. In the case of the border crossing between St. Stephen and Calais, then, these agents played a critical mediatory role.

The importance of this mediation was evident in May 1918 when Ottawa sent two investigators – referred to by the *Saint Croix Courier* as "specials" – to evaluate the work of customs officers stationed in St. Stephen. These special investigators, whose names were never given by the *Courier*, aroused the indignation of the newspaper for enforcing federal customs regulations down to the colour of shoes worn by officers. It was not a friendly visit, and the language used by the *Courier* to describe the event reveals that residents of St. Stephen resented attempts by forces from outside the region to regulate cross-border traffic and disturb the permeability of the St. Croix Valley.

The arrival of these specials was not a surprise to St. Stephen's customs officers, who, told of the visit beforehand, carefully prepared for the investigators' arrival. Unfortunately, they made a few oversights. Several of the men wore "fancy colored shoes" and were told to immediately discard them in favour of plain black footwear. Others wore coloured ties and were told to discard them too, the specials preferring white. Officers who chose to wear their customs badges pinned to their vests rather than their coats were also corrected, told that, if people had problems with how the officers treated them, they needed to be able to easily make out the particular man's name and badge number. "Well now, that was something entirely new," quipped the *Courier,* "something 'quite novel,' for local officers have always been accustomed to exercising such courtesy to strangers and all others that the necessity for complaints had not been thought of."[50]

The investigation moved on to how St. Stephen's customs agents interacted with locals. The specials were shocked when a woman returning from Calais and recognized by local officers was allowed to march past, small package in hand, without so much as a scrutinizing glance. "It was explained that such things had come to be regulated by the custom of many years in a border community," noted the *Courier.* "If any person passed with a parcel of any size or of any apparent value, he or she was stopped and duty collected, but many of the parcels going past had not cost more than ten cents and the duty was difficult to appraise." But that was nonsense to the specials, and the St. Stephen customs officers were told to inspect each package and collect duty on every item – "no matter what the value, or what the consequence" – making its way back into Canada from Calais.[51]

Then an automobile approached. Filled with Calais residents known to the local customs agents, it was initially allowed to pass without inspection. "But the 'specials' could not see that at all," and the vehicle was taken aside and examined. The local agents were told that, like small packages carried by women, every automobile should be taken aside and thoroughly searched for dutiable goods. Even when the local officers explained that "some people do business in Calais and reside in St. Stephen, and that they had to cross and recross and there was no good reason to hold them up every time that they passed the custom house," the answer was the same. "Nothing doing with those specials, those very 'specials,'" the *Courier* seethed.[52]

The investigators' visit was deemed outrageous by St. Stephen's newspaper, which emphasized that the visitors, "clothed with a little temporal authority but know[ing] nothing of border conditions," were out of their element. In condemning the specials' intransigence and ignorance, the *Courier* also turned local officers' military and patriotic achievements into a form of moral currency, giving them a higher status than their unnamed superiors from distant Ottawa. "Nobody knows anything about the 'specials' who visited us or of what they or theirs have done for Canada," the *Courier* noted.

> But of the "locals" involved, one has given his eldest son to the cause of Empire to "sleep in Flanders field," and two others have risked their lives in the cause of Empire and returned ... They did this for Canada, and it is safe to assume that the interests of Canada will not suffer at their hands, whether they wear black shoes or tan shoes, white ties or verigated [*sic*] ties, part their hair on one side or in the middle.

In concluding, the *Courier* emphasized that the people of St. Stephen and Calais who "suffer inconvenience" in the days, weeks, and months following the specials' visit should not "unjustly" blame the local customs officers for the new regulations.[53]

Not all perceived threats to the border-crossing culture of the St. Croix Valley were related to customs and immigration regulations. As in Windsor, residents of St. Stephen were also unsure about the daylight saving time scheme, first discussed on a national basis in 1916. Most worried that the plan, which would see St. Stephen's time advanced an hour, might negatively affect a region where people crossed the international boundary for work, school, and pleasure. If implemented, the plan would increase the time division to two hours because of the Canadian town's traditional use of Atlantic Time and the American community's use of Standard Time. For most residents of St. Stephen, this was unacceptable. Given the circumstances, the change to DST, which some towns and cities in New Brunswick were already considering in the spring of 1916, "will not be adopted in this section," the *Courier* noted, because to expand the time difference between Calais and St. Stephen would "result in endless discomfort owing to the close business and social relations of the two municipalities."[54]

Although a number of major Canadian centres – including Saskatoon, Saskatchewan; Winnipeg, Manitoba; and Brantford, Ontario – made the time change in 1916, St. Stephen refused to implement DST.[55] It was hardly alone; farmers across Canada thought that the adjustment made little sense since their days revolved around nature's time frame, not around that of the government or urban residents.[56] But border towns such as St. Stephen and Windsor suggested that the switch should not be made because of its negative impact on a long-running economic, social, and cultural relationship with a neighbouring American community.

Despite these kinds of protests, in April 1918 the federal government, believing that it could improve worker efficiency and safety with daylight saving time, introduced the measure on a national scale. St. Stephen made the change later that month.[57] Immediately, a number of protests were raised. Employees of the Milltown Cotton Mill complained that they were getting up before sunrise and eating breakfast in the dark. That meant using more coal and candles to light the home and became expensive for some working-class households.[58] St. Stephen residents soon began making similar complaints, some literally counting down the days until the end of DST in late October.[59] When that time finally neared (and unknown to most just a few weeks before the war ended), the *Courier* suggested that some arrangement be made whereby Calais and St. Stephen were placed on the same time and remained there permanently. "It would be a very convenient arrangement for the people on the border," the *Courier* insisted, "if the new time was continued in Maine and New Brunswick was allowed to go back to Atlantic standard for the communities would then have the same standard of time."[60] As much as such a change might have meant to the people of the St. Croix Valley, it never took place. To this day, St. Stephen residents get up and go to work an hour ahead of their Calais counterparts.

Many of these initiatives affecting the border and pursued by the federal government during the First World War were seen as meddling by outsiders who, as the *Courier* insisted, "know nothing of border conditions."[61] Some locals were willing to make these kinds of sacrifices – paltry as they were compared with the horrors facing soldiers in the trenches overseas – but for many residents of this border region the new rules went too far. For people accustomed to moving across the boundary at a moment's notice, it did not make much sense to prevent a man from visiting his Calais sweetheart simply because he had enlisted or was of an age suitable for enlistment. For most of the war, residents of St. Stephen and Milltown, New Brunswick, were not concerned that their border was under threat, and they made little attempt to organize a home guard, even though enemy aliens regularly tried to cross at sections of the line in this region and, in one case, did target a nearby community. People were not particularly patient when the government insisted that customs officers inspect purses, packages, and cars owned by locals coming across the line. They also did not like the idea of tinkering with local clocks. They were not the only people to complain about government measures designed to help the war effort but, in many cases, annoying for one reason or another. But what set the people of this region apart were the reasons why they protested increased border security or the DST scheme: it threatened to erode the border-crossing culture of their international community.

Part 3
White Rock, British Columbia, and Blaine, Washington

In 1910, the people of Blaine, Washington, which sits just south of the BC border, voted to "go dry." The hope of prohibitionists, as elsewhere, was that eliminating the production, sale, and consumption of alcohol would make the local community safer and more productive – in short, a better place to live. But there was one problem: just steps across the Canadian border and a short jaunt from Blaine stood the St. Leonard Hotel, a towering saloon. The hotel's owner, Richard Asbeck, soon found himself at the centre of a fierce debate between residents of Blaine and the Canadian municipality of Surrey.[1]

In Surrey, there was little interest in shutting down the St. Leonard. Several factors can explain this reluctance. First, Asbeck paid considerable liquor licensing fees to the municipality. Second, he had improved the property a great deal since taking it over, adding telephone and electric connections, flush toilets, a stable, and grass.[2] Overall, his hotel was one of the first modern business establishments in all of Surrey, and since – as nearby White Rock, British Columbia's, *Semiahmoo Gazette* reminded its readers – the hotel was breaking no Canadian laws, it would be a shame to shut it down.[3]

But everything changed in early 1913 when salmon offal dumped in Semiahmoo Bay by Blaine's canneries began washing up onto White Rock's pristine beaches. With a diphtheria outbreak partially attributed to the dumping by Surrey's medical health officer, White Rock residents immediately began pressing Surrey Council to address the issue.[4] Unfortunately for White Rock, Surrey Council had as much power to stop the salmon dumping as Blaine had to cancel the St. Leonard liquor licence. The result was a standoff between White Rock and Blaine, with residents of the American community agreeing to stop the dumping only when the St. Leonard Hotel doors were closed for good.[5] Canadian and American newspaper editors lashed out at one another in angry editorials for more than a year before Surrey Council finally agreed to cancel the St. Leonard liquor licence in the spring of 1914.[6] Although the *Blaine Journal* rejoiced on hearing the news and credited Surrey residents with shutting down what it repeatedly referred to as the "snake ranch" on the border, White Rock's *Semiahmoo Gazette* offered no such happy sentiment, neglecting to comment on the hotel's closing.[7] And though the Blaine salmon dumping

FIGURE 19 The infamous St. Leonard Hotel just before the First World War. Located only steps from the Canada–US border, it aroused anger and consternation in Blaine, which began its experiment with prohibition in 1910. *Source:* White Rock Museum and Archives.

ended shortly thereafter, prohibition continued to be a point of debate between the two communities for years to come.[8]

Such episodes revealed to residents of White Rock and Blaine that the nearby international boundary existed and mattered, even if (unlike in Windsor and Detroit or St. Stephen and Calais) no visible geographic feature clearly divided American and Canadian territory. Although a few miles separated downtown Blaine from downtown White Rock, the major border-crossing points between them – in the west the Douglas area surrounding the St. Leonard and in the east the Pacific Highway, completed in 1913 – were marked by little more than tiny customs sheds or tents in the middle of fields. But in spite of the primitive quality of this border region's customs and immigration service and open territory at the forty-ninth parallel, by the outbreak of war in Europe the boundary between White Rock and Blaine was firmly cemented in the minds of local residents. In Blaine, a town first populated in the 1870s and 1880s, it was an important line separating the progressive-minded community from British Columbia and its booze. In White Rock, residents hoping to see the community boom as a resort destination for residents of Vancouver and New Westminster showed little interest in prohibition, which might discourage tourists from visiting.

White Rock and Blaine are small communities. Today the population of White Rock stands at nearly 20,000, a significant increase from a handful of families at the turn of the twentieth century.[9] Blaine has seen its population remain fairly stagnant, from an estimated 1,800 in 1889 to roughly 4,100 in 2012.[10] These days there is little indication that the communities are, or ever were, socially, culturally, or economically bound together. Evidence of just such a community once existed between Windsor and Detroit, and St. Stephen and Calais, and one could argue that it still exists in the latter two towns. But, as the following section demonstrates, such a community never truly existed along Semiahmoo Bay, for a number of reasons.

First, and most importantly, settlement did not precede the introduction of a modern, bureaucratized border in this region. Along the Detroit and St. Croix Rivers, farms, ferries, lumber mills, and shipyards had existed for generations prior to the introduction of immigration policy in the early twentieth century that led to the inspection of travellers at popular border-crossing sites. That was not the case at the section of the international boundary between White Rock and Blaine, where the populations of both communities remained small until the late nineteenth century (and, in the case of White Rock, would not surpass a few dozen families until the eve of the First World War). Whereas border-crossing cultures had become entrenched in Detroit, Windsor, St. Stephen, and Calais, and were the basis for locals defending the border's permeability during the First World War, in White Rock and Blaine the push was often in the opposite direction, toward cementing the international boundary as a way to protect area residents from a number of perceived threats.

Second, in a wider Pacific coast region fixated on race and specifically the local population of "Asiatics," the border became a necessary filter for monitoring the movement of people born in China, Japan, and India. Starting with the Fraser River gold rush in 1858, Asians – at that time mostly Chinese – moved in large numbers to Washington Territory and land loosely controlled by Britain's Hudson's Bay Company.[11] Upon arriving in the region, most Chinese were relegated to positions that whites refused (or at least detested), from operating laundries to laying railway tracks. Although they worked harder and longer shifts than their white counterparts, the Chinese rarely earned more than half a white man's wage. The cultural habits of the Chinese, deemed strange by their white counterparts, hardly endeared them to the Americans or British living in the wider Pacific region. Making them even less popular in the late nineteenth century was their tendency to send earned wages back home to families in China, giving the impression that they were not interested in contributing their share to the local economy.[12] These factors, together with Anglo-Saxon conceptions of a racial hierarchy gleaned from a selective reading of Charles

Darwin's *Origin of Species* (published in 1859), made tensions between Asians and whites more than a little rancorous in the Pacific Northwest.[13] In contrast, race was not such a major concern in central Canada or the Maritimes (and their neighbouring American regions), where the influx of Asians through border-crossing points was comparatively meagre.

But race was not the only factor setting this border region apart from the Detroit River area and St. Croix Valley before and during the First World War era. Social, cultural, and economic factors also reinforced the need to monitor and control activity at the international boundary. One factor was that in 1910 Blaine enacted prohibition at the local level, whereas the neighbouring Canadian municipality of Surrey, of which White Rock was a part, refused to follow suit. Taking advantage of this situation was Richard Asbeck, owner of the St. Leonard Hotel, which operated within walking distance of downtown Blaine. The issue highlighted not only the need to monitor and enforce border regulations but also key differences between Canadians and Americans living in this border region.

These towns were also fundamentally different in an economic sense. Although residents of both communities depended heavily on lumbering for steady wages in the early twentieth century, by the First World War White Rock was rapidly evolving into a resort community that depended more on its beaches and fair climate than on its fir and cedar trees. In contrast, Blaine remained committed to more traditional industries, including lumbering and salmon canning. These factors served to distinguish Blaine from White Rock, where locals focused on making their community as attractive to summer visitors as possible and showed little interest in prohibition.

Unlike residents of Windsor, those of White Rock shared a more visible economic connection with other Canadian cities in the immediate region. Most tourists visiting the seaside town during the summer months were from Vancouver and New Westminster, not the United States. This meant that the vast majority of White Rock's early investors were Canadian, not American. In addition, the town's focus on tourism in the early twentieth century made it dependent on federal and provincial representatives who helped to expand the community's primitive infrastructure during the war years. And though White Rock's economic development owed a great deal to the decision of the American-owned Great Northern Railway (GNR) to connect Seattle with Vancouver through the community in 1909, an acrimonious relationship with the GNR did not engender the kind of cross-border good feeling seen in Windsor, where locals expressed deep attachment to US firms such as Ford.

All of these factors served to shape a cross-border relationship between White Rock and Blaine that, though mostly friendly (at least after

FIGURE 20 White Rock, which grew rapidly during the first decades of the twentieth century, from a collection of shacks along the hillside in 1900 to a bustling resort town by 1920. *Source:* White Rock Museum and Archives.

the St. Leonard Hotel closed in 1914), was distinct from relations between Windsor and Detroit or St. Stephen and Calais.

54-40 or Fight!

This provocative campaign slogan captured the imaginations of thousands of Americans in 1844 and helped presidential candidate James Knox Polk to upstage his rivals in the federal election that fall.[14] The idea that the United States was willing to go to war with Britain in order to establish the fifty-fourth parallel as the official international boundary in the Pacific Northwest appeared to set the young republic and the British Empire on a collision course only a generation following the bitterly fought War of 1812. For its part, Britain believed that it held a legitimate claim to a much different boundary – one running along the Columbia River. Evidence of a British presence there prior to the establishment of Fort Astoria by the Americans in early 1811 was weak; in fact, it amounted to little more than British writers claiming that, at one point on his epic journey around the world in the late sixteenth century, Sir Francis Drake had made a brief stop along North America's Pacific coast at the forty-eighth parallel. Others in Britain argued that Captain George Vancouver, who had mapped a large part of the Pacific coast and interacted with its First Nations more than two centuries later, had established a British presence that allowed London to dictate where the international boundary lay.[15]

In the end, war was averted. In the spring of 1845, Polk turned his focus south, to the annexation of cotton-rich Texas. Mexico disputed the move, along with American claims to New Mexico and California, and throughout the year the two nations rattled their sabres.[16] When Mexico refused to negotiate on the matter, war became imminent. In May 1846, Mexican and American forces clashed along the Rio Grande.[17]

In spite of his bold campaign slogan, Polk could fight only one war at a time. And in the grand scheme of things, acquiring the densely forested backwoods of the Pacific Northwest was a lower priority for Washington.[18] As tensions with Mexico escalated in the summer of 1845, American and British representatives met to hammer out a compromise. It took nearly a year, but by June 1846 the two sides had come to agree on the forty-ninth parallel as the new boundary. Proponents of "manifest destiny" (a term coined by an American journalist the year of Polk's inauguration), rejected the measure, but nevertheless it passed through the US Senate with a vote of thirty-seven to twelve.[19] On June 15, 1846, the Oregon Treaty (known by many in the United States as the Treaty of Washington) was signed.[20]

Although the precise location of the sea boundary west of the coast would remain unclear for another quarter century, the Oregon Treaty firmly established the forty-ninth parallel as the land demarcation point from the sea to the Rockies, passing through bogs, forests, hills, streams, and meadows. But in a practical sense, the border remained invisible to anyone actually venturing across it in the 1840s and 1850s. The discovery of gold along the Fraser River in 1856 changed that; recognizing that an influx of California miners from the south could lead the United States to rethink its decision to compromise on the forty-ninth parallel, the Hudson's Bay Company alerted the British government to the situation, and the latter promptly sent troops to the vulnerable Victoria colony. Britain also requested that the United States appoint representatives to help survey the agreed upon boundary and map the frontier.[21]

The American Boundary Commission arrived at Victoria in June 1857 and was joined a year later by a contingent of Royal Engineers. The leaders of each boundary commission, US Chief Commissioner Archibald Campbell – whose name would eventually grace the river running through White Rock's southeastern section – and Captain John Summerfield Hawkins, first met along the shores of Semiahmoo Bay in mid-August 1858.[22] Although relations between the two groups were somewhat icy, for the next four years they went about the process of demarcating the line, pushing through oozing bogs, tall grasses, and mosquito-infested woods.[23] Across this vast expanse, from the shores of Point Roberts to the crest of the Rockies, they laid over 200 iron pillars and stone cairns.[24] With the land boundary laid, the commissioners went home, leaving their markers behind. And while thousands of American miners pushed through the boundary in search of fortune along the Fraser River, few settled along Semiahmoo Bay.

During the period that followed, the Semiahmoo First Nations remained the sole inhabitants of this land. Few recognized the boundary imposed by the survey crews (in fact, some of the Semiahmoo allegedly stole the crew's stone cairns and used them to construct traps for catching marten).[25] The problem for the Semiahmoo was that the new border ran between Aboriginal family networks, separating them from their traditional allies, the Lummi band of northern Washington. The process of delineating the boundary had begun with the Point Elliott Treaty, completed in 1855 and signed by representatives of the US government and Amerindian bands of the Puget Sound area.[26] The Semiahmoo never signed the treaty (ratified in 1859), though it did have important impacts on their relationships with bands that did recognize it.[27]

Because of years of raids by enemy tribes, the tiny Semiahmoo band – whose numbers dwindled from about 300 in the eighteenth century to just fifty in the 1850s – were unable to stand effectively against such action by the American and British governments.[28] With few alternatives, they appear to have quietly respected the imposition of the border as well as their relegation to a reserve of 392 acres between the White Rock beaches to the north and the international boundary to the south. In the years that followed, smallpox took its toll on the Semiahmoo; in 1890, Indian Agent Peter Byrne estimated their number at sixty, but by 1909 a new assessment placed their population at just thirty-eight.[29]

By most accounts – written by descendants of Europeans – the Semiahmoo got along with their white neighbours in White Rock and Blaine. The first church in the White Rock area, a tiny Roman Catholic chapel, was built in 1860 on the reserve and was successful in converting many of the local Aboriginal people to Christianity.[30] In interviews conducted in the mid-twentieth century by local historian Margaret Lang Hastings, early white pioneers recalled playing with Semiahmoo children and attending the band's potlatches along White Rock's beaches.[31] These children were invited to attend White Rock's first one-room schoolhouse, opened in 1910, and their parents worked alongside whites at the nearby Campbell River Lumber Company mill.[32] W.E. Johnson, a customs collector in White Rock during the Great War, later recalled his mother baking bread and trading it to the Semiahmoo in exchange for fresh fish.[33] The Semiahmoo also offered little protest when residents of White Rock and Blaine passed through their territory, the route bisecting the reserve being the quickest way to walk between the American and Canadian communities.[34] The relationship between the Semiahmoo and white settlers was by no means perfect, with the bitterest dispute – the appropriation of Semiahmoo land to construct an expanded customs facility at the border following the Second World War – simmering until a federal court decided in favour of the Semiahmoo in 1997 and the land was returned.[35] However, in the early twentieth century, the Aboriginal peoples of this region appear to have engaged in mostly friendly relations with their white neighbours.

The first white settlers to arrive in the Semiahmoo Bay area made their way to the location that would become Blaine in 1870. Initially named Semiahmoo, the town's first homesteaders – including the Dexters, Bobletts, and Richards – arrived on the steamboat *J.B. Libby* and quickly set to work building a school, sawmill, and church.[36] Most had come from the American Midwest; the Bobletts, for example, started their journey in Milwaukee before proceeding through Iowa, the Dakotas, Colorado, Arizona, California, and Oregon to board the *Libby* in Seattle. Early on, families survived on the profits of their farms or fishing boats, or on wages that fathers and sons earned in sawmills.[37] Some men found work across Semiahmoo Bay in Point Roberts, where salmon canneries were established in the 1880s. Within two decades of the arrival of the first white settlers, the newly established *Blaine Journal* newspaper predicted that the town's "rich farming," "geographical position," and "manufacturies [sic] of all kinds" would result in the rapid increase in local property values over the following years.[38]

Unfortunately, Blaine – renamed in 1884 for James G. Blaine, the former US secretary of state and unsuccessful Republican presidential candidate – did not immediately become the bustling town envisioned by its newspaper.[39] Setbacks were frequent in the late 1880s, notably the closing of a major sawmill and the destruction by fire of a shingle mill.[40] Margaret Stewart, whose family moved to the Hazelmere area east of White Rock in 1878, remembers desperate Americans coming across the border into the surrounding municipality of Surrey, where they fished trout and hunted grouse almost to the point of extinction. "They had nothing else to do for a while there," Stewart recalled. "And they fished ... awful hard, because things was tough."[41]

Across the border in White Rock, progress was even slower. Although the *British Columbia Directory* in 1879 predicted that White Rock was bound to become a popular summer resort sometime in the future, at the time it remained extremely isolated from burgeoning cities such as New Westminster,

Victoria, and Vancouver.[42] A road opened between tiny Surrey farming centres Cloverdale and Hall's Prairie shortly thereafter hardly helped the situation, though it did serve to bring a few more vacationers during the summer months.[43]

Although they faced an uphill battle, investors from both sides of the border did make an effort to develop White Rock in the late nineteenth century. In 1886, Englishman W.J. Smith bought up much of the local land but then sold it to a Blaine realtor today remembered only as "Gerbritsh." He subdivided the lands and sold lots for between $150 and $300, but few buyers actually developed their new properties. The most visible attempt to launch development in White Rock was the opening of a hotel by New Westminster businessman John Hendry in 1890, but with no easy way for potential visitors to reach it the establishment went out of business.[44] For the next two decades, White Rock's development remained at a standstill.

But Hendry was hardly fazed by the hotel failure. The head of a rising BC lumber empire and, for a time, the mayor of New Westminster, he played a key role in the promotion of a new railway that would provide valuable transportation links among his city, south Surrey, and Seattle.[45] Opened for service in February 1891, the New Westminster Southern linked Seattle with Brownsville, British Columbia, and provided Blaine, New Westminster, and south Surrey with important connections to nearby markets.[46]

The line had an immediate impact on the American border town's fortunes. That year New Westminster businessman Daniel Drysdale opened the first modern salmon cannery in Blaine, which in its inaugural year packed roughly 9,000 cases of sockeye and coho. By 1893, annual production had increased to 36,000 cases.[47] Salmon canning in Blaine was given another boost when the San Francisco–based Alaska Packers Association (APA) purchased Drysdale's company in 1894 and in turn infused substantial capital into expanding and modernizing the operation. Three major international conflicts in the next fifteen years – the Spanish-American War, South African Boer War, and Russo-Japanese War – served to increase demand for packed meat, such as canned salmon, and this demand not only helped the Blaine site of the APA but also led to the establishment of seven new canning operations.[48]

By 1913, Blaine was becoming well known not only for its salmon canning but also for its agricultural potential, with much of the harvest going across the border into British Columbia.[49] Blaine also boasted a number of lumber and shingle mills during this period.[50] Although the town's permanent population did not increase substantially between the late 1880s and 1910 (1,800 in 1889; 2,254 in 1910), the outlook of the community certainly improved with the addition and subsequent growth of these new industries.[51]

Across the border, the development of White Rock lagged behind its American neighbour. However, it too saw a population boost following the arrival of the New Westminster Southern in early 1891. From that point forward, more and more residents of New Westminster and Vancouver visited the local beaches, most taking the train to Blaine, disembarking, and then walking a few miles to White Rock.[52] Unfortunately, such transportation shortcomings prevented the growth of a permanent population.

The most important step toward White Rock's development was the rerouting of the Great Northern Railway track in 1909.[53] The route would wind its way around the coast of Semiahmoo Bay, proceeding from the western section of Blaine through White Rock, Blackie's Spit (later called Crescent Beach), Mud Bay, and on to New Westminster and Vancouver. The new route was not without its problems; the land across north Delta was extremely boggy, and preparing a satisfactory roadbed would be expensive.[54] Trestles would have to be built across the Nicomekl and Serpentine Rivers, with men posted to open swing spans for passing vessels. And though the land along Semiahmoo Bay was flat, the rising bluff next to it at what is now White Rock and Crescent Beach could lead to mudslides that would block or damage the tracks and even result in derailment and loss of life.[55] But there was one advantage that the new route offered that no one could ignore: it significantly shortened the distance between Vancouver and Seattle, reducing the time required to make the trip and, it was hoped, encouraging more passengers to come aboard.

By the end of 1908, construction was complete, and on March 15, 1909, the first trains made their way from Blaine north through the tiny hamlet of White Rock. Greeting them at the town's station was local customs collector W.E. "Fred" Johnson, who moved to Surrey from Halifax as a child. In 1909, Johnson and his wife were getting by like summer vacationers, living in a tent while they saved up their money to purchase a home.[56] In long-established communities such as Windsor and St. Stephen, the Johnsons' situation would have raised eyebrows, but not in primitive prewar White Rock, which Johnson described as a "mere handful of houses in the forest."[57]

Eventually, the coming of the Great Northern Railway would change all that. When the town's first post office was established in 1910, it serviced an estimated 200 people.[58] In 1912, New Westminster businessman Peter Greyell opened a new, fifty-room hotel on White Rock's seafront roadway, Washington Avenue (later renamed Marine Drive). It was a popular destination for both summer visitors and workers involved in constructing the town's new and improved rail depot, which also happened to be the site of the local customs and immigration office.[59] Separated by a breezeway, the depot featured offices and waiting rooms for GNR agents and passengers on one side and workspace for customs and immigration officials (including a lockup) on the other. The new facility, which also included a small shed where veterinarians inspected livestock being imported from the United States (much to the disgust of nearby swimmers), officially opened on New Year's Day 1913.[60]

By the beginning of the First World War, White Rock's development was well under way. Cottages popped up fast along the towering bluff opposite Semiahmoo Bay.[61] Thousands visited the seaside town (which many likened to the Bay of Naples) during the summer months, and an estimated 430 made it their year-round place of residence.[62] Most of the traffic came from Canadian cities rather than American cities or Blaine. In an April 1911 article on the community's steady growth, the *Blaine Journal* noted that White Rock was becoming the "future summer resort of the New Westminster and Vancouver people."[63] Indeed, many residents of these cities boarded one of the four GNR trains that made their way to White Rock each day during the summer months. Holidays brought special rates, and travellers could buy packages in bulk that reduced each round trip to less than a dollar.[64] All in all, it meant that White Rock was far more accessible than it had been just a few years earlier, when getting to the town's beaches from Vancouver meant boarding a train, a ferry, a train again, and then walking several miles from Blaine. In March 1913, the *Semiahmoo Gazette* estimated that a businessman from Vancouver or New Westminster in need of a day's vacation could board a train from his city in the morning, "be on the beach at White Rock before 2 p.m., spend several hours by the sea and be home again before bedtime."[65]

Cheap rail packages were not solely responsible for the rapid development of White Rock. It also helped that some of the province's most influential political figures, including MP J.D. Taylor and MPP Frank J. MacKenzie, had summer homes in White Rock.[66] Their presence and political influence brought the community government money used to expand the town's primitive infrastructure.[67] In fact, in 1914, White Rock became the home of the South Surrey Conservative Association (SSCA) – whose membership included Taylor and MacKenzie – which constantly lobbied all levels of government for support in making their community the province's most eminent resort area.[68] For example, in 1914, Taylor and the SSCA were instrumental in acquiring more than $10,000 in government funds for a long-sought-after pier.[69] It is little surprise, then, that at a Conservative Party rally in White Rock in 1917, Taylor – who became a senator that year – was introduced as "the man who put White Rock on the map."[70]

In reality, it was the American-owned Great Northern Railway's decision to reroute the line from central Surrey to the shores of Semiahmoo Bay that truly initiated White Rock's rapid development. In an economic sense, the

FIGURE 21 White Rock's pier, built in 1914 with federal funding secured by MP J.D. Taylor and the South Surrey Conservative Association. *Source:* White Rock Museum and Archives.

GNR offered White Rock as many advantages as Ford offered Windsor – both brought business to these communities in bundles, the GNR in the form of American and Canadian tourists, Ford in the form of actual employment – but the St. Paul, Minnesota–based railway never received much credit from the people of White Rock.

The poor reputation of the GNR was primarily the result of its apparent uninterest in the growth of White Rock. Unlike Henry Ford, who paid Windsor workers a high wage and organized vacation days to Detroit River resort destinations, the GNR rarely showed any interest in the long-term economic development of White Rock. For example, when it bought up much of the land in White Rock in 1906, it refused to maintain or improve the properties in the years that followed. One major problem for residents was the poor condition of railway crossings, critical in a situation in which the track divided the beaches and sea on one side from Washington Avenue businesses and private dwellings on the other.[71] White Rock's *Semiahmoo Gazette* excoriated the GNR management, insisting that locals "have a most serious grievance" against the company.[72]

FIGURE 22 Looking south along the Great Northern Railway track, which separated White Rock from its pristine beaches. White Rock residents often expressed frustration with the American railway company's resistance to building or improving track crossings. *Source:* White Rock Museum and Archives.

GNR management responded by promising repairs at the crossing sites, making the access point between beaches and businesses safer.[73] But this did not satisfy the *Gazette,* which repeatedly referred to the company simply as a "foreign railway corporation" that had shown "carelessness" in its maintenance of the lands it owned in White Rock. There was little love between the Great Northern and White Rock five years after the relationship had begun with the rerouting of the line, even though that act had been the single most important development in the advancement of White Rock's population and economy.[74]

Instead, most of the credit for White Rock's development went to BC businessmen and politicians such as John Hendry, F.J. MacKenzie, and J.D. Taylor, who helped to transform the town from a backwoods lumber camp into a popular resort destination with a steadily growing permanent population by the summer of 1914.

Furthermore, both permanent and part-time residents arrived well after the establishment of Canadian and American immigration apparatuses in the first decade of the century, meaning that there was no border-crossing culture to defend once the war brought tightened border security. And though residents of White Rock and Surrey frequently shopped in Blaine prior to the establishment of general stores on the Canadian side of the line, unlike in Windsor and

Detroit or St. Stephen and Calais, there was little social or cultural integration between the two communities lining Semiahmoo Bay. There were no shared sports leagues there before the outbreak of war, nor were there local festivals widely attended by residents of both communities.[75] Utilities and services were also separate, with White Rock and Blaine acquiring their own water and electricity.[76] The only exception was fire protection, which until the Second World War was provided to White Rock by Blaine.[77] The Canadian community's telephone service was also routed through Blaine, though this ended during the First World War.[78]

5

"God Save the King"

Relations between White Rock and Blaine

As in Windsor, Detroit, St. Stephen, and Calais, news of Archduke Franz Ferdinand's assassination in Sarajevo in late June 1914 hardly affected the day-to-day routines of White Rock residents. The local *Semiahmoo Gazette*, at the time published and distributed by owner and editor Charles E. Sands on a bimonthly basis, neglected to mention the event in June or July.[1] Instead, as in the other communities, the *Gazette*'s focus was squarely on local events.[2] Across the border, the *Blaine Journal*, published on a weekly basis by owner and editor J.W. Sheets, recognized on July 31 that war was imminent between Europe's great powers but neglected to make such a prediction front-page news, relegating the story to its back section.[3]

Although the *Semiahmoo Gazette* showed little interest in the arms race or the assassination that triggered an epic conflict, there was little doubt in the summer of 1914 that, should war be declared, White Rock would be ready to aid the British Empire in its hour of need. That was made clear the year before when an anonymous local was reported to have remarked "the British navy, nothing. Why, if Japan or China sent a war boat to attack Victoria or Vancouver, Uncle Sam would soon settle the business."[4] The comment immediately elicited a response from editor Sands, who referred to it as "faulty, illogical," and "unpatriotic."[5] Later, in a letter to the editor, a *Gazette* reader called the original commenter a "parasite" and a "bad Canadian," suggesting that the United States would be more likely to invade and annex British Columbia than to protect it from enemies.[6]

The *Semiahmoo Gazette* was fiercely loyal to the British Empire from its first edition in March 1913 to the end of its short publication run in May 1918. In the days leading up to Victoria Day in May 1914, it commemorated the occasion with a selection from Pauline Johnson's poem "Canadian Born": "And we, the men of Canada, can face the world and brag; that we were born in Canada, beneath the British flag."[7] Months later, with Dominion Day approaching, the *Gazette* considered the idea of having to defend Britain in the event of war; referring to Canada as the "first of the dominions in the British Empire," it predicted that the country would "discharge that duty honourably."[8]

In August 1914, the residents of White Rock were asked to do just that. It was a challenge that the *Semiahmoo Gazette* believed all residents of Canada would be prepared to meet. "Canada, New Zealand, Australia, South Africa, and the Federated Malay States will prove, and indeed are already proving, their loyalty to the Great Mother Land in deeds – not words," the *Gazette* proudly declared.[9] Unlike Windsor's *Evening Record*, which viewed the war as a potential disaster for Canada, the *Gazette* saw the conflict as an opportunity for the young nation to prove its worth to the empire on the world stage.[10] "Canada as a nation has cause to be happy this Christmas," the *Gazette* insisted. "She has been given the opportunity to prove, by deeds, that she is loyal, true, and brave; that she stands for honour among nations as among individuals and that the trend of her young sturdy life is ordered and governed by an efficient [and] capable administration."[11]

The people of White Rock immediately embraced this sentiment. A town meeting was called once Britain's declaration of war became known; commencing with the singing of "God Save the King," it featured stirring speeches by local politicians, businessmen, and military figures. The addresses were "met with a most enthusiastic reception," according to the *Gazette,* and prompted five local men to volunteer with the 104th Royal Westminster Regiment in nearby New Westminster.[12] Ex-military men enthusiastic about doing their bit but too old to enlist joined the White Rock chapter of the Imperial Veterans' Association.[13] Many of these men also joined the local Imperial Reserve (IR), a home guard force designed to protect the local community from attacks along the coast or through the border with the United States. A month into the war the IR had already recruited more than forty members, meaning that nearly one in ten White Rock residents joined the unit within a few weeks.[14] (In comparison, Windsor's home guard unit was unpopular for most of the war, and St. Stephen residents neglected to organize such a force.[15]) During the war's early stages, members of the IR, including prominent businessman Henry Thrift, acted as fundraisers for various patriotic purposes, such as the Belgian Relief Fund. At a meeting in early September 1914, they raised seventy dollars with promises for more contributions on behalf of the town's major employer, the Campbell River Lumber Company. Thrift used the meeting to announce a similar commitment by the town's customs and immigration officials, who (unaware that the war would last four years) pledged to help local patriotic funds by setting aside 5 percent of their monthly salaries for "as long as necessary."[16]

This rapid adjustment to war conditions and the ready response of locals to defend the British Empire were the results of a deep cultural connection between the small Canadian border town and the British Empire. Although the Canadian census did not record tiny White Rock's ethnic breakdown in 1911 or 1921, stories from the community's original settlers reveal that many people moving to the area in the late nineteenth century and early twentieth century

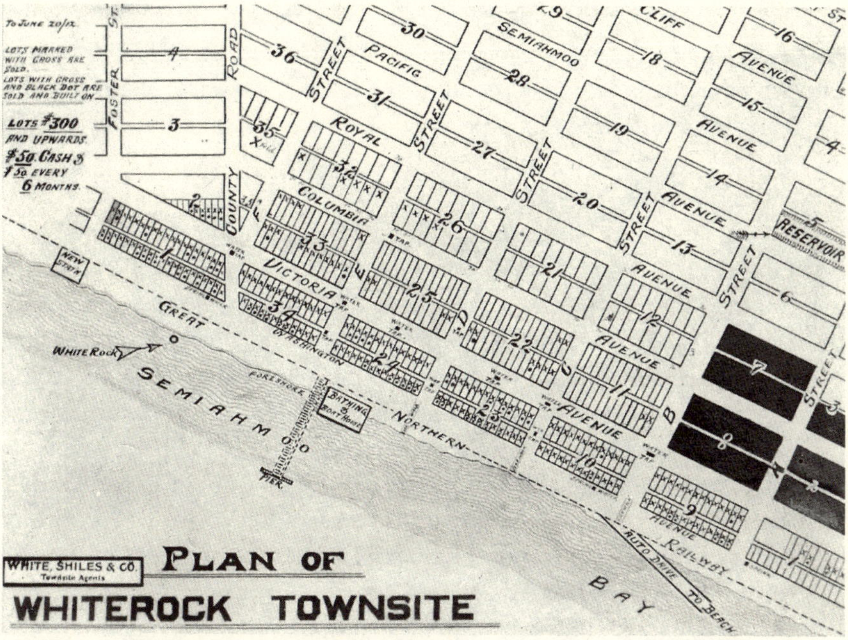

Figure 23 The White Rock townsite plan in 1912. At the time, lots went for roughly $300 – just over $6,000 today. The value of land in White Rock would skyrocket, however, as the area became an attractive resort destination during and after the First World War. *Source:* White Rock Museum and Archives.

were either born in Britain or the descendants of British immigrants. Most, if not all, were extremely proud of their imperial connection, which shaped their migration experiences.[17]

Several prominent residents were noteworthy examples. W.E. Johnson, a White Rock customs collector in 1914, was born in Nova Scotia in 1879 and moved with his family to Surrey in the 1880s. In an interview recorded years later, he recalled how his grandmother, when told that she had only six months to live by her Boston doctor, decided to move back to Halifax, where she had spent much of her life. She lived for five more years, not six months, and Johnson credited her decision to return to British soil as an explanation.[18] He later made a similar adjustment. When working as a customs collector for the US government at Blaine, he was asked to acquire American citizenship in order to secure a promotion. He balked at the idea and instead moved across the border, where he became White Rock's customs collector.[19]

Margaret Stewart, whose oral interviews provide some of the best glimpses of White Rock's early history, was born in 1876 to Scottish parents who met and married in Ontario before travelling west along American railways. Eventually, Stewart's family made their way north to British Columbia, where they settled at Hall's Prairie, just east of White Rock. Stewart remembers that her father refused to make a home for his family in Washington because "he said he never felt really at home in the US" and "felt better when he got under the Union Jack again."[20]

This deep attachment to the British Empire was a familiar theme in the recollections of many White Rock and area pioneers. The Loney brothers, including Edward, John, and James, were born in Carleton County, Ontario. Before pushing west in the 1880s, two of the brothers, Ed and John, explored the idea of acquiring plots of land for themselves in the United States. Upon learning that they would have to swear an oath of allegiance to the US government, the pair decided to return to Canada. Eventually, they travelled to British Columbia along the Canadian Pacific Railway, where they found work in Vancouver and New Westminster before establishing farms near White Rock.[21]

The story of White Rock pioneer Henry Thrift is very similar. During his years in White Rock, he worked tirelessly to promote not only the town's development but also its cultural links with the British Empire. Thrift's father, James, served in the British army from 1813 to 1822 and was present when the Duke of Wellington led Allied forces to victory over Napoleon at Waterloo. Henry followed in his father's footsteps, entering the army at a young age. According to his daughter, Mary, in recognition of his service, Thrift was presented with a Bible signed by the queen herself in 1872. When he moved to Canada a few years later, he hardly lost his sense of attachment to the monarchy. Donning the scarlet jacket, striped pants, and pillbox hat of his former unit, the Hampshire Regiment, he went to see the Duke and Duchess of Cornwall (later King George V and Queen Mary) upon their visit to Vancouver in 1901. Evidently stunned to see such a unique uniform in the crowd, the duke and duchess approached Thrift for a brief chat. "It was a great thrill to him!" Mary recalled in an interview years later.[22]

Thrift brought this pride in the imperial connection with him to White Rock, where he played a significant role in the town's economic and cultural development before and during the First World War. Within months of arriving in Surrey in 1882, he became the county's municipal clerk. Later he worked as a bricklayer and mail carrier and served for a brief period as Surrey's reeve. A successful businessman, Thrift was able to acquire substantial lands in White Rock in the 1890s, prior to its boom as a resort town.[23] But he was no absentee landowner – instead, he used his political clout to help steer the development of White Rock in the new century. In 1910, he helped in the construction of the community's first schoolhouse by donating the necessary land.[24] Two years later he worked with MP J.D. Taylor in a successful bid to win funds from the dominion government for the construction of a local pier.[25] In 1914, he led the push to shut down the St. Leonard Hotel.[26] During the war, he served on a number of local boards and committees, including the White Rock Ratepayers' Association, White Rock Improvement League, Imperial Reserve, South Surrey Conservative Association, and local Military Service Act exemption board.[27] He also served as an assistant constable and sanitation inspector.[28]

Thrift (along with his brother Colin and, later, his son Edmund) was also a prominent figure in the Semiahmoo chapter of the Loyal Orange Order.[29] As opposed to St. Stephen and Windsor, where the Orange Lodge – a Protestant fraternal organization that celebrated the imperial connection and condemned French and Roman Catholic values – had little influence over local affairs, the chapter in White Rock, established in May 1914, was active throughout the period.[30] Its membership included some of the most prominent members of the community, including the Thrift family, MP J.D. Taylor, MPP Frank J. MacKenzie, Surrey Councillor George Radford, and local Methodist minister William Pascoe Goard.[31] The Semiahmoo Orangemen were active throughout the war, from organizing a patriotic banquet attended by 100 members and guests in November 1914 to planning a community-wide celebration of the anniversary of the Battle of the Boyne on July 12, 1916.[32] This latter event included a baby beauty contest, a tug-of-war competition, a Boy Scout procession, an evening concert, and recruiting speeches made by Goard, Thrift, and MacKenzie. The women of White Rock also used the occasion to raise money for the local Red Cross fund.[33] As men began returning to White Rock later in the war, the Orange Lodge – along with the local Red Cross Society – played a key part in organizing "welcome back" events that featured patriotic speeches and musical concerts.[34] Many of these events, as well as other Orange Order celebrations, were held in White Rock's own Orange Hall.[35]

The presence of proud British residents and their formation of pro-British institutions such as the Imperial Reserve and Orange Lodge had significant impacts on White Rock's military effort. At no point during the war did the town struggle to find recruits, and upon imposition of the Military Service Act in 1917 the local newspaper proudly noted that not a single man of military age was left to be conscripted, all having already volunteered for service overseas.[36]

In contrast, across the forty-ninth parallel, Blaine residents rarely focused on the war during its first three years. As opposed to Calais and Detroit, its Red Cross Society was not active until after the US declaration of war.[37] Like many American communities, the town did raise money and goods for the Belgian Relief Fund, from cash to a ton of potatoes and even – rather oddly – dozens of woolen tam-o'-shanters.[38] But though White Rock's young men joined the colours and its older residents supported organizations such as the Orange Order and Imperial Reserve, the people of Blaine showed far more interest in beating booze than "the Hun." Even with the St. Leonard Hotel closed by the outbreak of war, liquor still made its way into the American border community.[39] That enraged J.W. Sheets, owner and editor of the *Blaine Journal.* Throughout the early years of the war, he focused most of his front-page headlines and editorials on the battle with the bottle.

Still, Blaine was hardly kept in a cocoon and learned of the war's impact on Canada through various avenues. Many Blaine residents continued to travel to British Columbia during the early years of the conflict, and they would have witnessed how the war affected their Canadian neighbours. Although there is no evidence of organized, cross-border sports leagues involving Blaine and White Rock representatives, the two towns did periodically engage in games of baseball.[40] Preachers from White Rock and nearby Cloverdale appeared before Blaine residents at various church services during the war's early stages, suggesting some level of religious uniformity.[41] Social organizations also featured a degree of integration, with Blaine women participating in White Rock's Ladies Aid events and White Rock women joining Blaine's chapter of Royal Neighbors, an American organization established in the late nineteenth century to provide its members, all of whom were women, with affordable life insurance.[42] There is little doubt that Blaine residents learned of the war's impact on White Rock upon interacting with their Canadian neighbours within these various forums.

And though war news rarely adorned its front page or received discussion in its editorial section, there was ample coverage of the European conflict in other sections of Blaine's newspaper during the period of American neutrality. For the most part, this coverage was neutral, though not necessarily in its tone and content. The *Journal* often presented its readers with reports from both German and Allied sources; in fact, in one issue, the newspaper provided two entirely different accounts of the same Eastern Front battle, one declaring a massive Russian victory ("Russians Defeat 400,000 Teutons"), the other indicating a significant Russian setback ("Russian Losses Are Huge").[43] The first story, originating from Petrograd, declared the battle a crippling defeat for the German forces, whereas the second article, written in Berlin, suggested that the Russians had lost at least half a million men over the course of the engagement.[44] The same strange contradictions were presented the following year when the *Journal* published conflicting reports from the Germans and British amid the bloody Battle of the Somme.[45]

Rarely did these articles show preference for the Allies, and in some cases they condemned British actions during the war. For example, in early 1916, the *Journal* published a Berlin story accusing the British navy of refusing to rescue drowning German seamen.[46] Even when the neighbouring Canadians were engaged, such as at the Second Battle of Ypres in April 1915, the *Journal* refused to take sides. "The battle of Ypres ended with the Germans consolidating most of the 20 square miles of territory they have won from the allies," it noted. "The engagement has had no result of major importance."[47] Across the border that month, the *Semiahmoo Gazette* noted that White Rock resident J.W. Robertson had been killed in the fighting at Ypres.[48] The *Blaine Journal*'s uninterest in major engagements involving neighbouring Canadians stands in stark contrast to how newspapers in Detroit and Calais covered these battles.[49]

Despite the impact of the conflict on neighbouring White Rock, the *Journal* directed few editorials toward the Canadian war effort. In fact, by the close of 1914, most stories associated with the fighting overseas had been pushed from the *Journal*'s front pages to its back sections. Not even the controversial sinking of *RMS Lusitania,* which took more than 100 Americans with it to the bottom of the Atlantic, elicited a passionate response. Although word of the May 1915 disaster received a prominent place on the paper's front page, Sheets provided no editorial on the subject, instead offering commentary on the reduction of whiskey production in Kentucky and Maryland.[50] In fact, the *Journal* rarely discussed the war in its editorial section, and when it did, as in July 1915, it condemned the conflict as "the greatest crime of any age" while calling on the Wilson administration to "initiate the movement for universal peace."[51] The *Journal* also provided readers with weekly sermons from Pastor Charles Taze Russell, who argued in doomsday-themed columns that the war was a sign of an impending class struggle that would end in global anarchy.[52] His controversial tirades rarely appeared in Detroit or Calais newspapers, and later in the war they were banned from Canada entirely by the country's main censorship apparatus.[53] There is little doubt that editorials condemning the war, whether written by Sheets or Russell, would have been considered offensive by White Rock residents sacrificing their time, money, and lives in search of victory.

But even anti-war editorials were rare in a newspaper focused almost entirely on prohibition during the period of US neutrality, as had been the case prior to August 1914. Local prohibitionists received a boost that fall when both Washington and Blaine voted overwhelmingly in favour of prohibition, the measure passing in the latter by a ratio of approximately two and a half votes to one.[54] This continued a trend already established in Blaine since 1910, when saloons were first banned. Like many progressives in favour of eliminating liquor, the *Journal*'s editor saw prohibition as a boon to the local community. Estimating that in 1909 the four local bars took in roughly $30,000,

Sheets asserted that, in late 1914, such money "now goes to buy food and clothing and build homes."[55]

To be fair, the *Blaine Journal* did not necessarily reflect the opinions of all residents of the American border community during the First World War. However, its preoccupation with prohibition and its relegation of war news to its back pages do suggest that people in the community – who would not have purchased the paper had its opinions not reflected those of the majority – were not particularly interested in the war or how it affected their neighbours in White Rock.[56] This is somewhat surprising if only for the fact that at least a few Blaine residents had joined various BC units earlier in the war and were with the Canadian Expeditionary Force overseas.[57]

The frayed relationship with White Rock was almost certainly a factor contributing to Blaine's relative uninterest in the war and specifically the Canadians' war effort. Relations between the two communities continued to be somewhat fractured after August 1914; for example, in February 1915, members of White Rock's South Surrey Conservatives Association discouraged local businesses from hiring Blaine residents in an effort to reverse the Canadian town's unemployment problem. It was an altogether ironic idea given that one of White Rock's biggest employers, the Campbell River Lumber Company, was owned by Blaine resident Harold Hunter.[58]

White Rock residents also pressured the local *Semiahmoo Gazette* (after June 1915 renamed the *Surrey Gazette*) to stop running ads for Blaine businesses, presumably because doing so discouraged readers from frequenting Canadian establishments during wartime. For some time, the *Gazette* had advertised widely for businesses based in the American border community. The State Bank of Blaine, Pastime Theater, Wolten and Montfort hardware store, and M.M. Barber Jewelers were just a few of the many Blaine enterprises that paid to advertise in White Rock's newspaper on a regular basis in 1914 and 1915.[59] For a newspaper that struggled financially throughout the war (and eventually collapsed in the spring of 1918), it must have been difficult to turn away such financing. As a result, *Semiahmoo Gazette* owner Charles Sands defended his decision to advertise Blaine businesses with this passionate appeal:

> White Rock employs many Blaine men for labour. White Rock people freely patronize Blaine merchants. White Rock men smoke and chew tobacco purchased in Blaine. White Rock ladies, in many instances, are adorned with millinery from Blaine. Articles of clothing from Blaine are worn by White Rock inhabitants. Blaine eggs and butter are found on many a White Rock breakfast table. The gasoline which will clean the ink from this type was purchased in Blaine by a White Rock merchant. The White Rock children, when sick, are invariably

dosed with drugs from Blaine stores. Even the agates from White Rock beaches are taken to Blaine to be polished and mounted.[60]

Given all of this interaction between Blaine and White Rock residents, Sands thought that he need not defend his decision to accept advertising revenue from American companies. Furthermore, troubling finances dictated that he accept that revenue since it cost him $600 to run the newspaper each year and Canadian subscriptions accounted for only $200 of his income.[61]

Despite Sands's fiery defence of his advertising practices, by mid-1915 the number of Blaine businesses advertising in the *Surrey Gazette* had been noticeably reduced. A year later there were virtually no Blaine firms placing ads in the Canadian paper. It remains unknown exactly why and whether or not it was associated with White Rock residents pressuring the *Gazette* to halt advertising of Blaine businesses. Sands was a prominent member of various community organizations that helped to raise funds for the war effort and had two brothers in the CEF, one recognized for "brave and efficient military service while under heavy fire"; perhaps, then, Sands faced more intense pressure than the typical newspaper owner to advertise "loyally."[62] Regardless, when the war started, many Blaine firms advertised in the *Semiahmoo Gazette*, but by the spring of 1916 not a single one continued to do so.

An editorial late in 1915 reveals that the *Gazette*'s initial defence of its practice of running ads for Blaine businesses was related, in all likelihood, to the newspaper's delicate financial situation rather than its editor's desire to maintain positive relations between residents of White Rock and Blaine. In an October editorial entitled "Border Towns," Sands openly discussed the advantages and disadvantages of living and working in a Canadian community located next to the international boundary. The advantages were almost wholly tied to the creation of local jobs through the establishment of customs and immigration offices. But Sands asserted that there were many disadvantages to residing in a Canadian border town, too, notably the fact that labour regulations concerning alien workers were not particularly well enforced, allowing Americans and Canadians to cross the border relatively easily in search of employment. In most cases, one side hired more than the other, and in the Semiahmoo Bay border region Sands held that the balance tipped in favour of Blaine: "As far as White Rock and practically the whole of Surrey municipality is concerned this latitude works out as 'give' on the part of the Canadian and 'take' on the part of our United States cousins immediately to the south of us."[63]

The US entry into the war in April 1917 evoked mixed emotions from the people of Blaine. Some met the news by travelling to nearby Bellingham, the nearest mid-sized US city, to mark the occasion.[64] The *Blaine Journal*, meanwhile, treated the task of sending local men off to Europe and supporting the American war effort as something of a chore – not at all desirable, though admittedly necessary. "What we had been sincerely hoping would not come is a reality," the *Journal* noted the day that Congress approved President Woodrow Wilson's request for a declaration of war on Germany. "The people of this country have not wanted war, and desired that we keep from it by ever self-respecting means, but we believe the time has come when the country must act."[65]

The American entry into the Great War does appear to have facilitated the improvement of relations between Canadians of White Rock and Americans of Blaine following several years of bitter disputes involving cross-border employment, liquor trafficking, and pollution of shared Semiahmoo Bay. In the pages of the *Blaine Journal*, earlier reports of German victories at the front were replaced with heroic tales of British, French, and Canadian successes, coupled with new condemnations of German diplomatic and military conduct.[66] Although most Blaine residents visited Bellingham to mark the country's declaration of war, a month later they joined their Canadian neighbours in commemorating Victoria Day. In fact, residents of Blaine did not merely attend the day's events in White Rock but actually had their own celebration, inviting their neighbours from British Columbia to participate. It was the first time in its history that Blaine had observed the late queen's birthday, and it marked the occasion by flying Union Jacks along with Stars and Stripes across town. White Rock businessman Henry Thrift was invited (along with the White Rock Boy Scouts) to participate in a special ceremony, whereby the Union Jack and Old Glory were raised together on the same flagpole.[67] Afterward, a Bellingham singer enticed Blaine men to join the colours with the song "Come Boys, Come." Written by a White Rock woman whose husband was stationed at the front, the song was a "beautiful piece" and "written from the heart."[68] Given the prominent role of White Rock residents in the day's events, it is little surprise that the *Journal* noted the large attendance of British Columbians.[69]

The display of positive cross-border relations, revealed for the first time in years by the American declaration of war, continued over the next few weeks. White Rock Boy Scouts were invited to Blaine to participate in its annual Memorial Day events, which included a service at the local Congregational church followed by a special musical program.[70] In June 1917, Blaine hosted the Chautauqua, a travelling circuit of events that featured musical performances as well as lectures and debates on popular social and political ideas.[71] Among the more popular attractions, as scheduled by the Blaine Chautauqua Association, were performances by Canadians, including baritone H. Ruthven

Macdonald and comedian Francis Labadie.[72] In one lecture, attendants sat riveted as a former chaplain of the Canadian Expeditionary Force discussed his harrowing experiences at the front.[73] No doubt White Rock inhabitants crossed the boundary to witness such proceedings. Blaine residents were also invited to attend social events on the Canadian side of the line following the US declaration of war. They participated in a "joint celebration" of Dominion Day in July 1917 and later that month joined White Rock residents in an evening dance designed to raise money for patriotic purposes.[74]

But the US declaration of war had a limited impact on the fractured relationship between White Rock and Blaine. There were no editorials in the *Surrey Gazette* or *Blaine Journal* declaring that the war was acting as a "renewal" of ties binding Americans and Canadians together. In White Rock, the *Surrey Gazette* greeted the American declaration of war with the tongue-in-cheek headline "The Stars and Stripes Are Now Worthy of Full Honours," suggesting that some residents of the Canadian border town regarded Old Glory as rather inglorious before April 1917.[75] White Rock residents also remained rather unsympathetic to Blaine's continued experiment with prohibition, even after British Columbia voted to go dry in 1916.[76] A year later booze continued to make its way across the international boundary from White Rock into Blaine, much to the frustration of the *Blaine Journal*.[77] Neither White Rock nor Surrey officials appear to have made any effort to prevent this kind of trafficking.[78]

These two communities continued to have fundamentally different priorities in 1917 and 1918, just as they had earlier in the war and before it. Blaine embraced moral reform beyond mere prohibition, instituting a number of strict ordinances in the war's latter stages. Young people were banned from visiting pool rooms and pawn shops and restricted from going out late at night by a community-wide curfew.[79] One ordinance banned the sale of fireworks for the Fourth of July, and another forced civilians to aid overwhelmed police officers.[80]

Residents of White Rock, meanwhile, expressed little interest in such reforms. When the rest of British Columbia voted for prohibition in 1916, White Rock sought to keep the beer taps flowing.[81] This was a visible divergence of interests between White Rock and its American neighbour; whereas the focus of Blaine Town Council meetings was often on the introduction of ordinances designed to limit how wild a summer weekend might become, discussions about White Rock at gatherings of Surrey Council typically involved lobbying by the White Rock Improvement League for funds to help enhance its appeal to out-of-town vacationers by expanding and improving road networks and upgrading sanitation facilities.[82]

Given these differences, it is not particularly surprising that news of the armistice failed to bring these distinct communities together. Since the *Surrey*

FIGURE 24 The large rock behind White Rock's name. Located along the beach and a short walk from the community's pier and railway station, the famous white rock weighs an estimated 486 tons. *Source:* White Rock Museum and Archives.

Gazette terminated publication earlier in 1918, examples of armistice celebrations in White Rock, unfortunately, are lacking. What we do know is that White Rock was hit hard by the Spanish flu in October and November 1918. Given such a dire situation, perhaps any celebration was a quiet and somewhat solemn one.[83]

In Blaine – seriously affected by the flu pandemic the following year – news of the armistice was happily met, but residents did not engage in the community-wide or transnational celebrations seen in St. Stephen and Calais or Windsor and Detroit.[84] People awoke on November 11 to pleasing news that the war was over, but many continued with their daily routines and went to work. In fact, the only unique feature of the day was the brief blaring of Blaine's fire siren to relay word of Germany's defeat. However, "aside from that there was little evidence of the receipt of such joyous news," the *Blaine Journal* reported.[85]

The war did not dramatically alter the relationship between White Rock and Blaine before or after the American entry into the conflict in April 1917, and they continued to be distinct towns whose residents had relatively unique war experiences. Compared with other communities in this study, American neutrality appears to have been less of a divisive topic in White Rock and Blaine, perhaps precisely because the border-crossing culture there was not nearly as advanced as that in the St. Croix Valley or Detroit River region. In St. Stephen, there was a sense that Canada and the Canadians residing along the dividing

St. Croix River had somehow been betrayed by their American neighbours in Calais and beyond, contributing to the emergence of tensions between the two communities in 1915 and 1916. However, the American entry into the war in April 1917 ushered in a period of intense cross-border movement and social integration in the St. Croix Valley that was in no way matched by residents of White Rock and Blaine.

The next chapter moves on from the relationship between the people of White Rock and Blaine to the way that the border was practically administered shortly prior to and during the First World War. As will be seen, there was no opposition to the implementation of strict border-crossing regulations by the residents of either White Rock or Blaine because, as opposed to Windsor and Detroit or St. Stephen and Calais, a bureaucratized border was introduced to this region prior to the emergence of a visible border-crossing culture.

6

Booze and Bandits

Administering the White Rock–Blaine Border

From the late nineteenth century onward, White Rock and the surrounding area of south Surrey were considered a particularly sensitive section of the international boundary. Like any other point along the Canada–US border, however, this was a reflection of circumstances unique to the wider region and not the surrounding localities, in this case White Rock and Blaine. This part of the boundary – far more than those sections dividing Windsor and Detroit or St. Stephen and Calais – was a critical crossing point for people of "undesirable" races, including East Indians, Chinese, and Japanese.

Throughout the late nineteenth century and early twentieth century, the people of British Columbia and Washington were fixated on race, specifically on keeping out Asians. The real concerns for immigration officials in Ottawa and along the BC–Washington border were Chinese and Indian nationals; the former were considered undesirable since completion of the Canadian Pacific Railway in 1885, the latter since the emergence of a North American wing of their homeland's anti-colonial movement in the early twentieth century.[1] Both had customs and cultures that, in the minds of many white Canadians and Americans, threatened each nation's Anglo-Saxon heritage.[2] The Chinese were deemed a particular menace, however, because they worked longer hours and for 30 to 50 percent lower wages than their white counterparts, making them a threat to white employment during economic crises.[3] These concerns were hardly limited to North America's west coast – both federal governments expressed a desire to limit Asian immigration nationwide in the late nineteenth century – but the focus of anti-Asian legislation was certainly on the Pacific region. Given the proximity of British Columbia (relative to the other provinces) to Asia, it is little surprise that, according to the Canadian census of 1911, more than 17,000 Chinese-born people resided in British Columbia, compared with just over 2,600 in Ontario and fewer than 100 in New Brunswick.[4] South of the border, the 1910 US census showed more than 25,000 East Indian, Chinese, and Japanese nationals living in Washington, compared with 7,700 in Michigan and 1,000 in Maine.[5]

Monitoring the movements of these undesirable races became a key part of immigration inspection at the BC–Washington border shortly after the expansion of American and Canadian immigration departments. Several of the most popular crossing points were in south Surrey: Douglas, on Blaine's west side, approximately five kilometres from downtown White Rock and directly adjacent to Semiahmoo Bay; Pacific Highway, on Blaine's east section and across from farmers' fields of the Hall's Prairie area; and at rail depots in downtown White Rock and Blaine, a few miles north and south of where the Great Northern Railway crossed the forty-ninth parallel.

Watching over this territory was an enormous task for the four Canadian immigration agents hired to patrol an expanse stretching from Semiahmoo Bay's shores to the Pacific Highway, a distance of roughly six kilometres east to west. In 1913, two inspectors were stationed at White Rock to monitor activity along nearby roads, the GNR line, and across Semiahmoo Bay. Another inspector was stationed at the Pacific Highway crossing, and a final agent acted in a relief and patrol role, covering territory in between.[6] The task was not made any easier by the federal government's constantly fluctuating immigration policy; for example, when railway companies in British Columbia required labourers, certain standards – such as a qualification that all immigrants have twenty-five dollars on them – were waived, meaning that the emphasis on keeping out poor central and eastern Europeans was relaxed.[7] Immigration inspectors were also expected to be aware of labour conditions in various parts of British Columbia; where workers threatened to strike, any immigrant admitting the place as his or her destination was supposed to be rejected.[8] Although this was policy for immigration agents nationwide, it was seen as particularly pressing on the west coast, where the Industrial Workers of the World (IWW), or "Wobblies," had a significant impact on organizing labour protests among railway employees prior to the First World War.[9]

The two immigration officers stationed at White Rock spent virtually all of their time inspecting trains stopped at the local railway depot while moving between Seattle and Vancouver in 1912 and 1913, leaving them with few opportunities to patrol the international boundary. Instead, that task was left to two other agents, one stationed at the Pacific Highway and a second patrolling the territory near and behind the line on his horse. The difficulty in keeping out undesirables with so few men was alleviated, however slightly, by regular communication with American immigration agents stationed at Blaine; according to department policy at the time, both were required to alert their American and Canadian counterparts when a traveller was rejected.[10] Blaine immigration agents also tipped off Canadian inspectors at White Rock when they suspected that undesirables were preparing for an illegal move across the boundary; this was the case in March 1913 when Blaine officials revealed to Canadian inspectors that a group of thirteen Greek travellers had gathered at the boundary and were suspected of preparing for an overnight infiltration

FIGURE 25 Visitors to White Rock's beaches who travelled north across the border were stopped for questioning by immigration inspectors operating out of the railway station, visible here. *Source:* White Rock Museum and Archives.

of Canada, presumably because they feared being rejected by Canadian immigration authorities. All available inspectors were called on, with the four Canadian agents fanning out across the territory between Semiahmoo Bay and the Pacific Highway. Unfortunately for the inspectors, they saw only shadows moving that night and were unable to apprehend a single individual. The following morning, they found that only five of the original thirteen Greeks remained in Blaine.[11]

This was not the only case in which aliens unlikely to gain legal entry into British Columbia crossed the international boundary. For years following the rerouting of the Great Northern Railway track to White Rock, the easiest way to get into Canada illegally was to board a northbound train in Seattle. Because there were only two immigration agents stationed at White Rock to inspect passengers – and they had only minutes to do so because of tight scheduling by the railway – these inspectors relied on GNR porters to report anyone who might be considered undesirable by the immigration authorities.[12] This was an incredibly flawed system for a couple of reasons. First, porters were not familiar with the Immigration Act, knowledge of which became a requirement for all men hired to work as Canadian inspectors after 1913.[13] Second, since most porters were poorly paid African Americans, they were easily and often paid off by men and women who suspected that, for whatever reason, they might be rejected by the immigration authorities.[14]

This tactic worked well for some groups, notably prostitutes, but was hardly a viable option for more visible undesirables such as Chinese labourers. But they also found ways to get around immigration inspections; they simply got off a GNR train at an American town near the border, such as Blaine, and then moved across the boundary under the cover of darkness.[15] Another tactic was to take a boat to Point Roberts – American territory but connected by land to British Columbia – and cross the boundary there.[16]

The ease with which undesirables crossed the border into British Columbia led to a significant increase in their populations prior to the First World War. In 1913, the *British Columbian* newspaper of New Westminster noted the increased population of Chinese- and Japanese-born residents of the province between 1901 and 1911, with their numbers growing from 14,865 to 19,568 and from 4,597 to 8,587, respectively.[17] Furthermore, census figures (released in 1913) showed that in 1911 people of Chinese and Japanese descent accounted for roughly one-eighth of the entire population of Delta, the census district encompassing White Rock.[18] Had they formed their own ethnically homogeneous communities, separately the Chinese and Japanese of Delta would have outnumbered the permanent population of White Rock. In comparison, the number of people of Chinese heritage living in Windsor that year was just forty-two.[19] No Japanese were recorded living there. In St. Stephen, not a single person of Chinese or Japanese extraction lived within town limits.[20]

In White Rock, these trends were seen as alarming. Prior to the war, locals pointed to Japan and China, not Germany or Austria-Hungary, as the most likely countries to attack British Columbia, and many locals might have looked on Chinese and Japanese immigrants as if they were advance spies of an enemy nation.[21] But the greater fear was that "Asiatics" would simply displace Anglo-Saxon British Columbians as the province's dominant race. In an April 1914 sermon, Methodist minister and local Orange Lodge executive member W.P. Goard admitted his fear that the invasion of British Columbia by the "Oriental nations" would soon lead to the province's Anglo-Saxon population being "driven out," not unlike the way that European immigration contributed to the decline of Canada's Aboriginal peoples. "Canada holds the fate of the whole Anglo-Saxon race within her grasp and British Columbia especially is the bulwark for the rest of the Dominion and for the continent of Europe against the onward march of the Oriental," Goard insisted. Dramatically pointing to the Union Jack hanging above the platform on which he spoke, Goard encouraged the Anglo-Saxon residents of White Rock to "Go Forth and Possess ... by might of arms as well as by right of occupation." With that, his listeners rang out their support for his message with booming applause and the singing of "God Save the King."[22]

White Rock was home to perhaps a few dozen Chinese and Japanese labourers employed by the local Campbell River Lumber Company, located on the town's eastern periphery. Most resided in shacks next to the mill or along nearby Parker Street. White Rock resident Carrie Moffatt, whose father was chief engineer at the mill, recalled years later that East Indians were also employed by the company.[23] Moffatt, however, does not discuss whether tensions between Asian and white workers were high during the war years or whether they were affected by the nativism of community leaders such as Goard. At no point during its publication did the *Surrey Gazette* discuss frictions between white and Asian residents of White Rock, though this does not necessarily mean that people of Chinese, Japanese, or East Indian descent were treated like valuable members of the community.

Across the boundary at Blaine, a town named for a presidential candidate who stood for Chinese exclusion, there was also concern about the movement of undesirable racial groups.[24] For years, the people of Washington, like their neighbours in British Columbia, had depicted Chinese labourers as opium-smoking, strange-looking, diseased people.[25] Despite these attitudes, many Asian workers were employed by Blaine's salmon canneries, though there was a concerted effort to have them replaced with white women during the late nineteenth century and early twentieth century.[26] As was the case north of the border, Asians were welcome in Blaine only when there was no white person willing to perform a necessary (if not particularly desirable) task, such as gutting fish.[27]

Residents of Blaine also saw many Asians pass through town before and during the war, a number attempting to cross the nearby international boundary illegally. Where possible, US and Canadian inspectors arrested not only these immigrants but also the individuals who tried to profit from their surreptitious passage into either country.[28] In one instance, two GNR employees were arrested for attempting to smuggle a pair of Chinese men into Canada in a large toolbox.[29] Before transferring from Blaine to White Rock, immigration inspector W.E. Johnson became familiar with a number of "Chink Runners," as they were called, from the "Cloverdale Smuggler" to "Chinese Kelly."[30]

With the outbreak of war in 1914, a growing number of European immigrants also began making their way from British Columbia into Washington via Blaine. Although Canada would not pursue conscription until 1917, many ethnic groups fled the country out of fear that they would be drafted into the Canadian Expeditionary Force. This traffic was not limited to enemy aliens:

in fact, the flow of Greeks and Russians into the United States was so intense that it forced US immigration authorities to post additional inspectors to various points near the international boundary.[31] The following year even more immigration inspectors were hired to help deal with an influx of Austrians and Germans who, according to the *Blaine Journal*, "evidently don't like the atmosphere up there."[32]

Although the heavy traffic of immigrants raised alarms at the local level, Blaine's support for increased border security during the war was primarily associated with its fight against booze. Following the town's decision to go dry in 1910, the *Blaine Journal* lobbied for the hiring of more US officials at the international boundary to monitor cross-border movement and limit liquor trafficking. In 1913, it lamented the US government's decision to move customs inspectors from the Douglas area, on Blaine's west side, closest to White Rock and directly opposite the St. Leonard Hotel, to the Pacific Highway location a few miles to the east. The fear, of course, was that Douglas would now become a major crossing point for drunks and their liquor:

> It is hoped that [Douglas] station will not long be left without attention, a station that is today next to the Great Northern railway, the most travelled along the border for many miles. We are reliably informed that the average number of vehicles crossing the line at this point daily is above 100 and a great many fail to report after crossing.[33]

Indeed, these were extremely busy crossing points prior to the outbreak of the First World War. Customs reports show that 19,934 people were recorded passing through the Douglas station in vehicles in 1913, the vast majority crossing to visit rather than settle permanently in British Columbia. The White Rock immigration office, headed by Inspector-in-Charge H.G. Lawrence, reported 94,655 passengers in transit across the GNR tracks that year, with approximately 4,736 intending to stay in the province. Of them, an estimated 1,231 were rejected, with another seventy-two prosecuted for attempting to enter the country illegally. Of course, given that there were so few inspectors appointed to guard the boundary in this busy border region, the true number of aliens entering the country surreptitiously was impossible to calculate.[34]

Therefore, in their first years of operation in south Surrey, immigration authorities faced the imposing task of keeping out thousands of undesirable immigrants with only a handful of inspectors. These men and the department for which they worked also faced unique challenges in this part of the long international boundary: unlike other points along the border, this was a key crossing point for people of undesirable races, particularly Asians. In communities such as New Westminster and White Rock, concern about the constantly growing population of Chinese, Japanese, and East Indians served to arouse unique attitudes toward the international boundary not seen in Windsor or St. Stephen, where border permeability was viewed as advantageous to the local economy and culture and where fewer people worried that Anglo-Saxons were about to become outnumbered by Asians. Liquor trafficking, though a concern along the Detroit and St. Croix Rivers, did not arouse as much anxiety in these areas during the war because Canadian and American opinions of prohibition were far less divergent than those at White Rock and Blaine.[35] Finally, even the matter of pollution was handled differently; whereas White Rock, Surrey Council, and Blaine failed to work together effectively to find a peaceful solution to the dumping of salmon offal in shared Semiahmoo Bay, community leaders in Windsor and Detroit came together in 1912 to discuss complaints that factories on the American side of the border were polluting the shared Detroit River.[36] As a result, at no point before or during the war did Windsor and Detroit newspapers engage in a bitter dispute over pollution such as that seen in the pages of the *Semiahmoo Gazette* and *Blaine Journal*.

Unlike in Windsor and St. Stephen, immediately following the declaration of war, White Rock prepared for trouble at the border. Whereas the local home guard remained understaffed and unpopular in Windsor throughout the war, and St. Stephen never saw the need to organize such a force, in White Rock the Imperial Reserve attracted forty members within weeks of Britain's entrance into the European conflict.[37] Many of the town's most visible community leaders, such as businessman and politician Henry Thrift, played important roles in the Imperial Reserve, whose membership included men who had military experience but were unfit for duty in 1914.

Also unlike Windsor's home guard, White Rock's IR got its first taste of action almost immediately after being formed when a Russian gang known as the Sedro-Woolley Bandits robbed several banks in Washington and British Columbia before moving into south Surrey.[38] The case left a long-lasting impression on residents of White Rock and the surrounding area when the bandits, in a shootout with authorities in the Canadian border town, killed customs inspector Clifford Adams.[39] Blaine's sheriff worked with Canadian customs and immigration inspectors, New Westminster police, MPP Frank J. MacKenzie, and White Rock's IR to track down the bandits, most of whom were eventually found and shot dead at various points around the municipalities of Surrey and Whatcom County, Washington.[40] Only the group's leader escaped with his life and made off with most of the booty.[41]

There were also local and personal links with the movement of enemy aliens – including Germans, Austrians, and Hungarians – following the declaration of war. Shortly before the war, the *Semiahmoo Gazette* noted that the local White Rock Hotel had just been leased by Anthony Kengyel, a Vancouver businessman with experience in managing just such establishments. "The White Rock hotel is therefore in good hands and patrons can rely upon quick, efficient service, an excellent table and all home comforts," the *Gazette* reported.[42]

Imagine the town's shock, then, when shortly after the declaration of war Kengyel abandoned his business and fled across the border to Washington, apparently en route to his Austrian homeland. Initially prevented from crossing by American immigration authorities at Blaine, the undeterred Kengyel backtracked to Vancouver and eventually made it to Seattle.[43] In a letter written from Portland, Oregon, and acquired by New Westminster's *British Columbian*, Kengyel proclaimed that he was on his way back to Austria-Hungary to join the army.[44]

There was considerable movement of enemy aliens across this part of the boundary during the first year of the war. Although White Rock immigration inspectors reported working closely with customs officers to keep German and Austro-Hungarian army reservists such as Kengyel from fleeing Canada via the United States for Europe, in early 1915 the *Blaine Journal* noted that there had been an influx of just such reservists since the beginning of the war.[45] Evidence suggests that in July Germans living in Hall's Prairie (roughly five kilometres east of White Rock) had aided many of these reservists in getting across the line. Ernst Hamel and David Kitzel, having been suspected by White Rock immigration officials of smuggling enemy aliens into the United States, were arrested after a brief but successful undercover scheme executed by Stephen Raymer, an agent working for the Vancouver immigration office. Raymer, who pretended to be a German reservist seeking help in making his way to Washington undetected, was taken in by Hamel and Kitzel and eventually shown a forest path that led to Blaine, where he was to contact a tailor known only as "Uhrrman." Initially charged with high treason (an offence punishable by death), the accused were eventually prosecuted for the lesser crime of aiding and abetting enemy aliens in illegally crossing the border.[46] Although Raymer's testimony appeared to be strong enough to secure a conviction, defence attorney Joseph Martin was successful in bringing the character of the star witness into question.[47] Because all other evidence was circumstantial, two separate trials in the summer and fall of 1915 ended in hung juries, in each case eight jurors standing for conviction and four for acquittal.[48] As a result, in November Hamel and Kitzel were freed on their own recognizance, no doubt to the frustration of Raymer and the prosecuting attorneys, who had succeeded in convincing two-thirds of the appointed jurors that the accused were guilty.[49]

Despite the failure of the Crown to secure a conviction, the trial of Hamel and Kitzel revealed that the BC–Washington border was in danger of becoming a site for the widespread smuggling of enemy aliens. In Blaine, but especially in White Rock, it almost certainly stirred up feelings of paranoia, particularly since both men had deep roots within the wider border region: Hamel had once been elected to the Surrey Council, and Kitzel had family members across the boundary in Birch Bay, Washington, roughly ten kilometres south of Blaine. The latter man had ten children, including seven with his first wife, Catherine (who died in 1900), and three more with Amaliza Seeling (also known as Emilie Seline), who spent some time in Blaine (and was well known throughout the community) before marrying Kitzel and moving north of the border to Hall's Prairie.[50] Both of Kitzel's wives had been born in Germany, though all ten children lived in the United States and Canada.[51] According to the *British Columbian*, Hamel had lived in Hall's Prairie for about fifteen years, Kitzel thirty.[52]

During the years that followed, immigration and customs officers stationed at White Rock and the surrounding area aggressively patrolled the boundary in an attempt to limit the cross-border movements of enemy aliens.[53] Inspector-in-Charge Lawrence, after years of requesting more manpower from the federal government, finally saw more inspectors hired to patrol this part of the boundary. By 1918, the staff at White Rock had increased from two to four men, with a man added to the Douglas station (previously unattended by immigration officials) and four more posted to the Pacific Highway station (previously overseen by a single inspector).[54] At the railway depot in White Rock, their strategies also changed: rather than hastily inspecting passengers on GNR cars at the local station, two inspectors now rode the train to Seattle and back each day, one in the morning, the other in the evening.[55] This solved the earlier problem of porters – expected to report travellers likely to be rejected – being paid off by passengers nervous about their ability to enter the country legally.

Still, these officials faced the enormous task of preventing the cross-border movement of enemy aliens, people of undesirable racial groups, and, after conscription came into effect in 1917, men of military age. The number of people crossing the border in White Rock and area late in the war was staggering, with an estimated 55,000 making their way along the GNR tracks between March 31, 1917, and March 31, 1918, and another 7,000 crossing in automobiles at the Pacific Highway station in May 1918 alone.[56]

That traffic remained a point of serious concern in both White Rock and Blaine. South of the border, the *Blaine Journal* continued to fret over the movement of alcohol from Canada into town. A newspaper that gleefully met news of British Columbia's move to prohibition on October 1, 1917, by declaring the date "British Columbia Day" was soon disappointed to find that alcohol could still easily be acquired. Christmas Eve 1917 was particularly ugly for Blaine prohibitionists, with intoxicated locals stumbling about town and engaging in fistfights.[57] According to the *Journal*, part of the problem was that US customs officials were woefully inconsistent in how they followed the state's prohibition laws; in Blaine, some customs officers allegedly allowed travellers entering the country to carry one quart of liquor with them.[58] Elsewhere along the border, officials were not so lenient; in 1918, *Journal* editor J.W. Sheets commended Canadian and American customs officials at Sumas, Washington, and Huntingdon, British Columbia, for seizing several cases of cognac and whiskey. At the same time, Sheets suggested that the US customs department would do well to move some of those capable officers to Blaine, where they could help to prevent liquor trafficking.[59] These incidents indicate that not everyone in Blaine fully supported local prohibition, and their behaviour only reinforced demands by the town's majority (who supported the measure) that the border be closely monitored to prevent BC alcohol from being distributed throughout the community.

As Blaine prohibitionists continued to fight liquor late in the war, in White Rock the *Surrey Gazette* expressed concern over the growing population of non-whites in the province. With reports that the ratio of Asians to whites had increased from 1:7 prior to the war to 1:3.5 in 1917, the *Gazette* suggested immediately conscripting Chinese men into labour battalions to perform manual tasks, such as harvesting wheat or cutting timber.[60] In this way, their numbers could be monitored and their behaviour controlled by military authorities. Preventing more Asians from entering the province through strict enforcement of immigration regulations was thus a major concern in White Rock in 1917, as it had been prior to the war.

There were also concerns in White Rock about the movement of cheaper American goods across the border into Surrey from Blaine. Specifically, the problem was with Blaine's butchers: because meat could be acquired much more cheaply in the US border town, any attempt to open a butcher's shop in White Rock failed.[61] In 1918, intrepid White Rock customs official W.E. Johnson investigated the matter.[62] He found that all meat purchased in Blaine and headed for White Rock needed to be stamped by the United States Department of Agriculture (USDA) if it was to avoid a duty. Smaller cuts of meat meant for household consumption usually did not carry this stamp. For years, Canadian customs officials had either overlooked the rule or been unaware of it; regardless, Johnson began to insist that anyone bringing meat not stamped by the USDA across the line into British Columbia pay duty. The duty effectively

FIGURE 26 White Rock's customs and immigration team. Inspector W.E. Johnson, seated in the middle of the front row, lived in a tent along the Canada–US border when he and his wife first moved to the area. *Source:* White Rock Museum and Archives.

eliminated the differential between BC and Blaine meat prices, stopping the flow of such products north across the boundary.

In an oral interview conducted years later, Johnson expressed great pride in this achievement, suggesting that his actions did not make him an outcast in the community.[63] Indeed, he would go on to become one of White Rock's most popular figures, serving as customs collector and president of the White Rock Waterworks Company. Later in life he was recognized by the city of White Rock and municipality of Surrey for his contributions to the region's development.[64] His actions, then, were not seen to be detrimental to relations with Blaine or the economic advancement of White Rock. This stands in stark contrast to Windsor, where retailers were verbally attacked by locals angry over the allegation that store owners had requested Ottawa to send a "lady searcher" to prevent the smuggling of goods purchased in Detroit at Easter 1915, and to St. Stephen, where the arrival of federal customs investigators intent on preventing local officials from bending the rules aroused a vitriolic response from the *Saint Croix Courier.*[65]

As they had prior to the war, both White Rock and Blaine saw the border as a tool that, if administered properly, could improve the lives of locals. This attitude was much different from that held by residents of the Detroit and St. Croix River regions, where being able to cross the boundary easily was seen as key to maintaining a strong economy and positive relations with neighbouring communities.

This kind of border-crossing culture did not exist in White Rock and Blaine during the First World War. In its early stages, the attention of locals was drawn to the dangers posed by border permeability, including the movement of Asians, criminals, and enemy aliens. Unlike Windsor and Detroit or St. Stephen and Calais, these fears were not overcome as the war progressed but contributed to pre-existing concerns about border permeability, including the surreptitious movements of unwanted goods and people of undesirable racial groups. As a result, there was no protest over the implementation of stricter customs and immigration standards as the war continued. In fact, local citizens called for greater regulation of immigration and goods such as liquor and groceries. And though the previous chapter showed that the American entry into the war served to increase cross-border social integration ever so slightly, it did not change attitudes toward the border's desired function in this part of the continent.

Conclusion

The modern border between the United States and Canada was established over a century ago as both countries attempted to limit the number of undesirable immigrants entering the country. Initially, the focus was on keeping out people who would tax the system by entering state-run prisons, hospitals, and asylums. But by the turn of the twentieth century, immigration policy had expanded to exclude people of undesirable races, particularly those from Asia. After 1908, both Canada and the United States placed agents at popular land-crossing sites to ensure that these immigration policies were followed.

But it is important to note that these guidelines were often adjusted and manipulated by local immigration inspectors who, being from the communities where they were posted, administered policies in ways that suited local attitudes toward border permeability. This was also the case for customs agents, who in places such as Windsor, Ontario, and St. Stephen, New Brunswick, were rarely aggressive in their inspections, recognizing that doing so would be unpopular and might negatively affect an inspector's social status within the wider community. In contrast, in White Rock, British Columbia, immigration and customs inspectors were considerably more thorough, precisely because residents of nearby communities believed that the close monitoring of goods and people crossing the boundary would be to their benefit.

In essence, attitudes toward the international boundary varied from place to place. In Windsor and St. Stephen, residents had shared for generations close economic and social ties with American neighbours in Detroit and Calais. An open border was considered beneficial to the local community because it allowed residents to find work and purchase cheaper goods across the boundary. But it also allowed locals to reach and interact with their friends and family members across the border on a regular basis, and in both Windsor and St. Stephen these kinds of transnational social networks had existed for generations by the turn of the twentieth century. Many of these people recognized that the Detroit and St. Croix Rivers represented international points of demarcation, but few saw that as a reason to impede the flow of friendly travellers.

In White Rock, these cross-border ties, whether economic or social, were not in place by the outbreak of the First World War. As opposed to the Detroit River and St. Croix Valley borderlands, most settlers did not share cherished

FIGURE 27 Visitors, many of them from Vancouver, Victoria, and New Westminster, enjoyed White Rock's beaches during the summer months. *Source:* White Rock Museum and Archives.

memories with their American neighbours in Blaine, Washington. Economic and social dynamics also played a major role in determining attitudes toward the boundary in this border region. Although both White Rock and Blaine were founded upon similar industries (lumbering in particular), north of the border there was a distinct push toward tourism in the early twentieth century. Unlike Windsor and St. Stephen, in White Rock Americans were not credited for helping the growth of the community, even if the decision of the Great Northern Railway, based in St. Paul, Minnesota, to lay track around Semiahmoo Bay in 1909 was the central factor in its early development. Instead, BC investors and politicians from New Westminster and Vancouver reaped much of the praise for the community's steady population growth between the turn of the twentieth century and the end of the First World War. This divergence of interests was reflected elsewhere in local society as residents of Blaine embraced social reform while those of White Rock showed no interest in moral governance, particularly prohibition. Finally, on both sides of the border, there was concern about the movement of undesirable races, including Chinese, East Indian, and Japanese immigrants, found in much greater numbers in the Pacific Northwest than in central Canada and the American Midwest or northeast.

Although the First World War is often characterized as a watershed moment by Canadian historians, every community – including those along the

FIGURE 28 Windsorites decorate the cenotaph – built and unveiled in 1924 – following the death of King George V in 1936. The original plan for Windsor's Great War monument involved building a memorial tunnel under the Detroit River, but budget issues prevented the project from moving forward. *Source:* Jonathan Vance.

international boundary – had its own wartime experience.[1] In Windsor, many people reacted to the British declaration of war in August 1914 in a way similar to that of their countrymen in Toronto – in other words, they openly celebrated Canada's opportunity to demonstrate its value to the empire on the world stage. But others, including staff of the *Evening Record*, were not so sure that the conflict would benefit Canada.[2] Across the international boundary, newspapers such as the *Detroit Free Press* and *Detroit News* expressed their disgust with events occurring in Europe in the late summer and fall of 1914.[3] There the costly American Civil War remained a critical part of local memory, particularly as Detroit prepared to host the national meeting of the Grand Army of the Republic that year.[4] There is little doubt that the people of Windsor, who shared workplaces, baseball diamonds, and marriages with the people of Detroit, adopted or at least appreciated their neighbours' feelings about the emerging European conflict.

When news of the war reached the Canadian shore of the meandering St. Croix River, the people of St. Stephen carried on with their plans for the day. In a town with few British-born residents and deep transnational connections to nearby Calais, reactions to the motherland's declaration of war were hardly boisterous. It would be nearly a year before the war took hold of the St. Croix Valley.

Nevertheless, residents of Windsor and St. Stephen did support the war effort and received considerable encouragement from their American neighbours, some of whom joined the Canadian Expeditionary Force or contributed money and goods to various patriotic organizations, even if they did not wholeheartedly approve of the war. In both the Detroit River and the St. Croix Valley border regions, US neutrality created tensions between Canadians and Americans, though these episodes were often brief and more than balanced by demonstrations by American residents of support for the Allied war effort. Finally, when the United States declared war in April 1917, the news was welcomed in both St. Stephen and Windsor as a watershed moment that would lead to closer and better relations between Canadians and Americans at both the local level and the national level.

In White Rock and Blaine, demonstrations also revealed that locals were pleased to see Canada and the United States fighting together against a common foe. But in communities where economic and social dynamics pulled locals away from the border and into closer ties with their respective national societies, there were no declarations that the war would usher in a new and prosperous age of Canadian-American relations. Ultimately, celebrations of the new military alliance in White Rock and Blaine were as fleeting as tensions over American neutrality in St. Stephen and Calais and Windsor and Detroit.

This, too, was the result of prewar factors, including an absence of transnational economic and social exchanges across this section of the BC–Washington border. Furthermore, in White Rock, many locals continued to identify closely with the British Empire, many having moved from US soil to south Surrey because they did not feel comfortable living under the Stars and Stripes. White Rock residents demonstrated their loyalties during the First World War by joining the Imperial Reserve and Loyal Orange Lodge, organizations that did not exist or were considerably less popular in both Windsor and St. Stephen, either because British-born residents accounted for only a small percentage of the wider population or because economic and social ties to an American community diminished emotional ties to the British Empire.[5]

The war also had a dramatic impact on attitudes toward the state in these communities, but again each town's reaction differed. This also had much to do with prewar circumstances; for example, in White Rock and St. Stephen, the majority of residents supported the incumbent Conservative Party, meaning that they were arguably less likely to criticize the government.[6] In Windsor, in contrast, there was substantial support for the Liberal Party in 1914, particularly at the provincial level, meaning that city residents might have been more likely to point out perceived faults in the formulation of federal and provincial policies drawn up by the ruling Conservative governments.[7] In each case, local newspapers (the *Semiahmoo/Surrey Gazette, Saint Croix Courier,* and *Windsor Evening Record*) reflected the political attitudes of the majority.

Given the brevity of their prewar transnational experience and their support for the federal Conservatives, it is little surprise that residents of White Rock approved of changes by Ottawa to the border's administration during the war years. In comparison, there was outrage in Windsor when the federal government in 1915 sent a lady searcher who inspected local women and seized smuggled goods purchased in Detroit. Windsorites again protested when Ottawa introduced new border-crossing regulations that required men of military age to acquire a passport in 1917. Windsorites also voiced their disapproval of the daylight saving time scheme imposed by the federal government in 1918, with many politicians, business leaders, and labourers expressing their concern that it would negatively affect economic relations between their city and Detroit. Windsorites eventually, and only after loud protests, acquiesced to the order to make the time change. When the change was finally made, the Ontario border community was the last in the country to do so. Finally, Windsor residents vehemently opposed the provincial government's introduction of new parameters to the Lord's Day Act in 1916, which prevented them from acquiring Sunday newspapers printed in Detroit.

Attacking the provincial and federal governments during wartime, however "unpatriotic," did not set Windsor apart. As historians of other Canadian communities have shown, the government did face criticism for a number of reasons, particularly as the war progressed. In Quebec, French Canadians fiercely opposed conscription, and in the west (where the number of munitions contracts awarded by the federal government was paltry compared with those granted to central Canadian manufacturers) there was a demand for "conscription of wealth."[8] But what distinguished Windsor from Regina, Winnipeg, Toronto, and Montreal was the reason that residents criticized the government and the language that they used to formulate their critique. In every one of the above cases – the lady searcher episode, the Sunday newspaper debate, the passport debacle, and the DST controversy – border residents expressed their dissatisfaction with the government by dismissing policies that negatively affected traditional economic and social relations with Detroit. Windsorites rebuffed "outside influences" from Ottawa or Toronto, arguing that politicians from those cities were not in a position to understand the unique cross-border ties between Windsor and its American neighbour. In some cases, frustration with government policy led Windsorites to make startling comments that simply do not fit with traditional conceptions of wartime Canada, for example the suggestion by Windsor's newspaper that Canada and the United States eliminate the boundary so as to abolish immigration inspection or the proposal by Robert Timms that Windsor replace its very British name with South Detroit (or, as George Bouteiller suggested, simply Detroit).[9]

In the northeast, the people of St. Stephen were less vitriolic in their opposition to government policy. But they, too, expressed concern when men in uniform were prevented from visiting Calais, when the DST scheme was first discussed in 1916 (and then implemented two years later), and most visibly when Ottawa sent "special" customs investigators to examine the practices of local agents at the Ferry Point Bridge.[10] Much like the *Evening Record*, the *Saint Croix Courier* suggested that official protocol did not fit with local conditions and that the investigators sent by Ottawa were ignorant of the border-crossing culture of the St. Croix Valley.

There are a number of reasons why these findings are important. First, they emphasize that the border was not uniformly conceptualized in each of the regions through which it ran. The implementation of border controls aroused distinct responses in communities where a border-crossing culture already existed and where such transnational ties were absent or undeveloped. In places where settlement long predated the implementation of centralized immigration bureaucracies, there was significant apprehension about the changes

FIGURE 29 The St. Croix River, which divides St. Stephen and Calais was the site of vibrant and profitable lumbering and shipbuilding operations for much of the nineteenth century. Unfortunately, by the First World War, these heady days were little more than a distant memory. *Source:* Provincial Archives of New Brunswick, Isaac Erb Fonds, P11–153.

introduced when the previously distant federal government began making an appearance in the lives of people accustomed to a transnational environment. And though the presence of customs and immigration officials at the boundary was not new in 1914, during the Great War era inspectors were expected, for the first time, to act with the best interests of the nation, rather than the local community, in mind when carrying out their tasks.

Second, this book reveals how Canadians reacted to expansion of the state in the early twentieth century. Before the First World War, most Canadians would have viewed their relationship to the government in very different terms than when the conflict ended. In August 1914, few citizens had sacrificed their money, time, and lives for Canada. There was no income tax system in place, with the federal government relying on customs and excise duties for support.[11] Women could not vote, and Aboriginal, Asian, and black Canadians were barred from entering the military.[12] As for Canada's army, it was comprised of just 3,110 professionals on the eve of war out of roughly 1.95 million men of military age.[13] But the war changed all that. Eventually, men of all colours joined the armed forces, and women made such valuable contributions to the war effort that they won the federal (and in most cases provincial) vote.[14] For years after the armistice, these people viewed their relationship with the state as a reciprocal one; in time, they would expect the government to pay them back for their service to the country.[15]

But changes in the relationship between citizen and state did not come to pass without substantial criticism. In Canadian border communities St. Stephen and Windsor, there was anger directed toward a government that implemented policies associated with the international boundary as if such legislation affected all citizens equally. In truth, the overnight introduction of Order-in-Council PC 1433, which required all men of military age to carry photo identification when crossing the international boundary, did not affect the people of Windsor or St. Stephen in the same way as it did residents of Toronto or Ottawa. In these latter communities, such a policy might have been frustrating for a few hundred people on a handful of days over the course of a year. But in Windsor and St. Stephen, PC 1433 (or other government actions affecting the border) altered life for all residents immediately and dramatically. Reactions to legislation of this kind in these two border towns varied from extreme to moderate alarm, but in both cases there was an expression that what was good for the national community was not necessarily in the best interests of the locality.

Third, this book shows that the social, economic, and communications networks of the early twentieth century played an essential role in how border communities identified and interacted with their local, extranational, provincial, and national neighbours. In Windsor and St. Stephen, interaction with extranational neighbours in Detroit and Calais was frequent, mostly because of efficient and reliable ferry and bridge links, which carried people to factories, theatres, dance halls, and baseball diamonds across the international boundary. However, because of relatively primitive or expensive rail, road, telegraph, and telephone systems, rarely did residents of these communities interact with provincial neighbours in cities such as Chatham and London or Fredericton and Saint John. Sporting activity offers a glimpse of this condition: in Windsor, local baseball, soccer, and basketball teams regularly competed against clubs from surrounding Essex County and Detroit but rarely engaged in matches with squads from outside the wider Detroit River region. The same was true in St. Stephen, where leagues most often included teams hailing from American and Canadian communities within a roughly fifty-kilometre pocket of the dividing St. Croix River known as the St. Croix Valley. Distance was a major issue in both cases: roughly 80 and 180 kilometres separate Windsor from Chatham and London, respectively, and St. Stephen is located approximately 100 and 120 kilometres from Saint John and Fredericton. In contrast, White Rock is just 25 and 40 kilometres from New Westminster and Vancouver, making transportation quicker and cheaper. As a result of these geographical factors, Windsor and St. Stephen maintained strong local (and by extension transnational) identities during the First World War, whereas White Rock was easily absorbed by nearby provincial centres that offered residents of the BC border community greater economic opportunities and cultural attractions than the quiet industrial town of Blaine. All of these factors affected how the people of each community felt about border permeability and the importance of maintaining social, cultural, and economic links with their American neighbours. These factors also shaped whether and to what extent residents of border communities thought that they were part of a distinct community that transcended the international boundary.

And fourth, this book reveals the many identities worn by Canadians during the First World War era. Historians have explored how people in Canada shed their imperialist ties and came to articulate a distinctly Canadian national identity as a result of the country's contribution to the war effort, and in the years following the conflict that might have been the case.[16] But when the war was actually being fought, the hierarchy of identities was constantly in flux. In Windsor, St. Stephen, and White Rock, people fought to defend Canada, the British Empire, the Allies, and their hometowns, and not necessarily in that (or any) order. Windsorites were proud of their transnational links to Detroit but not necessarily more so than their connections with the national community. However, if their transnational way of life was threatened by legislation haphazardly introduced by the federal or provincial government, then complaints arose that meddling outsiders did not understand that Windsor was "part and parcel of the city of Detroit."[17] St. Stephen residents clashed with their American neighbours in Calais when the sizes and ages of local recruits were criticized by the *Calais Advertiser* in early 1915.[18] But that criticism was forgotten when the United States entered the fray two years later, the *Saint Croix Courier* proclaiming the occasion "a renewal and strengthening" of the ties binding the people of the United States, Canada, and specifically the St. Croix Valley together.[19] The people of St. Stephen also viewed their place within the British Empire differently as the war progressed, from virtually ignoring Victoria Day in 1914 to organizing a large celebration in 1916.[20] In the American community of Blaine, people fêted Victoria Day for the first time ever in 1917 and invited their White Rock neighbours to observe as the Stars and Stripes was raised along with the Union Jack in a special and, to that point rare, transnational ceremony.[21]

Although 9–11 has significantly affected how Canadians and Americans view the international boundary between them, it was during the First World War that the border we know today began to take shape. Although both American and Canadian governments had placed immigration officials at popular land-crossing sites from coast to coast in the decade before the First World War, the heightened paranoia of the years 1914–18 led to the implementation of legislation that completely changed the border-crossing experience. In Canadian border communities such as Windsor and St. Stephen, they were viewed as unwanted challenges to a deeply ingrained border-crossing culture based on years of transnational trade and social exchange. But reactions to changes at the border varied and were largely dependent on the existence of these economic and social ties prior to the early twentieth century.

This study demonstrates that, though the First World War has been considered a defining moment in the development of a distinct Canadian identity, the conflict and its meaning were interpreted in very different ways, depending on the community in question. As historians Robert Rutherdale, Ian Miller, James Pitsula, and Jim Blanchard have shown, there was no single home-front experience during Canada's Great War. This book supports that idea. In communities straddling the boundary with the United States, toeing the official line sometimes meant compromising transnational traditions. For some, it was a steep price for victory, and it ultimately changed life along the Canada–US border forever.

Notes

Introduction

1 "Border Annoyances," *Windsor Evening Record,* December 5, 1916.

2 *Fifth Census of Canada 1911: Religions, Origins, Birthplace, Citizenship, Literacy, and Infirmities, by Provinces, Districts, and Sub-Districts, Volume II* (Ottawa: C.H. Parmlee, 1913), Table XIV, 391; Table XV, 403–4.

3 Gregory P. Marchildon, "From Pax Britannica to Pax Americana and Beyond," *Annals of the American Academy of Political and Social Science* 538 (1995).

4 Bowlby Estate Collection, Acc. No. 1995/7, Windsor Public Library; "Board of Trade Visits School," *Windsor Evening Record,* February 5, 1915.

5 See William Oxford, *The Ferry Steamers: The Story of the Detroit–Windsor Ferry Boats* (Erin, ON: Boston Mills Press, 1992).

6 Thomas Klug, "The Immigration and Naturalization Service (INS) and the Making of a Border-Crossing Culture on the US–Canada Border, 1891–1941," *American Review of Canadian Studies* 40, 3 (2010).

7 Ibid.

8 Quoted in Reginald Stuart, *Dispersed Relations: Americans and Canadians in Upper North America* (Baltimore: Johns Hopkins University Press, 2007), 9.

9 Jonathan Vance, *A History of Canadian Culture* (New York: Oxford University Press, 2009), vii.

10 Andrew R. Graybill and Benjamin H. Johnson, *Bridging National Borders in North America: Transnational and Comparative Histories* (Durham: Duke University Press, 2010), 2.

11 Victor Konrad and Lauren McKinsey, *Borderlands Reflections: The United States and Canada* (Orono, ME: Borderlands Project, 1989), 21.

12 Melissa Gauthier and Fayuca Hormiga, "The Cross-Border Trade of Used Clothing between the United States and Mexico," in *Borderlands: Comparing Border Security in North America and Europe,* ed. Emmanuel Brunet-Jailly (Ottawa: University of Ottawa Press, 2007), 95.

13 According to a study of the American news media, "when fear is the prevailing framework for looking at social issues, then other competing frames and discourses lose out." In comparing the two, it would be hard to suggest that the US–Canada border aroused as much fear in the United States as the often violent US–Mexico boundary, at least prior to 9–11. David L. Altheide and R. Sam Michalowski, "Fear in the News: A Discourse of Control," *Sociological Quarterly* 40, 3 (1999).

14 For more on European borders, see Emmanuel Brunet-Jailly, *Borderlands: Comparing Border Security in North America and Europe* (Ottawa: University of Ottawa Press, 2007); Alexander V. Prusin, *The Lands Between: Conflict in the East European Borderlands, 1870-1992* (Oxford: Oxford University Press, 2010); David H. Kaplan, *Boundaries and Place: European Borderlands in Geographical Context* (Washington, DC: Rowman and Littlefield Publishers, 2002); and Mark von Hagen, *War in a European Borderland: Occupations and Occupation Plans in Galicia and Ukraine, 1914–1918* (Seattle: University of Washington Press, 2007).

15 For more on the US–Mexico border, see Rachel St. John, *Line in the Sand: A History of the Western US–Mexico Border* (Princeton: Princeton University Press, 2011); Kelly Lytle Hernandez, *Migra! A History of the US Border Patrol* (Oakland: University of California Press, 2010); and Mae M. Ngai, *Impossible Subjects: Illegal Aliens and the Making of Modern America* (Princeton: Princeton University Press, 2005).

16 Canada–US trade reached $577 billion in 2006, with $1.6 billion in goods crossing the international boundary each day. John B. Sutcliffe, "Neoliberalism in a Small Canadian City? Windsor City Council and the Reform of the Detroit River Border Crossing," *American Review of Canadian Studies* 41, 3 (2011).

17 Chantall Allan, *Bomb Canada, and Other Unkind Remarks in the American Media* (Edmonton: Athabasca University Press, 2009), 79–81; David Stirrup and Gillian Roberts, "Introduction to the ARCS Special on Culture and the Canada–US Border," *American Review of Canadian Studies* 40, 3 (2010).

18 Smith wrote his book in the late 1880s, a scary time for Canadian nationalists. The country was wracked by internal divisions following the 1885 Northwest Rebellion, during which a largely English-speaking federal government suppressed an uprising fomented by the French-speaking Roman Catholic Métis population of the South Saskatchewan River valley. In Quebec, French Canadians sympathetic to the Métis cause rioted when Métis leader Louis Riel was executed in November.

19 Goldwin Smith, *Canada and the Canadian Question* (London: Macmillan, 1891), 2.

20 Unsurprisingly, Smith's book aroused considerable consternation among Canadian nationalists. According to Carl Berger, Canadian historian Arthur Lower attributed Canada's unique identity to a combination of its frontier experience, British traditions, and American influences, particularly the Rebellions of 1837–38, in which Canadians began to challenge traditional notions of elite rule in favour of responsible government. Meanwhile, Canadian historian and social critic Frank Underhill pointed to Canada's Great War experience, which he saw as a unifying era in the country's past, as evidence of a distinct nationalism that could be identified and nurtured. Carl Berger, *The Writing of Canadian History: Aspects of English-Canadian Historical Writing: 1900–1970* (Toronto: Oxford University Press, 1976), 121, 58.

21 Marcus Lee Hansen, *The Mingling of the Canadian and American Peoples* (New York: Arno Press, 1940), v.

22 Although I find these books the most relevant, a number of other texts focused on Canadian-American relations and the administration of the Upper North American border are worth considering. Particularly useful works include Reginald Stuart's *Dispersed Relations: Americans and Canadians in Upper North America*; Jacques Poitras's *Imaginary Line: Life on an Unfinished Border*; James Laxer's *The Border: Canada, the US, and Dispatches from the 49th Parallel*; and Marian Botsford Fraser's *Walking the Line: Travels along the Canadian/American Border.*

23 Bruno Ramirez, *Crossing the 49th Parallel: Migration from Canada to the United States, 1900–1930* (Ithaca: Cornell University Press, 2001), 6.

24 Ibid., 26.

25 See the success story of Ontario-born James Pappa in Randy Widdis, *With Scarcely a Ripple: Anglo-Canadian Migration into the United States and Western Canada, 1880–1920* (Montreal: McGill-Queen's University Press, 1999), 3.

26 Ibid., 11.

27 Prior to Liberal Prime Minister Wilfrid Laurier's election in 1896, Canadian immigration policy was fanatically pro-British. Asians, blacks, and central and southern Europeans were discouraged from migrating to the new country. This policy reflected the popular attitudes of Canadians, most of whom were of Anglo-Saxon heritage. See Ninette Kelley

and Michael J. Trebilcock, *The Making of the Mosaic: A History of Canadian Immigration Policy* (Toronto: University of Toronto Press, 1998).

28 Quoted in Thomas Thorner, "'Let Someone Else Have a Taste of Our Good Life': The Immigrant Experience," in *"A Country Nourished on Self-Doubt": Documents in Canadian History, 1867–1980*, ed. Thomas Thorner (Peterborough: Broadview Press, 1998), 81.

29 David R. Smith, "Structuring the Permeable Border: Channeling and Regulating Cross-Border Traffic in Labor, Capital, and Goods," in *Permeable Border: The Great Lakes Basin as Transnational Region, 1650–1990*, ed. John J. Bukowczyk (Pittsburgh: University of Pittsburgh Press, 2005), 124.

30 Klug, "The Immigration and Naturalization Service."

31 Marian Smith, "The Immigration and Naturalization Service (INS) at the US–Canadian Border, 1893-1993: An Overview of Issues and Topics," *Michigan Historical Review* 26, 2 (2000).

32 Kelley and Trebilcock, *The Making of the Mosaic*, 109–10.

33 Ibid., 113.

34 Sifton resigned from Laurier's cabinet over a dispute with the prime minister regarding separate school legislation in the new provinces of Alberta and Saskatchewan. Robert Craig Brown and Ramsay Cook, *Canada, 1896-1921: A Nation Transformed* (Toronto: McClelland and Stewart, 1974), 75–77.

35 Kelley and Trebilcock, *The Making of the Mosaic*, 116–17.

36 Klug, "The Immigration and Naturalization Service."

37 Ibid.

38 Canadian Great War military history first reached a wider audience with the release of Colonel F. Duguid's *Official History of the Canadian Forces in the Great War, 1914–1919*. Duguid published just the first volume (covering August 1914 to September 1915) before his project was forever delayed by Canada's entry into the Second World War. A second official history, *Canadian Expeditionary Force, 1914–1919*, written by Colonel G.W.L. Nicholson, was published in 1962. It is a top-down analysis that has provided scholars with an important chronological groundwork upon which to lay new, and more specific, analyses. Studies emerging from this model include Nicholson's *The Gunners of Canada* (1967), J.A. Swettenham's *To Seize the Victory* (1965), and S.F. Wise's *Canadian Airmen and the First World War* (1980). The 1980s and 1990s proved to be a boom era for Canadian military history, highlighted by several important book releases, including Pierre Berton's *Vimy* (1986), Desmond Morton and J.L. Granatstein's *Marching to Armageddon* (1989), Bill Rawling's *Trench Warfare* (1992), and Morton's *When Your Number's Up* (1994), just to name a few. In recent years, the primary focus of Canadian military history has continued to be on the life of the average dominion recruit, with Tim Cook's two volumes, *At the Sharp End* (2007) and *Shock Troops* (2009), achieving critical acclaim for blending passionate and haunting letters and diary entries with an accessible narrative account of the fighting.

39 Ian Hugh Maclean Miller, *Our Glory and Our Grief: Torontonians and the Great War* (Toronto: University of Toronto Press, 2002); Robert Rutherdale, *Hometown Horizons: Local Responses to Canada's Great War* (Vancouver: UBC Press, 2004); James M. Pitsula, *For All We Have and Are: Regina and the Experience of the Great War* (Winnipeg: University of Manitoba Press, 2008); Jim Blanchard, *Winnipeg's Great War: A City Comes of Age* (Winnipeg: University of Manitoba Press, 2010).

40 Christopher Capozzola, *Uncle Sam Wants You: World War I and the Making of the Modern American Citizen* (New York: Oxford University Press, 2008), 13.

41 Craig Robertson, *The Passport in America: The History of a Document* (Oxford: Oxford University Press, 2010), 36.

42 For more on the subject of Canada's expanding state during wartime, see Jeffrey Keshen, *Propaganda and Censorship during Canada's Great War* (Edmonton: University of Alberta Press, 1996); Desmond Morton, *Fight or Pay: Soldiers' Families in the Great War* (Vancouver: UBC Press, 2004); and two articles by Gregory S. Kealey, "State Repression of Labour and the Left in Canada, 1914–20: The Impact of the First World War," *Canadian Historical Review* 72, 3 (1992), and "The Surveillance State: The Origins of Domestic Intelligence and Counter-Subversion in Canada, 1914–21," *Intelligence and National Security* 7, 3 (1992).

43 Windsor City Council Minutes, November 20, 1916, Windsor Public Library Archives, RG 2 AIV-1.

44 In addition to other nearby ports of entry, including Douglas, British Columbia, Walkerville, Ontario, and Milltown, New Brunswick.

Part 1: Windsor, Ontario, and Detroit, Michigan

1 Richard Cavendish, "The Founding of Detroit," *History Today* 51, 7 (2001).

2 "Building Fort Ponchartrain, History of Detroit," http://historydetroit.com/places/fort_ponchartrain.php.

3 Clarence Monroe Burton, *When Detroit Was Young: Historical Studies* (Detroit: Burton Abstract and Title, c. 1950), 73.

4 By 1750, its population was 900; amid the American Revolution in 1773, it was 1,367 (excluding soldiers). David Lee Poremba, *Detroit: A Motor City History* (Chicago: Arcadia, 2001), 22, 42.

5 Burton, *When Detroit Was Young*, 28.

6 Don Lochbiler, *Detroit's Coming of Age: 1873 to 1973* (Detroit: Wayne State University Press, 1973), 28.

7 When Detroit was devastated by fire in 1805, with only a handful of buildings still standing, it was the city of Montreal (Detroit's sister city) that contributed the lion's share of relief. Burton, *When Detroit Was Young*, 30.

8 R. Alan Douglas, *Uppermost Canada: The Western District and the Detroit Frontier, 1800-1850* (Detroit: Wayne State University Press, 2001), 6–7; Kevin R. Shackleton and Sandy Antal, *Duty Nobly Done: The Official History of the Essex and Kent Scottish Regiment* (Walkerville, ON: Walkerville, 2006), 19, 54.

9 Dennis Carter-Edwards, "The War of 1812 along the Detroit Frontier: A Canadian Perspective," *Michigan Historical Review* 13, 2 (1987).

10 Shackleton and Antal, *Duty Nobly Done*, 54, note that the French of Essex shared "little attachment to King George III or the republic. They identified more closely with friends and kinsmen across the Detroit River."

11 The Western District encompassed present-day southwestern Ontario and the entire area west of the Great Lakes. Douglas, *Uppermost Canada*, 6–7.

12 Like many Americans, Hull feared and loathed the Aboriginal allies of the British in 1812. Saving Crown lands in Upper Canada was not the focus of those warriors fighting alongside Major-General Isaac Brock, but they were ready to fight to the death to protect their own territory against further American encroachment. Robert S. Allen, "His Majesty's Indian Allies: Native Peoples, the British Crown, and the War of 1812," *Michigan Historical Review* 14 (1988).

13 Shackleton and Antal, *Duty Nobly Done*, 57.

14 In early 1814, the Americans toyed with the idea of dispatching a force to the Western District that would force the removal of all residents in order to create a "desert" buffer between Detroit and the British forces stationed farther northeast. Carter-Edwards, "The War of 1812 along the Detroit Frontier"; Shackleton and Antal, *Duty Nobly Done*, 60.

15 In subsequent engagements, Americans would enter battle under the charge "Remember the Raisin!" in reference to the Raisin River at Frenchtown. "River Raisin Battlefield – City of Monroe," http://www.co.monroe.mi.us/government/departments_offices/museum/docs/River_Raisin_Battlefield_Brochure.pdf.

16 Carter-Edwards, "The War of 1812 along the Detroit Frontier."

17 For instance, the American force that wreaked considerable destruction in passing through the Western District during the fall 1813 campaign was comprised of Kentucky volunteers almost exclusively. Kentuckians were also responsible for the recapture of Michigan earlier in the year. Ibid.; Shackleton and Antal, *Duty Nobly Done,* 74.

18 Jane Errington, *The Lion, the Eagle, and Upper Canada: A Developing Colonial Ideology* (Montreal: McGill-Queen's University Press, 1987), 84.

19 C.H. Gervais, *The Border Police: One Hundred and Twenty-Five Years of Policing in Windsor* (Windsor: Penumbra Press, 1992), 12.

20 The main thrust of the Fenian campaign lasted just one year, 1866, but further attacks were threatened until 1870. Despite an initial setback for the Fenians at Campobello in the northeast, their later success in the Niagara region aroused widespread fear in Canada West. The most disturbing setback for the Canadians was at the Battle of the Ridgeway in early June 1866, when a Fenian force scattered a company of the Queen's Own Rifles before retreating to American territory. Thereafter, the Fenian threat petered out but not before arousing considerable consternation at points all along the international boundary. Despite ultimate failure, the Fenian invasions revealed major weaknesses in the defence capabilities of Britain's North American colonies. Hereward Senior, *The Last Invasion of Canada: The Fenian Raids, 1866–1870* (Toronto: Dundurn Press, 1991), 88–89.

21 Frederick Neal, *The Township of Sandwich, Past and Present* (Windsor: Record Printing, 1909), 76.

22 Neil F. Morrison, "Essex County, Province of Ontario: A Geographical Study" (PhD diss., University of Michigan, 1944), 37.

23 For a time, it appeared that nearby Amherstburg might become the region's dominant economic centre; however, because ice tended to build up to impassable levels at this particular point along the Detroit River, Windsor emerged as the better choice. Completion of the Essex "Cut-Off" line in 1883 linking the town of Essex and Windsor directly and circumventing Amherstburg unceremoniously ended dreams that the latter town might act as the county's commercial and industrial hub. Neil F. Morrison, *Garden Gateway to Canada: One Hundred Years of Windsor and Essex County, 1854–1954* (Windsor: Herald Press, 1954), 123.

24 Ibid., 39.

25 Not only did they proliferate in number, but also steamers ferrying passengers and goods across the Detroit River grew in size and extravagance after the 1850s. In 1857, the Great Western Railway Company unveiled the steamer *Union,* which featured a large cabin, an enormous side-wheel, twin smoke stacks, and a dining room on its upper deck. Powered by condensing engines and sophisticated steering technology, it moved passengers back and forth much faster than its predecessors. F.J. Holton et al., *History of the Detroit and Windsor Ferries* (Detroit: University of Michigan Library, 1918), 6.

26 William Oxford, *The Ferry Steamers: The Story of the Detroit–Windsor Ferry Boats* (Erin, ON: Boston Mills Press, 1992), 12.

27 Ibid., 15.

28 Holton et al., *History of the Detroit and Windsor Ferries,* 6–14.

29 For most of the mid- to late nineteenth century, the charge for a one-way ticket had been ten cents, but in 1892 a "monthly ticket book," containing 100 one-way passes, could be purchased for $1.50. Oxford, *The Ferry Steamers,* 64.

30 The current between Glengarry Avenue in Windsor and the American shore was so fast that this corridor rarely froze over, even after the rest of the waterway was frozen solid. Ibid., 35.
31 "Detroit Lake and River Steamers Carry 44,000 Passengers," *Windsor Evening Record*, July 3, 1914.
32 Oxford, *The Ferry Steamers*, 35–39.
33 "Michigan Central Station" Historic Detroit.org, http://www.historicdetroit.org/building/michigan-central-station/; Morrison, *Garden Gateway to Canada*, 237.
34 Gregory P. Marchildon, "From Pax Britannica to Pax Americana and Beyond," *Annals of the American Academy of Political and Social Science* 538 (1995): 155.
35 Morrison, *Garden Gateway to Canada*, 49.
36 In Toronto, in comparison, there was a US branch plant for every 4,255 city residents. In Windsor, the ratio was 1:769. David Roberts, *In the Shadow of Detroit: Gordon M. McGregor, Ford of Canada, and Motoropolis* (Detroit: Wayne State University Press, 2006), 4.
37 F. Maclure Schlanders, "A Little History of the Border Cities," Windsor Border Chamber of Commerce Pamphlet, September 1, 1920, Windsor Public Library Archives, Bowlby Estate Collection, Acc. No. 1995/7.
38 Although Ford of Canada's assistant general manager, Wallace Campbell, would deny that his company was a branch plant before a Canadian Tariff Inquiry Commission in 1920, the company's early management, engineering, and real and imagined figurehead were all American in origin. Dimitry Anastakis, "From Independence to Integration: The Corporate Evolution of the Ford Motor Company of Canada, 1904–2004," *Business History Review* 78, 2 (2004): 213.
39 According to an account from Ford of Canada supervisor George Dickert, McGregor and Ford got along well, meeting regularly in an often informal fashion. Roberts, *In the Shadow of Detroit*, 43.
40 Ibid., 88.
41 Morrison, *Garden Gateway to Canada*, 179.
42 Roberts, *In the Shadow of Detroit*, 25.
43 Essex County's temperate climate and level geography, both of which facilitated the construction of roads, might also have been important factors in Ford's decision to establish an automotive assembly plant in Windsor. Ibid., 25–29.
44 Morrison, *Garden Gateway to Canada*, 178.
45 Roberts, *In the Shadow of Detroit*, 31.
46 Ibid., 57.
47 Ibid., 86.
48 When it was first incorporated in 1912, Ford City's population was just 600. By July 1914, the local newspaper estimated nearly 3,000 people living within its boundaries. "City Briefs – Ford Wants Long Pants," *Windsor Evening Record*, July 13, 1914.
49 "Ford Motor Seeks Permission to House Employees in Tents," *Windsor Evening Record*, May 21, 1913.
50 Roberts, *In the Shadow of Detroit*, 122.
51 "Ford Married Men Lose Out," *Windsor Evening Record*, June 23, 1914.
52 With an entire municipality named for him, Henry Ford was the spiritual leader of Ford Canada. The magazine *Industrial Canada* in its January 1915 issue ran this ad for Ford's Canadian operations: "Ford Motor Cars are now made in Canada under the direct supervision of Mr. Henry Ford, the most successful designer of automobiles in America." Roberts, *In the Shadow of Detroit*, 35.
53 Morrison, *Garden Gateway to Canada*, 64.

54 One of Windsor's most prominent families was the Bowlbys. Records show that Hellen Bowlby graduated from the Detroit School of Elocution and English Literature in 1890 and that Edith Margaret Bowlby graduated from Detroit's McDonald School of Music in 1919. Diaries of Hellen Bowlby and Edith Margaret Bowlby, Windsor Public Library Archives, Bowlby Estate Collection, Box 1, Acc. No. 1995/7. The May 1924 issue of the *Crier*, Windsor Collegiate Institute's magazine, reveals that several alumni were then studying at postsecondary institutions in the Detroit area, including Detroit City College and the University of Michigan. Windsor Public Library Archives, Hallam Collection, MS 5 I/7.

55 Morrison, *Garden Gateway to Canada*, 90.

56 For more on this subject, see Thomas Sugrue, *The Origins of the Urban Crisis: Race and Inequality in Postwar Detroit* (Princeton: Princeton University Press, 1996).

57 Estimates of the total black population in Detroit between 1900 and 1910 vary widely, with some sources suggesting that it was about 5,000 and others placing it closer to 10,000. Regardless, blacks did not represent a prominent ethnic group prior to the First World War. "Reminiscences, 30th Anniversary," Detroit Public Library, Burton Historical Collection Manuscripts Collection, Detroit Study Club Records, Lillian Johnson Collection, Box 2:2; "Populations of Various Ethnic Groups," History Detroit, 1701–2001, http://historydetroit.com/statistics/index.php.

58 *Thirteenth Census of the United States 1910, Volume 3: Reports by States, Alabama–Montana* (Washington, DC: Government Printing Office, 1912–14); "Populations of Various Ethnic Groups," History Detroit, 1701–2001, http://historydetroit.com/statistics/index.php.

59 Census statistics show that just 2 percent of all residents of Windsor proper had been born in continental Europe. *Fifth Census of Canada 1911: Religions, Origins, Birthplace, Citizenship, Literacy, and Infirmities, by Provinces, Districts, and Sub-Districts, Volume II* (Ottawa: C.H. Parmlee, 1913), Table XVI, 391.

60 According to the 1911 census, approximately 76 percent of all Windsor residents had been born in Ontario. Ibid.

61 Ibid., Table II, 50–51.

62 Census reports after the war note that 451,579 of the city's 755,572 churchgoers reported being Catholic. Given these statistics, it is safe to assume that Roman Catholicism was Detroit's dominant religion throughout the early twentieth century. Brian Wilson, "The Spirit of the Motor City: Three Hundred Years of Religious History in Detroit," *Michigan Historical Review* 27, 1 (2001); Matthew Pehl, "The Remaking of the Catholic Working-Class: Detroit, 1919-1945," *Religion and American Culture* 19, 1 (2009).

63 Approximately 29 percent of Torontonians had been born in Britain. Just 60 percent had been born in Ontario, a substantially lower percentage than in Windsor. *Fifth Census of Canada 1911,* Table XV, 403–4.

64 Ibid., Table VII, 214–15.

65 Ibid., Table II, 80–81.

Chapter 1: "Brothers Once More"

1 "Whitney Government Returned to Power with 83 Members in Legislature," *Windsor Evening Record,* June 30, 1914.

2 "Thousands on Streets Celebrate Liberal Sweep in Essex County," *Windsor Evening Record,* June 30, 1914.

3 "Diversity in Our Industries," *Windsor Evening Record,* July 6, 1914; "Horlick's Malted Milk Co. to Establish Plant in Windsor," *Windsor Evening Record,* July 4, 1914; "Business Revival," *Windsor Evening Record,* July 18, 1914.

4 "See Ford Plant," *Windsor Evening Record,* July 18, 1914.

5 As usual, Henry Ford and not Ford of Canada General Manager Gordon McGregor received credit for the generosity. "The reduction [in price] is made by Mr. Ford himself and applies to the Detroit factory as well as the Canadian branch at Ford," the *Evening Record* declared. "Ford Price Drops; Profit Sharing Plan Announced," *Windsor Evening Record,* August 1, 1914.

6 In July 1914, the number of people living in Windsor and working daily in Detroit was pegged at 2,500, about 10 percent of the city's population. "Wilcox Brings Up Income Tax," *Windsor Evening Record,* July 14, 1914; "Border Towns Celebrate Fourth of July," *Windsor Evening Record,* July 6, 1914.

7 Canadian Club whiskey was produced by Hiram Walker Distilleries in Walkerville, adjacent to Windsor. Its founder lived in Detroit but commuted daily to the border cities region. The company was founded in 1857 and by the turn of the twentieth century had become an industry leader. Walker's nephew, Hiram A., would become Windsor's first mayor, and the importance of the distillery to economic growth in the region would seriously limit the effectiveness of prohibition in the Detroit River region during and after the war. Carl Morgan, *Birth of a City: Commemorating Windsor's Centennial, 1992* (Windsor: Benchmark, 1991), 65–69.

8 "Border Towns Celebrate the Fourth of July," *Windsor Evening Record,* July 6, 1914.

9 "Citizens Desert Windsor July 1st," *Windsor Evening Record,* June 30, 1913; "Excursions Draw Thousands from City on Dominion Day," *Windsor Evening Record,* July 2, 1914.

10 "Windsor Was Able to Handle Record Crowd," *Windsor Evening Record,* July 16, 1914.

11 Neil F. Morrison, *Garden Gateway to Canada: One Hundred Years of Windsor and Essex County, 1854–1954* (Windsor: Herald Press, 1954), 286.

12 "A Ferry for Automobiles," *Windsor Evening Record,* July 16, 1914.

13 "Pirates Meet Moonshiners," *Windsor Evening Record,* June 19, 1914.

14 "Walkerville Plays Detroit Athletics," *Windsor Evening Record,* July 10, 1914.

15 "Pirates Add Another to Their Lead," *Windsor Evening Record,* July 13, 1914.

16 "At Wigle Park," *Windsor Evening Record,* May 19, 1913.

17 Winters might be mixing up the Revolutionary War and the War of 1812, but the sentiment remains intact. "Yankees Hate to Admit Welsh Is an Englishman," *Windsor Evening Record,* July 10, 1914.

18 The War of 1812 remained a very sensitive topic in many circles, particularly in Toronto. For instance, R.S. Neville, the Empire Club president and a close friend of Ontario Premier Sir James P. Whitney, said that the latter was among several prominent citizens who indicated that any cooperation with the United States in commemorating the war would be distasteful. Joseph Pope to Sir Robert Borden, December 2, 1911, Library and Archives Canada (LAC), RG25, Box 1116, File 1255.

19 Plans to build an international automobile tunnel under the Detroit River were devised shortly after the creation of the American Peace Centenary Committee and Canadian Peace Centenary Association in 1911 and 1912, respectively. LAC, RG25, Vol. 1116, File 1255; "Peace Centenary," *Windsor Evening Record,* June 18, 1914; "Windsor Men Join Peace Centenary Association," *Windsor Evening Record,* July 3, 1914.

20 "Subway as Peace Memorial," *Windsor Evening Record,* July 31, 1914.

21 Jonathan Vance, *Death So Noble: Memory, Meaning, and the First World War* (Vancouver: UBC Press, 1997), 208.

22 One of these men, Hospital Sergeant Harry Bayard Barr, had studied medicine in Detroit before volunteering for active service. He later died of fever while treating the wounded. Kevin R. Shackleton and Sandy Antal, *Duty Nobly Done: The Official History of the Essex and Kent Scottish Regiment* (Walkerville, ON: Walkerville, 2006), 148–55.

23 Ibid., 158.

24 "The German Menace," *Windsor Evening Record,* July 5, 1913.
25 Robert Borden, prime minister from 1911 to 1920, later wrote that "the assassination of Archduke Franz Ferdinand at Sarajevo on June 28th, had been alarming, but on both sides of the Atlantic none, I imagine, believed that the situation would develop, with such startling suddenness, into a war that in its effect upon both belligerent and neutral nations would almost shatter the very framework of modern civilization." Henry Borden, *Robert Laird Borden: His Memoirs* (Toronto: Macmillan, 1938), 210.
26 "Heir to Austrian Throne and Wife Assassinated," *Windsor Evening Record,* June 29, 1914.
27 "World War Is Feared," *Windsor Evening Record,* July 24, 1914.
28 "War Will Have Little Effect on Canada," *Windsor Evening Record,* July 27, 1914.
29 "No Canadians at Maneuvers," *Windsor Evening Record,* July 24, 1914.
30 "Crisis in Europe," *Windsor Evening Record,* July 30, 1914.
31 James L. Stokesbury, *A Short History of World War I* (New York: William Morrow 1981), 20.
32 Keith Robbins, *The First World War: The Outbreak, Events, and Aftermath* (Oxford: Oxford University Press, 1984), 7.
33 See Gerhard P. Groβ, "There Was a Schlieffen Plan: New Sources on the History of German Military Planning," *War in History* 15, 4 (2008).
34 Barbara Tuchman, *The Guns of August* (New York: Ballantine Books, 1962), 118–58.
35 Terry Copp, "The Military Effort, 1914–1918," in *Canada and the First World War: Essays in Honour of Robert Craig Brown,* ed. David Mackenzie (Toronto: University of Toronto Press, 2005), 111–30.
36 In his famous response to cousin Captain Talbot Papineau's open letter accusing him of turning the country against the war effort from its beginning, Henri Bourassa replied, "my first pronouncement on the intervention of Canada in the war is dated September 8th, 1914 ... I pronounced myself in favour of the intervention of Canada, *as a nation,* for the defence of the superior interests uniting Canada with France and Britain." LAC, MG30-E52, Vol. 03294; Arthur Hawkes, *Canadian Nationalism and the War* (Montreal: n.p., 1916); Sandra Gwyn, *Tapestry of War: A Private View of Canadians in the Great War* (Toronto: HarperCollins, 1992), 316.
37 Stokesbury, *A Short History of World War I,* 102.
38 "What War Will Do," *Detroit Free Press,* August 3, 1914.
39 "Believes Great War Will Be Long Drawn Struggle," *Detroit News,* September 2, 1914.
40 "Canadian Contingent," *Windsor Evening Record,* August 1, 1914.
41 "The One Voice of Canada," *Globe,* August 3, 1914.
42 "Keep Neutrality All US Can Do," *Detroit News,* August 1, 1914.
43 Journal of the Common Council, City of Detroit, July 28, 1914, Detroit Public Library, Burton Historical Collection.
44 "The Horrible Cost," *Detroit News,* August 1, 1914.
45 "What War Will Do," *Detroit Free Press,* August 3, 1914.
46 Later in the war the appointment of an Irish Canadian to the position of local bishop would threaten to destabilize Windsor's delicate ethnic balance. In 1917, Ford City's French Canadian population protested the appointment of Bishop Michael Fallon, an Irish Canadian with pro-Regulation 17 sympathies. Michael Power, "Bishop Fallon and the Riot at Ford City, 8 September 1917," Occasional Paper No. 3, Essex County Historical Society, 1986, 1.
47 "Americans Hasten to Aid of Britain," *Detroit News,* August 5, 1914.
48 Ibid.
49 Ibid.
50 "Twenty-First May Be Asked to Send 100 Men to the Front," *Windsor Evening Record,* August 5, 1914.

51 For more on eugenics, see Thomas C. Leonard, "Mistaking Eugenics for Social Darwinism: Why Eugenics Is Missing from the History of American Economics," *History of Political Economy* 37 (2005).

52 "Size of Our Soldiers," *Windsor Evening Record,* August 8, 1914.

53 James W. Walker, "Race and Recruitment in World War I: Enlistment of Visible Minorities in the Canadian Expeditionary Force," *Canadian Historical Review* 70, 1 (1989).

54 Robert Brown and Donald Loveridge, "Unrequited Faith: Recruiting the CEF, 1914–1918," *Revue internationale d'histoire militaire* 51, 54 (1982).

55 "Windsor Sends 197 Volunteers for the Canadian Contingent," *Windsor Evening Record,* August 11, 1914.

56 "Twenty-Five Thousand Pack Windsor Streets When Volunteers Parade," *Windsor Evening Record,* August 12, 1914.

57 "Stick to Volunteer System," *Windsor Evening Record,* December 16, 1914.

58 Copp, "The Military Effort, 1914–1918," 37–38.

59 The American Legion, a contingent of battalions organized specifically for the recruitment of Americans during the period of US neutrality, recruited hundreds of men in the Windsor region. Eric Smylie, "Americans Who Did Not Wait: The American Legion of the Canadian Expeditionary Force, 1915-1917" (MS thesis, University of North Texas, 1996), 68–69. On the CEF's recruiting struggles by 1916, see Ronald G. Haycock, *Sam Hughes: The Public Career of a Controversial Canadian, 1885-1916* (Waterloo, ON: Wilfrid Laurier University Press, 1986), 198.

60 Morrison, *Garden Gateway to Canada,* 254.

61 "Women of Windsor Show True Patriotism," *Windsor Evening Record,* August 11, 1914.

62 "Generous Response for Hospital Ship," *Windsor Evening Record,* August 14, 1914.

63 "Detroit Ladies Give Supplies," *Windsor Evening Record,* March 15, 1915.

64 "Social and Personal," *Windsor Evening Record,* April 3, 1915.

65 In May 1916, it was estimated that Detroit members of the St. Andrew's Society supported forty Canadian families at a cost of $700 per month. Detroit Public Library, Burton Historical Collection, St. Andrew's Society Records, Series 6, Subseries D, Box 20:13.

66 Displays for the event represented Canada, Scotland, England, France, Wales, Belgium, Bohemia, Serbia, Armenia, and Poland. Detroit Public Library, Burton Historical Collection, St. Andrew's Society Records, Series 1, Box 1:10, 1916.

67 "Saturday Will Be 'Canadian Day' at Allies Bazaar," *Windsor Evening Record,* November 17, 1916.

68 "Posters Attract Much Attention at Allies Bazaar," *Windsor Evening Record,* November 24, 1916.

69 "Three Detroit Boys Are Killed in Action; Enlisted in Windsor," *Windsor Evening Record,* March 20, 1915.

70 "Detroiters' Names on Casualty List," *Windsor Evening Record,* September 27, 1916.

71 "Veteran Added to Recruiting Staff," *Windsor Evening Record,* July 14, 1916.

72 "Went Broke at Races; Enlisted," *Windsor Evening Record,* July 20, 1916.

73 "Recruiting Men Here for Many Branches of Army," *Windsor Evening Record,* November 17, 1916.

74 In December 1916, the *Evening Record* lamented that there "are a number of Scotch slackers." "Conscription," *Windsor Evening Record,* December 19, 1916.

75 Although Tuson estimated in his speech that one in five 241st recruits were Americans, the number was actually closer to one in four. "Throng Bids Farewell to 241st Batt.," *Windsor Evening Record,* April 24, 1917; Shackleton and Antal, *Duty Nobly Done,* 327.

76 "Rovers Trim the Wolverines," *Windsor Evening Record,* March 15, 1915; "Border City Team Takes Soccer Cup," *Windsor Evening Record,* June 11, 1915.

77 "Crescents Will Play Strong Detroit Team," *Windsor Evening Record,* June 9, 1916; "Wanderers May Enter Baseball League in Detroit," *Windsor Evening Record,* June 29, 1916; "Large Crowd in Attendance at Inaugural Meeting of Windsor's New Track," *Windsor Evening Record,* September 5, 1916; editorial, *Windsor Evening Record,* September 6, 1916.
78 "Windsorite Takes 7 Prizes at Dog Show," *Windsor Evening Record,* June 30, 1916; "Horseshoe Team to Play Detroit Ball Tossers," *Windsor Evening Record,* July 14, 1916; "City Briefs – Friendly Match," *Windsor Evening Record,* July 17, 1916.
79 "Amusements," *Windsor Evening Record,* February 13, 1915.
80 "Detroit Preacher at Meetings Tonight," *Windsor Evening Record,* February 4, 1915; "Social and Personal," *Windsor Evening Record,* February 19, 1915; "Social and Personal," *Windsor Evening Record,* January 6, 1917.
81 "Social and Personal – Lemieux-Wallis," *Windsor Evening Record,* February 5, 1915; "Social and Personal – Crandell-Gottschalk," *Windsor Evening Record,* December 5, 1916.
82 "Hockey versus Huns," *Windsor Evening Record,* January 23, 1917.
83 "Curtain Will Be Rung Down on Canadian Racing with Running of Tuesday's Program," *Windsor Evening Record,* July 30, 1917.
84 "Assumption Team Preparing for Ypsilanti Game," "Collegiate Team Defeats Detroiters," *Windsor Evening Record,* October 8, 1917; "Formidable Team Wears Uniform of Windsor Collegiate," *Windsor Evening Record,* October 17, 1917; "W.C.I. Team to Meet Detroit Team," *Windsor Evening Record,* November 8, 1918.
85 Editorial, *Windsor Evening Record,* January 15, 1917.
86 "Renounces His Country; Seeks to Revenge Kin," *Windsor Evening Record,* March 30, 1917.
87 "Wilson's War Address," *Windsor Evening Record,* April 3, 1917.
88 "Help from the United States," *Windsor Evening Record,* April 5, 1917.
89 "Views of Readers – International Bridge to Succeed Ferry," *Windsor Evening Record,* April 19, 1917.
90 "Border Welcomes US Entry in War," *Detroit Free Press,* April 18, 1917.
91 "Parade Witnessed by Great Throng," *Windsor Evening Record,* April 16, 1917.
92 Shackleton and Antal, *Duty Nobly Done,* 327.
93 "Kilties Had Time of Their Careers," *Windsor Evening Record,* April 17, 1917.
94 Windsor military officers appeared before several meetings of the SAR in 1917 and 1918. Detroit Public Library, Burton Historical Collection, Marquis E. Shattuck Papers, Series 2, Box 11:4.
95 "The Canadians at Vimy," *Detroit Free Press,* April 15, 1917.
96 Journal of the Common Council, City of Detroit, September 17, 1918, Detroit Public Library, Burton Historical Collection.
97 Ibid., July 2, 1918.
98 "Veterans Appear in Detroit Parade," *Windsor Evening Record,* April 11, 1918.
99 "Directors Decide to Go On with Windsor Fair," *Windsor Evening Record,* June 1, 1918.
100 "Americans Organize to Aid in Welcome of Troops En-Route," *Windsor Evening Record,* June 4, 1918.
101 "Duke of Devonshire Pays Tribute to Doughboys," *Windsor Evening Record,* June 6, 1918.
102 "Fourth of July Welcome Given Sammies Here," *Windsor Evening Record,* July 5, 1918.
103 "News and Views of the Border – Invite War Veterans," *Windsor Evening Record,* July 26, 1918.
104 "Border Cities Go Wild When News of Truce Comes," *Windsor Evening Record,* November 11, 1918.
105 "Wild Parade Greets Truce," *Detroit News,* November 12, 1918.

106 Clarence M. Burton to Clyde J. Carpenter, November 13, 1918, Detroit Public Library, Burton Historical Collection, Clarence M. Burton Papers, Box 11.

107 Windsor City Council Minutes, November 25, 1918, Windsor Public Library Archives, RG2 AIV-1; Journal of the Common Council, City of Detroit, November 19, 1918, Detroit Public Library, Burton Historical Collection.

108 "Council Votes Armistice Day Legal Holiday," *Detroit Free Press,* November 10, 1921.

Chapter 2: "Part and Parcel"

1 The *Windsor Evening Record* reported that 800 cars and 15,000 people – many of them Detroiters headed to Windsor's horse-racing venues – could be found in the vicinity of Ouellette Avenue and Sandwich Street on July 16, 1914. "Windsor Was Able to Handle Record Crowd," *Windsor Evening Record,* July 16, 1914.

2 "City Briefs – Do It in the Morning," *Windsor Evening Record,* July 13, 1914.

3 In July 1914, it was estimated that the armada of ferry steamers operating on the Detroit River could carry 44,000 people in a single day. "Detroit Lake and River Steamers Carry 44,000 Passengers," *Windsor Evening Record,* July 3, 1914.

4 The 1910 US census found 43,542 Germans living in Detroit, though an August 1914 *Detroit Free Press* story suggested that the number was closer to 130,000; Olivier Zunz, *The Changing Face of Inequality: Urbanization, Industrial Development, and Immigrants in Detroit, 1880-1920* (Chicago: University of Chicago Press, 1982), 106; "Detroit Germans Mostly Peaceful, Declares Leidich," *Detroit Free Press,* August 3, 1914.

5 "Gossip of two good German housewives in an apartment house on Duffield street ... revealed a dark plot on the part of German sympathizers in the United States to destroy by aerial bombs the Windsor armory, the Remington Arms company factory in Windsor, and the Walkerville distillery," reported the *Detroit Free Press* on November 4. "Has Detroit a 'Bombbund' to Blow Up Windsor? Nurse Who Heard Women Gossip Says So," *Detroit Free Press,* November 4, 1914.

6 "Recruits Drill in Armories Tonight," *Windsor Evening Record,* November 24, 1914.

7 Colonel L.W. Shannon, OC MD1, to Secretary of the Militia Council, Ottawa, August 13, 1914, LAC, RG24, Vol. 4262, File C-13.

8 Report of F.R.J., October 22, 1914, LAC, RG24, Vol. 4262, File C-13.

9 Ibid., October 23, 1914.

10 "Militiamen Will Have Preference," *Windsor Evening Record,* November 27, 1914; "Sports Committee Meets Next Week," *Windsor Evening Record,* November 27, 1914; "Indoor Game for Thursday," *Windsor Evening Record,* December 16, 1914.

11 Indeed, in 1915, the City of Windsor would spend $5,000 on rifles and uniforms for these men. "Can't Aid Home Guards," *Detroit Free Press,* December 13, 1914; "War Expenditures of City Council Total $11,128.37 [sic; the total was actually $114,128.37]," *Windsor Evening Record,* December 19, 1916.

12 "No Need to Fear German Invasion," *Windsor Evening Record,* December 8, 1914.

13 Graeme S. Mount, *Canada's Enemies: Spies and Spying in the Peaceable Kingdom* (Toronto: Dundurn Press, 1993), 30.

14 "Warning of Bomb Plot Received by Windsor's Mayor," *Detroit Free Press,* June 22, 1915.

15 "War across the Border," *Detroit Free Press,* June 22, 1915.

16 "Warning of Bomb Plot Received by Windsor's Mayor," *Detroit Free Press,* June 22, 1915.

17 Mount, *Canada's Enemies,* 30.

18 In August 1915, former Invincible Machine watchman William Lefler was tried in Canada and sentenced to ten years in prison for his part in the attack. Charles Respa, who provided Lefler with the dynamite, was tried in Canada and received a life sentence. The

plot's main conspirator, Albert Kaltschmidt, was tried in the United States and sentenced to four years in prison in December 1917. "Lefler Begins 10 Years' Term as Dynamiter," *Detroit Free Press,* August 14, 1915; "Swears Detroiters Brought Dynamite for Windsor Jobs," *Ludington Daily News,* March 7, 1916; "The Kaltschmidt Sentence," *Detroit Free Press,* December 24, 1917.

19 "Eerie Plane Flits Over Lefler's Cell," *Detroit Free Press,* August 12, 1915.

20 Residents of Windsor were not the only Ontarians who feared a German attack from the air. Between 1914 and 1916, the people of Toronto, London, Niagara Falls, Hamilton, Sault Ste. Marie, Sweaburg, Tillsonburg, Petrolia, Oil Springs, Aylmer, and Port Stanley all reported seeing mysterious aircraft in the skies, many fearing that they were being piloted by Germans. "Windsor in Panic When 'Bird Man' Flies Over Border," *Detroit Free Press,* September 5, 1915.

21 "Report on Dynamite Plot Scares Sandwich," *Detroit Free Press,* September 21, 1915.

22 For more on fears associated with aerial bombardments, see Robert Bartholomew, "Phantom German Air Raids on Canada: War Hysteria in Ontario and Quebec during the First World War," *Canadian Military History* 7, 4 (1998).

23 "Beautiful New Waists"; "2,000 Extra Fine Panamas!"; "Clearing Out Trimmed Hats at $1.00 & $3.00," *Windsor Evening Record,* July 17, 1914; "Summer Shoe Sale"; "The New Tango and 'Castle' Punys"; "Pumps and Oxfords," *Windsor Evening Record,* July 25, 1914.

24 "Extra Special Values in Jewelry," *Windsor Evening Record,* July 24, 1915.

25 Dave McIntosh, *The Collectors: A History of Canadian Customs and Excise* (Toronto: NC Press, 1984), 300.

26 "Windsor and Vicinity Rapidly Becoming the Pittsburg of Canada," *Windsor Evening Record,* May 6, 1913.

27 "Another Windsor Youth Caught with Chinaman," *Windsor Evening Record,* July 27, 1914; McIntosh, *The Collectors,* 252.

28 "1,200 Women Searched in Custom Raid," *Detroit Free Press,* March 27, 1915.

29 Ibid.

30 "Crusade on Smuggling Causes Excitement," *Windsor Evening Record,* March 27, 1915.

31 "1,200 Women Searched in Custom Raid," *Detroit Free Press,* March 27, 1915.

32 "Politics in Complaints for Windsor Smuggling," *Detroit Free Press,* March 28, 1915.

33 "Women Officers Inspect Shoppers," *Detroit News,* March 27, 1915.

34 "Political Plot Seen in Customs Quiz in Windsor," *Detroit News,* March 28, 1915.

35 "1,200 Women Searched in Custom Raid," *Detroit Free Press,* March 27, 1915.

36 "Crusade on Smuggling Causes Excitement," *Windsor Evening Record,* March 27, 1915; "No Politics in Customs Smuggling," *Windsor Evening Record,* March 29, 1915.

37 "Views of Readers – The Lady Searcher," *Windsor Evening Record,* March 30, 1915.

38 "Views of Readers – That Customs Raid," *Windsor Evening Record,* April 1, 1915.

39 Before the introduction of income tax in Canada in 1917, approximately 75 percent of the Canadian government's revenue, before and after Confederation, was through customs and excise duties. McIntosh, *The Collectors,* 7.

40 "Crusade on Smuggling Causes Excitement," *Windsor Evening Record,* March 27, 1915.

41 "Veteran Customs Official Passes," *Windsor Evening Record,* March 26, 1917.

42 "Injuring Recruiting," *Windsor Evening Record,* November 17, 1916; "Views of Readers – Sunday Papers," *Windsor Evening Record,* November 17, 1916.

43 "Views of Readers – Exclusion of Sunday Papers," *Windsor Evening Record,* November 20, 1916.

44 "A Meddlesome Reformer," *Windsor Evening Record,* November 21, 1916.

45 Windsor City Council Minutes, November 20, 1916, Windsor Public Library Archives, RG2, AIV-1.

46 "Board of Trade Protests Ban on Sunday Papers," *Windsor Evening Record*, November 22, 1916.

47 "Canadians Protest Sunday Labor Law," *Detroit Free Press*, November 19, 1916.

48 "Seek to Raise Ban on Sunday Papers," *Detroit Free Press*, November 25, 1916.

49 Unfortunately, it remains unclear how Detroit's religious community reacted to Rochester's plea. "Other Dry States Combed for Model of Michigan Law," *Detroit News*, December 11, 1916.

50 "Voice of Readers – Sunday Paper Embargo," *Windsor Evening Record*, November 23, 1916.

51 "Border Annoyances," *Windsor Evening Record*, December 5, 1916.

52 In late December, local police were told that they must forcibly stop the distribution of weekend American newspapers. Constables were placed near the ferry docks at Sandwich Street and Ouellette Avenue, where they seized these papers and forced the newsboys carrying them to disperse. "Stops Newsboys Selling Journal with Scare Head," *Windsor Evening Record*, December 23, 1916.

53 "Sunday Paper Clubs Doomed?," *Windsor Evening Record*, January 15, 1917.

54 "The Tyranny of Rochester," *Windsor Evening Record*, April 10, 1917.

55 "Mercy! Rochester Loose Again!," *Windsor Evening Record*, November 2, 1917.

56 D.H. Reynolds to J.S. Austin, November 27, 1915, LAC, RG76 MF C-10616, File 801552, Part 3.

57 In October 1915, the immigration authorities in Ottawa berated Austin and his team for allowing Bert Harris (a.k.a. Albert Ashburner) into the country sometime between February and June; within months, he was an inmate at the Ontario Reformatory in Guelph. W.D. Scott to J.S. Austin, October 4, 1915, LAC, RG76 MF C-10616, File 801552, Part 3.

58 W.D. Scott to J.S. Austin, July 23, 1915, LAC, RG76 MF C-10616, File 801552, Part 3.

59 To put this into perspective, consider that Ford Canada employees – in most cases unskilled or semi-skilled labourers with little education – were paid after 1915 four dollars per day: twenty-four dollars per week or approximately $1,248 per year.

60 F. Wensley to D.H. Reynolds, November 1, 1915, LAC, RG76 MF C-10616, File 801552, Part 3.

61 W.D. Scott to W.W. Cory, Deputy Minister of the Interior, February 28, 1916, LAC, RG76 MF C-10616, File 801552, Part 3.

62 Percy Reid to W.D. Scott, March 29, 1916, LAC, RG76 MF C-10616, File 801552, Part 3.

63 Ibid.

64 For more on Detroit's manpower shortage in early 1917, see "Our Canadian Newcomers," *Windsor Evening Record*, January 5, 1917, 4. Similar problems in Windsor were revealed in a report by the city's Fire Committee on April 15, 1918, when it was discovered that the local fire department could not keep its men from leaving for better-paying positions in the region's factories. Report of the Fire Committee, April 15, 1918, Windsor City Council Committee Records and Reports, Windsor Public Library Archives, RG2 A, Box 14, Unit 28.

65 M.B. Scarth, Travelling Immigration Inspector, to W.D. Scott, November 1, 1916, LAC, RG76 MF C-10616, File 801552, Part 3.

66 W.D. Scott to Captain Padden, November 21, 1916, LAC, RG76 MF C-10616, File 801552, Part 3.

67 Windsor's returned soldiers were virtually guaranteed employment by the City of Windsor. In June 1914, city council passed a resolution "in favor of making every reasonable provision for the employment of any and all men who return and do not find their former or other positions open to them." Windsor City Council Minutes, June 14, 1915, Windsor Public Library Archives, RG2, AIV-1.

68 D.H. Reynolds to W.D. Scott, October 27, 1917, LAC, RG76 MF C-10616, File 801552, Part 3.
69 W.D. Scott to O.G. Adams, December 3, 1917, LAC, RG76 MF C-10616, File 801552, Part 3.
70 O.G. Adams to W.D. Scott, December 15, 1917, LAC, RG76 MF C-10616, File 801552, Part 3.
71 D.H. Reynolds to W.D. Scott, December 27, 1917, LAC, RG76 MF C-10616, File 801552, Part 3.
72 W.D. Scott to W.W. Cory, June 24, 1918, and W.D. Scott to W.W. Cory, April 5, 1918, LAC, RG76 MF C-10616, File 801552, Part 3.
73 W.D. Scott to W.W. Cory, April 5, 1918, LAC, RG76 MF C-10616, File 801552, Part 3.
74 "200 Draft Evaders in Essex, Estimated," *Detroit Free Press,* March 8, 1918.
75 Gregory S. Kealey, "The Surveillance State: The Origins of Domestic Intelligence and Counter-Subversion in Canada, 1914-21," *Intelligence and National Security* 7, 3 (1992).
76 "Two Alleged Slackers Arrested in Detroit," *Detroit Free Press,* March 16, 1918, 8; "Slacker Hunt Halts Dances," *Detroit Free Press,* March 17, 1918.
77 "Slacker Hunt Halts Dances," *Detroit Free Press,* March 17, 1918.
78 The years 1917 and 1918 saw a number of reports in Detroit and Windsor newspapers about the activity of US–based German American terrorists. "Canada 'Raid' from Detroit Revealed," *Windsor Evening Record,* June 6, 1917; "Federal Agents Arrest Michigan Bomb Plotters," *Windsor Evening Record,* March 1, 1918; "Plot to Invade Canada," *Windsor Evening Record,* April 17, 1918.
79 "Windsor Troops in Detroit," *Detroit News,* April 6, 1915.
80 "Woman Dragged on Board Ferry at Detroit Side," *Windsor Evening Record,* August 1, 1916.
81 "Canadians Free from US Head Tax," *Windsor Evening Record,* April 2, 1917; "Voice of Readers – New Immigration Law," *Windsor Evening Record,* April 12, 1917.
82 "Canadians Pay $20,000 Head Tax," *Detroit Free Press,* August 1, 1917.
83 "Ottawa Refuses 241st Permission to Cross River," *Windsor Evening Record,* April 12, 1917.
84 "Parade Witnessed by Great Throng," *Windsor Evening Record,* April 16, 1917.
85 "Kilties Had Time of Their Careers," *Windsor Evening Record,* April 17, 1917.
86 "President Wilson's Proclamation Establishing Conscription, 28 May 1917," First World War.com, http://www.firstworldwar.com/source/usconscription_wilson.htm.
87 A.M. Willms, "Conscription 1917: A Brief for the Defence," in *Conscription 1917,* ed. Ramsay Cook et al. (Toronto: University of Toronto Press, 1969), 8.
88 "Ban at Border Halts Throngs," *Detroit Free Press,* May 26, 1917.
89 "Thousands Detained at Ferry Dock," *Windsor Evening Record,* May 25, 1917.
90 Ibid.
91 "Ban Temporarily Lifted Pending Arrival of Forms," *Windsor Evening Record,* May 26, 1917.
92 "Ban at Border Halts Throngs," *Detroit Free Press,* May 26, 1917.
93 "Order Detaining Americans Not Received as Yet," *Windsor Evening Record,* June 1, 1917.
94 "Passport Order Being Strictly Enforced To-Day," *Windsor Evening Record,* June 9, 1917.
95 Ibid.
96 "Ban at Border Halts Throngs," *Detroit Free Press,* May 26, 1917.
97 "Views of Readers – Men on Guard Duty," *Windsor Evening Record,* April 5, 1917.
98 "Home Guard Unit Idea Abandoned," *Detroit Free Press,* May 25, 1917.
99 In spring 1918, several new German American plots against Canada were discovered. In early March, US Department of Justice agents discovered a terrorist cell based in Brighton, Michigan, producing bombs intended for Canadian munitions factories. In

April, a Syracuse University professor alleged that as many as 500,000 German reservists in the United States were preparing for an invasion of Canada. "Federal Agents Arrest Michigan Bomb Plotters," *Windsor Evening Record,* March 1, 1918; "Plot to Invade Canada," *Windsor Evening Record,* April 17, 1918.

100 "Those Dominion Police," *Windsor Evening Record,* April 2, 1918.

101 Editorial, *Windsor Evening Record,* April 18, 1918.

102 Windsor City Council Minutes, June 11, 1918, Windsor Public Library Archives, RG2, AIV-1.

103 David Prerau, *Seize the Daylight: The Curious and Contentious Story of Daylight Saving Time* (New York: Thunder's Mouth Press, 2005), 97.

104 "Old Time and New Time," *Windsor Evening Record,* April 16, 1918, 4; Windsor City Council Minutes, April 15, 1918, Windsor Public Library Archives, RG2, AIV-1.

105 "Walkerville Indorses 'Daylight Saving' Plan," *Detroit Free Press,* April 20, 1918.

106 Ibid.

107 "Voice of Readers – What O'Clock Is It?," *Windsor Evening Record,* April 27, 1918.

108 Ibid.

109 "Mayor Is Blamed for Time Squabble," *Detroit Free Press,* April 24, 1918.

110 "Mayor Would End Confusion in Time," *Detroit Free Press,* April 27, 1918.

111 "Ford Motor Co. Adopts New Time," *Windsor Evening Record,* April 27, 1918.

112 "Ford Plant Will Set Time Ahead," *Detroit Free Press,* April 28, 1918.

113 "Border City Turns to 'Daylight Time,'" *Detroit Free Press,* April 30, 1918.

114 Ian Hugh Maclean Miller, *Our Glory and Our Grief: Torontonians and the Great War* (Toronto: University of Toronto Press, 2002), 16.

115 William Oxford, *The Ferry Steamers: The Story of the Detroit–Windsor Ferry Boats* (Erin, ON: Boston Mills Press, 1992), 6, 23.

116 "South Detroit," *Windsor Evening Record,* May 23, 1917.

117 "Suggests 'South Detroit' as Name for Border Towns," *Windsor Evening Record,* November 2, 1917.

118 "Voice of Readers – Prefers 'Detroit, Canada,'" *Windsor Evening Record,* November 12, 1917.

119 For more on the South Detroit debate and the use of isolationist rhetoric in Windsor during the war, see Brandon Dimmel, "South Detroit, Canada: Isolation, Identity, and the US–Canada Border, 1914-1918," *Journal of Borderlands Studies* 26, 2 (2011).

Part 2: St. Stephen, New Brunswick, and Calais, Maine

1 Carl Benn, "A Brief History of Fort York," Friends of Fort York, http://www.fortyork.ca/history-of-fort-york.html.

2 According to legend, once the war was over, British colonial authorities requested that the gunpowder, which had been stored at St. Stephen, be sent to Fredericton. However, the same authorities found the gunpowder missing, locals admitting that they had given the entire batch to their Calais neighbours. Edward Boyd, ed., "The Days before Yesterdays in the St. Croix Valley," manuscript, St. Croix Public Library, 2001, Chapter 3, Section 9.

3 Harold Davis, *An International Community on the St. Croix, 1604-1930* (Orono: University of Maine Press, 1950), 3.

4 In 1969, researchers unearthed twenty-three bodies from the French expedition. Archaeological investigations on the island are ongoing. Andrew Rankin, "Researchers in a Race against Time on Historic Island," *Toronto Star,* August 16, 2011; William Francis Ganong, *Champlain's Island: St. Croix (Dochet)* (Saint John: New Brunswick Museum, 1945), xviii.

5 A “Father Baird” studied the Passamaquoddy peoples in the early seventeenth century and estimated their numbers (including those along the St. Croix and Saint John Rivers) to be around 1,000. Davis, *An International Community on the St. Croix*, 6.

6 St. Stephen received its name in the 1780s, and Calais was named in 1806 out of respect for the French De Monts expedition. Doug Dougherty, *St. Stephen Yesteryear* (St. Stephen: Parsons Printing, 2000), 10; William Wallace Brown, “Pioneers of Calais,” in *Calais Centennial, 1909* (Calais: St. Croix Historical Society, 2009), 34.

7 Brown, “Pioneers of Calais,” 33; Davis, *An International Community on the St. Croix*, 83.

8 During and after the Revolutionary War, both Americans and Loyalists acquired contracts to produce masts and lumber for sale in the British Empire. Francis M. Carroll, “Drawing the Line,” *Beaver* 83, 4 (2003); Davis, *An International Community on the St. Croix*, 41.

9 Davis, *An International Community on the St. Croix*, 63.

10 Ibid., 64–67.

11 Dougherty, *St. Stephen Yesteryear*, 10.

12 Aubrey G. Davies, “International Frontier Week,” in “The Days before Yesterdays in the St. Croix Valley,” ed. Edward Boyd, manuscript, St. Croix Public Library, 2001, Chapter 4, Section 2.

13 Ronald Rees, *Historic St. Croix: St. Stephen – Calais* (Halifax: Nimbus, 2003), x.

14 Ibid., ix.

15 The Chesapeake Affair of 1807, in which American sailors were forcibly removed from the *USS Chesapeake* and then tried in Halifax for allegedly deserting the Royal Navy, was perhaps the most visible diplomatic offence by Britain against the United States prior to the War of 1812. John Boileau, *Half-Hearted Enemies: Nova Scotia, New England, and the War of 1812* (Halifax: Formac, 2005), 12–13.

16 Ibid., 15.

17 Grace Helen Mowat, *The Diverting History of a Loyalist Town: A Portrait of St. Andrews, New Brunswick* (Fredericton: Brunswick Press, 1953), 80.

18 Methodist Reverend Duncan McColl was the only minister present in the St. Croix Valley during the crisis and split his time between the American and British sides of the St. Croix River. For generations, local memory of McColl’s peacekeeping would evoke strong feelings from residents of St. Stephen and Calais. Davis, *An International Community on the St. Croix*, x-xi; Charles G. McCully, “Our Men and Women in the Past,” in *Calais Centennial, 1909* (Calais: St. Croix Historical Society, 2009), 51; “Biography of Rev. Duncan McColl,” St. Croix Public Library, Project Preservation File, Reel 2.

19 Richard Sassman, “A Borderline War,” *American History* 35, 6 (2001).

20 Scott Kaufman and John A. Soares, Jr., “Sagacious beyond Praise? Winfield Scott and Anglo-American-Canadian Border Diplomacy, 1837–1860,” *Diplomatic History* 30, 1 (2006).

21 Carroll, “Drawing the Line.”

22 Boyd, “The Days before Yesterdays in the St. Croix Valley,” Chapter 3, Section 9, supports this point when he notes that the issue “passed without dislocation of amity in the St. Croix Valley.” See also Davis, *An International Community on the St. Croix*, 145.

23 Mowat, *The Diverting History of a Loyalist Town*, 125.

24 Muriel H. Dixon, “The Story of Indian Island,” *Saint Croix Courier*, October-November 1977.

25 Mowat, *The Diverting History of a Loyalist Town*, 125.

26 Dougherty, *St. Stephen Yesteryear*, 107.

27 Ibid., 108.

28 Berla Short, "Short's Shipyards," Charlotte County Archives, Berla Short Collection, Box A787, 1.32.
29 Dougherty, *St. Stephen Yesteryear*, 38.
30 A last Short's residency remains unknown. Vincent Short and Edwin Sears, *Sail and Steam: Along the Maine Coast* (Portland, ME: Bond Wheelwright, 1955), 91–92.
31 According to the 1871 census, more than half of all New Brunswick residents were occupied in these three industries. Only 13.8 percent were employed in manufacturing, and only 2.9 percent were involved in trade and finance. Historian Erica Risberg notes that Maine was equally dependent on these three industries in the late nineteenth century. Joseph Richards Petrie, *The Regional Economy of New Brunswick: A Study Prepared for the Committee on Reconstruction* (Fredericton: n.p., 1944), 100; Erica Risberg, "The Hillbillies of Maine: Rural Communities, Radio, and Country Music Performers," *Maine History* 45, 3 (2010).
32 Petrie, *The Regional Economy of New Brunswick*, 107.
33 W.T. Easterbrook and Hugh G.J. Aitken, *Canadian Economic History* (Toronto: University of Toronto Press, 1988), 244.
34 Petrie, *The Regional Economy of New Brunswick*, 101.
35 New Brunswick was far more dependent on trade than the United Province of Canada on the eve of Confederation. According to Petrie, ibid., 107, New Brunswick's per capita trade in 1860 was $45.46, compared with $26.29 for Canada.
36 Ibid., 106.
37 Rees, *Historic St. Croix*, xiii, 40.
38 Petrie, *The Regional Economy of New Brunswick*, 146.
39 Between 1871 and 1941, New Brunswick's total population growth was 60.1 percent, compared with 211.9 percent throughout the rest of Canada. Ibid., 111.
40 Kris E. Inwood, "Maritime Industrialization from 1870 to 1910: A Review of the Evidence and Its Interpretation," in *Farm, Factory, and Fortune: New Studies in the Economic History of the Maritime Provinces*, ed. Kris Inwood (Fredericton: Acadiensis Press, 1993), 164.
41 Kenneth Norrie et al., *A History of the Canadian Economy* (Toronto: Nelson, 2002), 313; Charles E. Clark, *Maine: A History* (New York: W.W. Norton, 1976), 152–53.
42 Freight rate adjustments by the federal government's Board of Railway Commissioners in 1912 increased the cost of shipping goods from the Maritimes west, making the hope for industrial development comparable to that experienced in central Canada highly unlikely. Ken Cruikshank, "The Intercolonial Railway, Freight Rates, and the Maritime Economy," in *Farm, Factory, and Fortune: New Studies in the Economic History of the Maritime Provinces*, ed. Kris Inwood (Fredericton: Acadiensis Press, 1993), 171.
43 Rees, *Historic St. Croix*, xiii.
44 Jacques Poitras, *Imaginary Line: Life on an Unfinished Border* (Fredericton: Goose Lane Editions, 2011), 171.
45 Rees, *Historic St. Croix*, xiii; Trudy Irene Scee, *City on the Penobscot: A Comprehensive History of Bangor, Maine* (Charleston, SC: History Press, 2010), 152.
46 Neil S. Forkey, "Anglers, Fishers, and the St. Croix River: Conflict in a Canadian-American Borderland, 1867–1900," *Forest and Conservation History* 37, 4 (1993).
47 Rees, *Historic St. Croix*, xiii.
48 Boyd, "The Days before Yesterdays in the St. Croix Valley," Chapter 4, Section 10.
49 Davis, *An International Community on the St. Croix*, 275.
50 Dougherty, *St. Stephen Yesteryear*, 40.
51 Margaret McCallum, "Separate Spheres: The Organization of Work in a Confectionery Factory: Ganong Bros., St. Stephen, New Brunswick," *Labour/Le travail* 24 (1989); David

Folster, *The Chocolate Ganongs of St. Stephen, New Brunswick* (Toronto: Macmillan, 1990), 8.

52 "Ganong, Gilbert White," in *Dictionary of Canadian Biography Online*, http://biographi.ca/en/bio.php?id_nbr=7386.

53 Folster, *The Chocolate Ganongs of St. Stephen*, 18.

54 Ibid., 12.

55 Ibid., 30.

56 "Ganong, Gilbert White," in *Dictionary of Canadian Biography Online*, http://biographi.ca/en/bio.php?id_nbr=7386.

57 Davis, *An International Community on the St. Croix*, 295, estimates that the total number of Calais residents employed at the Ganong plant in the late 1880s was around 100. Dougherty and other local historians do not provide hard counts but insist that the number was considerable. Dougherty, *St. Stephen Yesteryear*, 43.

58 Rees, *Historic St. Croix*, 64.

59 Folster, *The Chocolate Ganongs of St. Stephen*, 30.

60 Although the Ganong brothers were initially seen as outsiders by residents of St. Stephen, upon the death of James in April 1888 the *Saint Croix Courier* referred to him as one of the town's "best citizens," and most businesses in the area closed on the day of his funeral. Ibid., 38.

61 "Ganong, Gilbert White," in *Dictionary of Canadian Biography Online*, http://biographi.ca/en/bio.php?id_nbr=7386.

62 McCallum, "Separate Spheres," 59.

63 The only drawback was that some Calais residents had sticky fingers in more ways than one. Folster, *The Chocolate Ganongs of St. Stephen*, 21.

64 Dougherty, *St. Stephen Yesteryear*, 44.

65 Folster, *The Chocolate Ganongs of St. Stephen*, 20.

66 Davis, *An International Community on the St. Croix*, 256.

67 Two Calais businessmen, L.G. Downes and A.E. Neill, reached out to Providence-based Lewis Dexter to help fund the construction and running of the facility, which would be based in Milltown, New Brunswick. Ibid., 258.

68 Boyd, "The Days before Yesterdays in the St. Croix Valley," Chapter 3, Section 9; Bill Eagan, *Woven in Time: An Oral History of the Milltown (St. Croix) Cotton Mill* (Bayside, NB: Korby, 2004), 7.

69 Davis, *An International Community on the St. Croix*, 259; "Canadian Royal Labor Commission," in *Index to the Miscellaneous Documents of the House of Representatives for the First Session of the Fiftieth Congress, 1887–1888* (Washington: Government Printing Office, 1889), 397.

70 In early 1886, the cotton mill's weavers went on strike to protest a pay cut and were eventually joined by other employees. The 700 workers participating in the walkout hired the Milltown, New Brunswick, band to play as they paraded to Calais and back. Davis, *An International Community on the St. Croix*, 259; Eagan, *Woven in Time*, 23.

71 Davis, *An International Community on the St. Croix*, 262.

72 Ibid., 295.

73 Ibid.

74 The Alien Contract Labor Law came into effect in February 1885. The primary purpose of the law was to prevent employers from hiring Chinese immigrants at low wages on a contract basis. As such, it was not originally designed to keep white Canadians out of American factories. However, as historian Thomas Klug has demonstrated, Detroit labourers later used the law to protest Canadian hires when jobs were in short supply during periods of economic depression in the 1890s. Samuel P. Orth, "The Alien Contract

Labor Law," *Political Science Quarterly* 22, 1 (1907); Thomas A. Klug, "The Detroit Labor Movement and the United States-Canada Border, 1885–1930," *Mid-America* 80, 3 (1998).

75 Davis, *An International Community on the St. Croix*, 295.

76 Isaac Case Knowlton, *Annals of Calais, Maine and St. Stephen, New Brunswick Including the Village of Milltown, Me., and the Present Town of Milltown, N.B.* (Calais: Sears, 1875), 97; "Orphan's Friend Lodge," Charlotte County Archives, Henry F. Eaton Steamer File, Box 9–12.

77 This practice appears to have continued into the twentieth century. At a council meeting held in St. Stephen in 1913, councillors openly discussed the "extras" that the local customs officer received as a supplement to his salary. "Matters of Importance Dealt with at August Meeting of Town Council," *Saint Croix Courier*, August 14, 1913; Dougherty, *St. Stephen Yesteryear*, 160.

78 "Calais Schools: Yesterday and Today," Charlotte County Archives, Box A796, 10–11; Dougherty, *St. Stephen Yesteryear*, 28; Davis, *An International Community on the St. Croix*, x.

79 Both baseball and horse racing were extremely popular in St. Stephen and Calais during the early twentieth century. The diamond jubilee festivities celebrating Queen Victoria's sixty years on the throne featured a parade that wound its way through all four communities. "Milltown Won from Calais," *Saint Croix Courier*, September 29, 1910; "Horse Races at the Fair Were Well Contested," *Saint Croix Courier*, October 6, 1910; Rees, *Historic St. Croix*, 74.

80 "General Directory of Calais and St. Stephen, 1890–1891," Charlotte County Archives, Box A792, 6–4 (2); "General Directory of Calais and St. Stephen, 1908-1909," Saint Croix Public Library.

81 Of the 492 marriages recorded between 1892 and 1899, 46 were cross-border marriages. Of the 456 recorded between 1910 and 1919, 78 involved a local Canadian wedding a local American. Calais Marriage Records, 1892–1955, Calais Free Library.

82 Dougherty, *St. Stephen Yesteryear*, 117–18.

83 The Calais-based St. Croix Gas and Light Company also supplied power to streetlights in Calais, St. Stephen, and Milltown, New Brunswick. Ibid., 116–17.

84 Ibid., 122.

85 In December 1913, the St. Stephen Fire Department reported having responded to sixty-one alarms during the year, including thirty-seven in Calais and twenty-four in St. Stephen. "Work of the Firemen during the Year Just Closed," *Saint Croix Courier*, December 13, 1913; Dougherty, *St. Stephen Yesteryear*, 125.

86 Dougherty, *St. Stephen Yesteryear*, 83; Davis, *An International Community on the St. Croix*, 299.

87 Census statistics show that 91 percent of Charlotte County residents and 86 percent of Washington County residents had been born in New Brunswick and Maine, respectively. Together, immigrants from Britain and continental Europe accounted for just 3 percent of Charlotte County's total population in 1911. *Fifth Census of Canada 1911: Religions, Origins, Birthplace, Citizenship, Literacy, and Infirmities, by Provinces, Districts, and Sub-Districts, Volume II* (Ottawa: C.H. Parmlee, 1913), Table XV, 381; *Thirteenth Census of the United States 1910, Volume 3: Reports by States, Alabama–Montana* (Washington, DC: Government Printing Office, 1912–14).

88 Editorial, *Calais Advertiser*, September 30, 1914.

Chapter 3: The "Ties that Bind"

1 "Peace Hath Her Victories Not Less Renowned than War," *Saint Croix Courier*, May 21, 1914.

2 Editorial, *Saint Croix Courier,* May 21, 1914.

3 Ibid.

4 In a May 1915 story written by a Canadian correspondent for the *Calais Advertiser,* the author noted that "no other holiday can take the place of the 4th. We remember when as a small boy we, with all the rest of the loyal Canadian boys, looked forward to the fourth of July with great longing ... One boy at scho[o]l used to say the day was just as much ours as it was the Yankee[s']." "Around the Union," *Calais Advertiser,* May 9, 1915.

5 "Canada's Natal Day Was Well Celebrated," "The Ball Game," and "Horse Races," *Saint Croix Courier,* July 3, 1914; "Dominion Day Celebration," *Calais Times,* July 3, 1914; St. Stephen Municipal Records, June 4, 1914, New Brunswick Provincial Archives, RS420, F81.

6 "Fourth of July in Calais," *Saint Croix Courier,* June 25, 1914; "The Fourth in Calais," *Saint Croix Courier,* July 3, 1914.

7 The *Courier*'s political slant reflected the voting habits of Charlotte County, which elected Conservative candidate Thomas Aaron Hart as MP in 1911 and 1917. In St. Stephen and area, voters elected Conservative candidate George Johnston Clarke MPP in 1903. He held the post until being appointed premier in 1914 amid a party scandal. "Charlotte County Government," http://www.heritagecharlotte.com/documents/CharlotteCo-Government.pdf.

8 Ronald Rees, *Historic St. Croix: St. Stephen – Calais* (Halifax: Nimbus, 2003), 93.

9 R. Peter Gillis and Thomas R. Roach, *Lost Initiatives: Canada's Forest Industries, Forest Policy, and Forest Conservation* (Westport, CT: Greenwood Press, 1986), 169; Harold Davis, *An International Community on the St. Croix, 1604-1930* (Orono: University of Maine Press, 1950), 274.

10 Murchie was buried in St. Stephen Cemetery. "George A. Murchie," *Calais Advertiser,* July 1, 1914.

11 "Austrian Archduke and Wife Victims of Assassins," *Saint Croix Courier,* July 2, 1914.

12 Not until July 30, 1914, did the *Saint Croix Courier* speculate that war would spread beyond the Balkans, and even then it was not convinced that Britain (and thus Canada) would be dragged into the fighting. Editorial and "All Europe Trembles on the Edge of War," *Saint Croix Courier,* July 30, 1914.

13 "Battle Was Disaster for Local Team" and "Charlotte County Sunday School Convention," *Saint Croix Courier,* August 6, 1914.

14 "Canada's Contingent Ready in a Fortnight," *Saint Croix Courier,* August 6, 1914.

15 Editorial, *Saint Croix Courier,* August 6, 1914.

16 "The Talk of the Town," *Saint Croix Courier,* August 6, 1914.

17 "We'll Eight [sic] for England[']s Glory, Lads," *Saint Croix Courier,* August 20, 1914.

18 The Canadian Patriotic Fund was designed to provide a regular stipend to the wives (and in some cases the mothers) of soldiers. Dependent fathers rarely received the stipend, no matter their need. Desmond Morton, *Fight or Pay: Soldiers' Families in the Great War* (Vancouver: UBC Press, 2004), 50.

19 "Preliminary Steps for Patriotic Fund Taken at Meeting of Thistles," *Saint Croix Courier,* September 3, 1914.

20 Ibid.

21 Editorial, *Saint Croix Courier,* September 3, 1914.

22 "Patriotic Fund Meeting Was Largely Attended," *Saint Croix Courier,* September 10, 1914; "Town Will Rebuild Shoe Factory and Contribute to Patriotic Fund," *Saint Croix Courier,* October 8, 1914.

23 Just 2 percent of Charlotte County residents reported being born in Britain in 1911. *Fifth Census of Canada 1911: Religions, Origins, Birthplace, Citizenship, Literacy, and*

Infirmities, by Provinces, Districts, and Sub-Districts, Volume II (Ottawa: C.H. Parmlee, 1913), Table XV, 381.

24 "All Europe in Turmoil," *Calais Advertiser,* August 5, 1914.

25 Canadians received most of their war news through the heavily censored United Press service. Prior to 1917, American newspapers were not censored. As a result, Canadians located near the border had access to much different accounts of the fighting than Canadians living farther from it. Even after the American declaration of war, the US government was comparably more lenient with censorship than Ottawa. "Allies Retreat," *Calais Advertiser,* August 26, 1914; Jeffrey Keshen, *Propaganda and Censorship during Canada's Great War* (Edmonton: University of Alberta Press, 1996), xiv, 112; Edward Costrell, *How Maine Viewed the War, 1914-1917* (Orono: University of Maine Press, 1940), 20.

26 Editorial, *Calais Advertiser,* September 30, 1914; "The War Losses," *Calais Advertiser,* October 28, 1914.

27 Ian Hugh Maclean Miller, *Our Glory and Our Grief: Torontonians and the Great War* (Toronto: University of Toronto Press, 2002), 34; "The War Losses," *Calais Advertiser,* October 28, 1914.

28 Editorial, *Calais Advertiser,* April 7, 1915.

29 Tim Cook notes that in February and March the Canadians lost only "a trickle of men" to casualties. Tim Cook, *At the Sharp End: Canadians Fighting the Great War, 1914–1916* (Toronto: Viking Penguin, 2007), 101.

30 "Brave St. Stephen Boy Tells of Terrible Ordeal," *Saint Croix Courier,* May 20, 1915.

31 "How Can Man Die Better," *Saint Croix Courier,* June 17, 1915.

32 "Around the Union," *Calais Advertiser,* May 12, 1915.

33 "Short Stories of Events in Town and Country," *Saint Croix Courier,* May 20, 1915.

34 "Just a Glance at What the 'Kids' Are Doing," *Saint Croix Courier,* July 15, 1915.

35 "Around the Union," *Calais Advertiser,* July 21, 1915.

36 "The Appeal for Men to Do Their Duty," *Saint Croix Courier,* June 3, 1915.

37 "Joining the 55th Battalion," *Saint Croix Courier,* June 3, 1915.

38 "To the Young Women of Charlotte County," *Saint Croix Courier,* June 3, 1915.

39 "How Can Man Die Better," *Saint Croix Courier,* June 17, 1915.

40 "Letters from the Soldiers in Camp at Salisbury," *Saint Croix Courier,* January 7, 1915.

41 "From Pte. Archie Connolly," *Saint Croix Courier,* August 12, 1915.

42 Ibid.

43 "The Talk of the Town," *Saint Croix Courier,* June 3, 1915.

44 "St. Stephen Council in Lengthy Session; Scott Act in Limelight," *Saint Croix Courier,* June 10, 1915.

45 "Ball League Ended," *Saint Croix Courier,* July 22, 1915.

46 "Short Stories of Events in Town and Country," *Saint Croix Courier,* May 18, 1916.

47 See, for example, "Milltown's Breezy Budget," *Saint Croix Courier,* May 25, 1916; "Junior Baseball," *Saint Croix Courier,* June 1, 1916; "Milltown's Breezy Budget," *Saint Croix Courier,* August 24, 1916; "Milltown's Breezy Budget," *Saint Croix Courier,* April 26, 1917; and "Of Local Interest," *Calais Advertiser,* July 11, 1917.

48 "Thirty Years Ago," *Saint Croix Courier,* May 25, 1916.

49 "The Talk of the Town," *Saint Croix Courier,* May 21, 1914.

50 "The Talk of the Town," *Saint Croix Courier,* May 27, 1915.

51 "Victoria Day Observance for the Boys in Khaki," *Saint Croix Courier,* May 18, 1916.

52 "The Talk of the Town," *Saint Croix Courier,* May 25, 1916.

53 "Victoria Day Observance for the Boys in Khaki," *Saint Croix Courier,* May 18, 1916.

54 "Short Stories of Events in Town and Country," *Saint Croix Courier,* August 3, 1916.

55 "Words of Eloquence and Inspiration Heard at Retail Merchants' Banquet," *Saint Croix Courier,* June 22, 1916.
56 Editorial, *Saint Croix Courier,* December 21, 1916.
57 "A New Club," *Saint Croix Courier,* April 8, 1915; "Empire Day Celebration Arranged for Tomorrow," *Saint Croix Courier,* May 20, 1915; "Burns Night Observed by Banquet at the Queen," *Saint Croix Courier,* February 1, 1917.
58 "A Fitting Observance of the Second Anniversary" and "Short Stories of Events in Town and Country," *Saint Croix Courier,* August 3, 1916; "The Second Anniversary Was Fittingly Observed," *Saint Croix Courier,* August 10, 1916; "Local and General," *Calais Advertiser,* August 9, 1916.
59 "Local and General," *Calais Advertiser,* August 9, 1916.
60 Editorial, *Saint Croix Courier,* May 13, 1915.
61 Editorial, *Calais Advertiser,* July 28, 1915; "The War," *Calais Advertiser,* August 4, 1915; Editorial, *Calais Advertiser,* September 22, 1915.
62 "Around the Union," *Calais Advertiser,* September 6, 1914.
63 "Of Local Interest," *Calais Advertiser,* September 30, 1914; "Patriotic Concert and Ball Thursday Evening, Sept. 24," *Saint Croix Courier,* September 17, 1914.
64 "St. Stephen," *Calais Advertiser,* May 5, 1915.
65 "Held a Bridge Party for Belgian Relief," *Saint Croix Courier,* November 12, 1914.
66 "Short Stories of Events in Town and Country," *Saint Croix Courier,* December 3, 1914.
67 "Calais Man Is Interested," *Saint Croix Courier,* September 16, 1915.
68 The Women's Canadian Club also invited Calais religious leaders to attend its meetings. Canadian Club Minutes, St. Croix Public Library, Reel 2, March 12 and 26, and November 24, 1913. The women of the WCC also raised $100 for the purchase of a machine gun in 1915 and refused to have the money spent on any other item. Canadian Club Minutes, St. Croix Public Library, Reel 2, November 7–24, 1914, and July 29, 1915; "The Talk of the Town," *Saint Croix Courier,* April 15, 1915.
69 By 1914, this had become something of a cross-border tradition in the St. Croix Valley. St. Stephen residents showed their support for Calais residents who headed off to fight during the American Civil War and then again during the Spanish-American War. "American Legion," *Calais Advertiser,* February 16, 1916; Rees, *Historic St. Croix,* 79–83.
70 Editorial, *Calais Advertiser,* May 5, 1915.
71 The idea for the American Legion was proposed by Minister of Militia Sam Hughes shortly after the war began. For more than two years, the legion recruited across Canada US citizens, most of whom were ex-servicemen. Unfortunately, pressure from the Wilson administration (concerned that deployment of the legion threatened US neutrality) led to dispersal of the unit in November 1916. For more on this subject, see Eric Smylie, "Americans Who Did Not Wait: The American Legion of the Canadian Expeditionary Force, 1915-1917" (MS thesis, University of North Texas, 1996).
72 "American Legion," *Calais Advertiser,* February 16, 1916.
73 "Around the Union" and "Of Local Interest," *Calais Advertiser,* February 23, 1916.
74 Recruiting: "Around the Union," *Calais Advertiser,* June 30, 1915; "Around the Union," *Calais Advertiser,* August 11, 1915; "Around the Union," *Calais Advertiser,* February 9, 1916. Casualties: "Of Local Interest," *Calais Advertiser,* October 4, 1916; "Of Local Interest," *Calais Advertiser,* October 11, 1916; "Of Local Interest," *Calais Advertiser,* October 18, 1916; "Local and General," *Calais Advertiser,* January 31, 1917.
75 Oddfellows: "The News from Calais," *Saint Croix Courier,* May 4, 1916. Ladies Friendship Club: "Milltown, Maine," *Saint Croix Courier,* November 25, 1915.
76 "The Talk of the Town," *Saint Croix Courier,* April 27, 1916.

77 "Big Woodworking Factory Is Consumed by Fire," *Saint Croix Courier,* October 19, 1916; "Milltown's Breezy Budget," *Saint Croix Courier,* May 23, 1918.
78 "The News from Calais," *Saint Croix Courier,* October 15, 1914; "The Talk of the Town," *Saint Croix Courier,* April 15, 1915; "The News from Calais," *Saint Croix Courier,* February 1, 1917; "The News from Calais," *Saint Croix Courier,* June 13, 1918.
79 "Funeral of John G. Murchie," *Saint Croix Courier,* January 13, 1916.
80 "The News from Calais," *Saint Croix Courier,* August 31, 1916.
81 "The News from Calais," *Saint Croix Courier,* December 14, 1916.
82 "St. Stephen's Greatest January Sale Starts with a Rush," *Calais Advertiser,* January 15, 1913; "St. Stephen Business College," *Calais Advertiser,* January 22, 1913; "Girls Wanted in Ganong Bros. Candy Factory," *Calais Advertiser,* January 12, 1916; "Calais Dollar Day" and "New York Store," *Saint Croix Courier,* June 3, 1915; "The Store that Saves You Money," *Saint Croix Courier,* March 1, 1917.
83 Editorial, *Saint Croix Courier,* August 31, 1916.
84 However, support for neutrality in other parts of the country was substantial enough to help Wilson eke out a narrow victory. "Bet Your Life, Says Hughes; Startled into Slang by Question about Preparedness," *New York Times,* July 26, 1916; "The News from Calais," *Saint Croix Courier,* November 23, 1916.
85 Donald Swartz, "A Young Man's Benefit: The Independent Order of Odd Fellows and Sickness Insurance in the United States and Canada," *Labour/Le travail* 48 (2001).
86 "The News from Calais," *Saint Croix Courier,* April 12, 1917.
87 "Help Wanted," *Saint Croix Courier,* April 26, 1917.
88 Ibid.
89 Editorial, *Saint Croix Courier,* April 26, 1917.
90 Editorial, *Saint Croix Courier,* June 4, 1917.
91 "Shoulder to Shoulder," *Calais Advertiser,* August 29, 1917.
92 In fact, in September 1917, the *Advertiser* suggested that Calais recruits were "lucky boys" about to embark "on an experience that will show its beneficial results through all their lives." "Off for Camp," *Calais Advertiser,* September 19, 1917.
93 "The War," *Calais Advertiser,* February 7, 1917.
94 "The War," *Calais Advertiser,* April 18, 1917.
95 "Canadian Cavalry Charge," *Calais Advertiser,* November 28, 1917.
96 "The Talk of the Town," *Saint Croix Courier,* May 17, 1917; "Calais Academy, Class of 1875," http://www.calaisalumni.org/class1875.htm.
97 "A Good Celebration of Dominion Day," *Saint Croix Courier,* June 28, 1917; "Dominion Day Races Were Well Attended," *Saint Croix Courier,* July 5, 1917; "Calais Races on July 4th," *Saint Croix Courier,* July 19, 1917.
98 "Meeting of the Great War Veterans Association, August 27, 1917," Royal Canadian Legion Records, St. Croix Public Library, Branch 9, Reel 1; "Only Three Weeks Now to the Big Fair Days," *Saint Croix Courier,* August 23, 1917.
99 "Big Military Features at Charlotte County Fair," *Saint Croix Courier,* August 30, 1917; "The Big Fair," *Saint Croix Courier,* September 13, 1917; "Short Stories of Events in Town and Country," *Saint Croix Courier,* September 20, 1917.
100 "The Big Fair," *Saint Croix Courier,* September 13, 1917.
101 According to US Army Colonel Hugh Drum, by late January 1918 there were roughly 180,000 American troops stationed in France. Gary Mead, *The Doughboys: America and the First World War* (New York: Overlook Press, 2000), 208.
102 "Calais Stands among First in Enlistments," *Saint Croix Courier,* March 14, 1918.
103 Editorial, *Saint Croix Courier,* May 2, 1918.

104 "Meeting of the Great War Veterans Association, May 23, 1918," Royal Canadian Legion Records, St. Croix Public Library, Branch 9, Reel 1; "Regular May Meeting Calais City Council" and "Getting All in Shape for Victoria Day," *Saint Croix Courier,* May 16, 1918.

105 "Victoria Day Celebration," *Saint Croix Courier,* May 30, 1918.

106 Ibid.

107 See, for example, "Programme Arranged for Memorial Day," *Saint Croix Courier,* May 29, 1913; "Memorial Day," *Calais Advertiser,* May 31, 1916; and "Flag Raising Feature for Memorial Day," *Saint Croix Courier,* May 24, 1917.

108 Unfortunately, the words of this poem are unknown. "Grand Army Observance of Memorial Day," *Saint Croix Courier,* June 7, 1918; "The News from Calais," *Saint Croix Courier,* June 20, 1918; "Calais Academy, Class of 1919," http://www.calaisalumni.org/class19.htm#Cobb.

109 Hew Strachan, *The First World War* (New York: Viking Penguin, 2004), 290–300.

110 "Dawn of Peace Brought Rejoicing," *Saint Croix Courier,* November 14, 1918.

111 Ibid.

112 Ibid.

113 "The News from Calais," *Saint Croix Courier,* November 14, 1918.

Chapter 4: "A Very Convenient Arrangement"

1 *Fifth Census of Canada 1911: Religions, Origins, Birthplace, Citizenship, Literacy, and Infirmities, by Provinces, Districts, and Sub-Districts, Volume II* (Ottawa: C.H. Parmlee, 1913), Table VII, 178–79.

2 Ibid., 170–71.

3 T.B. Willans to W.D. Scott, July 31, 1908, and John McDougall to W.D. Scott, October 2, 1908, LAC, MF C-10632, File 804947.

4 W.D. Scott to S.N. Hyslip, October 12, 1908, LAC, MF C-10632, File 804947.

5 W.D. Scott to W.W. Cory, April 16, 1914, LAC, MF C-10632, File 805189.

6 Harold Davis, *An International Community on the St. Croix, 1604-1930* (Orono: University of Maine Press, 1950), 295.

7 W.D. Scott to W.W. Cory, April 16, 1914, and W.D. Scott to Mr. Willans, October 28, 1914, LAC, MF C-10632, File 805189.

8 Cheryl MacDonald, "Spring Ahead," *Beaver* 81, 2 (2001).

9 "The Opening Games in St. Croix League," *Saint Croix Courier,* June 11, 1914; "The Talk of the Town," *Saint Croix Courier,* December 17, 1914; "The News from Calais," *Saint Croix Courier,* February 4, 1915; "Base Ball," *Saint Croix Courier,* June 3, 1915; "Of Local Interest," *Calais Advertiser,* June 23, 1915.

10 Woodland is located roughly 240 kilometres miles from Calais. W.D. Scott to Mr. Willans, October 28, 1914, LAC, MF C-10632, File 805189.

11 In late April 1914, Canadian Superintendent of Immigration W.D. Scott noted that neither US nor Canadian immigration inspectors stationed in St. Stephen, Calais, or the Milltowns refused admission to aliens crossing the border for work. There is no evidence in the immigration department's correspondence or local newspapers to suggest that this policy changed dramatically until 1917, when both countries began stopping men of military age from crossing the boundary. W.D. Scott to W.W. Cory, April 16, 1914, LAC, MF C-10632, File 805189.

12 "Short Stories of Events in Town and Country," *Saint Croix Courier,* August 27, 1914.

13 "Short Stories of Events in Town and Country," *Saint Croix Courier*, October 1, 1914.

14 "Of Local Interest," *Calais Advertiser,* August 26, 1914.

15 "German Raids from Maine?," *Saint Croix Courier,* August 20, 1914.

16 Ibid.
17 Ibid.
18 The distance between Vanceboro and Calais is approximately fifty kilometres if one cuts across Canadian territory.
19 "Plot to Embroil US with Britain, Canada's View of Bridge Attack," *Detroit Free Press*, February 3, 1915.
20 "C.P.R. Bridge over the St. Croix Dynamited by German Officer," *Saint Croix Courier*, February 4, 1915.
21 St. Croix, New Brunswick, resident John Rideout later told the *Saint Croix Courier* that he had seen Van Horn acting strangely near the railway bridge the day before the attack and warned local authorities. However, they dismissed his concerns. "Short Stories of Events in Town and Country," *Saint Croix Courier*, February 18, 1915.
22 Henry Landau, *The Enemy Within: The Inside Story of German Sabotage in America* (New York: Van Rees Press, 1937), 21.
23 Proof of von Papen's involvement in the Vanceboro bombing was later discovered when British authorities searched his luggage and found a chequebook showing that he paid Van Horn to blow up the bridge. According to Edward Costrell, *How Maine Viewed the War, 1914–1917* (Orono: University of Maine Press, 1940), 49, this kind of conduct did not help Germany's efforts to win the hearts and minds of Maine residents. Also see Graeme Mount, *Canada's Enemies: Spies and Spying in the Peaceable Kingdom* (Toronto: Dundurn Press, 1993), 32.
24 The United States was reluctant to extradite Van Horn because of his steadily worsening mental condition. According to American doctors, he suffered from syphilis and hallucinations and insisted that he was the natural son of the Grand Duke of Mecklenburg-Strelitz. Martin Kitchen, "The German Invasion of Canada in the First World War," *International History Review* 7, 2 (1985).
25 "Look on Strangers with Some Suspicion," *Saint Croix Courier*, February 11, 1915.
26 Ibid.
27 "Escaped German Prisoners Located Near Border," *Saint Croix Courier*, February 25, 1915.
28 "Around the Union," *Calais Advertiser*, March 17, 1915.
29 W.J. Bryan to Sir Cecil Spring Rice, February 27, 1915, LAC, RG25 1160, File 312.
30 Circular to Border Inspectors from W.D. Scott, Superintendent of Immigration, February 6, 1915, LAC, MF C-10632, File 805189.
31 "Look on Strangers with Some Suspicion," *Saint Croix Courier*, February 11, 1915.
32 Costrell, *How Maine Viewed the War*, 48, has noted that the Vanceboro bombing "was not taken too seriously" south of the border.
33 Editorial, *Saint Croix Courier*, February 11, 1915.
34 Close investigation of the *Saint Croix Courier* and St. Stephen Town Council minutes turns up no discussion of organizing such a force.
35 "Milltown Is Moving for Home Guard Company," *Saint Croix Courier*, April 6, 1916; "A Quiet Session of Milltown Council," *Saint Croix Courier*, May 4, 1916.
36 "House of Commons to F.M. Smith Esq., Town Clerk, Milltown, NB," May 16, 1916, Milltown Records, Charlotte County Archives, Box A787, File Wars 1.20.
37 The proposed manpower reduction was not passed by council, but the fact that the town was discussing reducing rather than increasing the number of night patrolmen suggests that few locals were worried that Germans or Austrians would soon attempt to invade from Calais and attack their town. "A Ghost Was Made to Walk at Town Council Organization," *Saint Croix Courier*, February 15, 1917; "St. Stephen Town Council Deals with Matters of Interest," *Saint Croix Courier*, March 8, 1917.

38 Only the night policeman noticed the problem. He immediately alerted the local customs officer, stationed at the St. Stephen end of the bridge, who, for whatever reason, had not heard the structure crumble. The *Courier* article covering the story does not mention an immigration agent, suggesting that none of the four men hired to inspect new arrivals was anywhere near this particularly sensitive section of the St. Croix River at the time of the incident. The bridge was still passable for automobiles, horse teams, and pedestrians. Only streetcar service between Calais and St. Stephen was affected by the issue. "An Accident Happened at Fortunate Time," *Saint Croix Courier*, August 17, 1916; W.D. Scott to W.W. Cory, February 6, 1917, LAC, MF C-10632, File 804948.

39 Although there were customs officers stationed at Milltown during the war, at no point did the immigration department hire a full-time inspector to patrol this part of the international boundary. John McDougald to Acting Deputy Minister of Immigration and Colonization, December 5, 1918, and T.B. Willans to Mr. Geska, December 17, 1918, LAC, MF C-10632, File 805189; "Of Local Interest," *Calais Advertiser*, February 14, 1917.

40 "The Talk of the Town" and "The News from Calais," *Saint Croix Courier*, April 4, 1918.

41 The *Courier* noted in a March 1915 article that customs collector W.L. Grant was a frequent curler in the community. "Some Lively Nights at the Curling Rink," *Saint Croix Courier*, March 11, 1915.

42 "Reached the Close of an Honourable Life," *Saint Croix Courier*, July 18, 1918.

43 W.D. Scott to W.W. Cory, February 6, 1917, LAC, MF C-10632, File 804948.

44 "The Talk of the Town," *Saint Croix Courier*, December 14, 1914.

45 "The Boys in Khaki Home for Christmas," *Saint Croix Courier*, December 31, 1914.

46 W.D. Scott to W.W. Cory, February 6, 1917, LAC, MF C-10632, File 804948.

47 "Of Local Interest," *Calais Advertiser*, August 30, 1916.

48 "Of Local Interest," *Calais Advertiser*, May 30, 1917.

49 Editorial, *Saint Croix Courier*, May 31, 1917.

50 "Great Differences between Understanding and Perception," *Saint Croix Courier*, May 9, 1918.

51 Ibid.

52 Ibid.

53 Ibid.

54 "The News from Calais," *Saint Croix Courier*, May 4, 1916.

55 MacDonald, "Spring Ahead."

56 Farmers complained that crops and livestock would not operate by an adjusted time. Ibid.

57 "Short Stories of Events in Town and Country," *Saint Croix Courier*, April 11, 1918.

58 "Milltown's Breezy Budget," *Saint Croix Courier*, April 18, 1918.

59 Editorial, *Saint Croix Courier*, May 23, 1918; "Milltown's Breezy Budget," *Saint Croix Courier*, August 29, 1918.

60 Editorial, *Saint Croix Courier*, October 17, 1918.

61 "Great Differences between Understanding and Perception," *Saint Croix Courier*, May 9, 1918.

Part 3: White Rock, British Columbia, and Blaine, Washington

1 For more on the St. Leonard Hotel debate, see Brandon Dimmel, "Shutting Down the Snake Ranch: Battling Booze at the BC Border, 1910-1914," in *Beyond the Border: Tensions across the Forty-Ninth Parallel in the Great Plains and Prairies*, ed. Kyle Conway and Timothy Patsch (Montreal: McGill-Queen's University Press, 2013).

2 Surrey Council Minutes, April 12, 1913, http://www.surrey.ca/bylawsandcouncillibrary/April-12-1913-RC-1A8C.pdf.

3 "The St. Leonard Hotel," *Semiahmoo Gazette,* November 8, 1913.

4 Surrey Council Minutes, January 6, 1913, http://www.surrey.ca/bylawsandcouncillibrary/January-6-1913-RC-CFA5.pdf.

5 "Surrey Has a Kick Coming," *Blaine Journal,* January 31, 1913.

6 Editorial, *Blaine Journal,* November 28, 1913.

7 "St. Leonard to Close Jan. 15," *Blaine Journal,* December 12, 1913.

8 In his January 1915 report, Surrey Medical Health Officer F.D. Sinclair noted that salmon offal was no longer washing ashore at White Rock. Surrey Council Minutes, January 18, 1915, http://www.surrey.ca/bylawsandcouncillibrary/January-18-1915-RC-1894.pdf. Although almost all BC communities voted in favour of prohibition in 1916, White Rock voted against the measure. "British Columbia Dry by 8,000," *Blaine Journal,* September 22, 1916. In the years following the war and British Columbia's return to alcohol, the Blaine chapter of the Women's Christian Temperance Union (WCTU) repeatedly filed complaints with the BC government for allowing saloons to operate near the international boundary. Stephen T. Moore, "Refugees from Volstead: Cross-Boundary Tourism in the Northwest during Prohibition," in *The Borderlands of the American and Canadian Wests: Essays on the Regional History of the 49th Parallel,* ed. Sterling Evans (Lincoln: University of Nebraska Press, 2006), 259.

9 Margaret Lang Hastings, *Along the Way: An Account of Pioneering White Rock and Surrounding District in British Columbia* (Cloverdale, BC: D.W. Friesen, 1981), 31; "About White Rock," http://www.whiterockcity.ca/EN/main/community/about-white-rock.html.

10 "Fires, Border Play Important Role in History of Blaine," *Blaine Journal,* July 30, 1959; "About Blaine," http://www.ci.blaine.wa.us/132/About-Blaine.

11 Jean Barman, *The West Beyond the West: A History of British Columbia* (Toronto: University of Toronto Press, 1991), 65–69.

12 See Yuen-fong Woon, "The Voluntary Sojourner among the Overseas Chinese: Myth or Reality?," *Pacific Affairs* 56, 4 (1983).

13 Barman, *The West Beyond the West,* 133–36; Seema Sohi, "Race, Surveillance, and Indian Anticolonialism in the Transnational Western US–Canadian Borderlands," *Journal of American History* 28, 2 (2011); "Silly Comment," *British Columbian,* July 6, 1915.

14 "54-40," or fifty-four degrees, forty minutes, north latitude, would have established the border at the Alaska panhandle and the edge of Russian America. Dave McIntosh, *The Collectors: A History of Canadian Customs and Excise* (Toronto: NC Press, 1984), 194.

15 Chad Reimer, "Borders of the Past: The Oregon Boundary Dispute and the Beginnings of Northwest Historiography," in *Parallel Destinies: Canadian-American Relations West of the Rockies,* ed. John M. Findlay et al. (Seattle: University of Washington Press, 2002), 232.

16 Sam W. Haynes, *James K. Polk and the Expansionist Impulse* (New York: Longman, 1997), 109–14.

17 Charles A. McCoy, *Polk and the Presidency* (Austin: University of Texas Press, 1960), 95–96.

18 Haynes, *James K. Polk and the Expansionist Impulse,* 118–22.

19 Charles Sellers, *James K. Polk, Continentalist, 1843–1846* (Princeton: Princeton University Press, 1966), 412.

20 George F.G. Stanley, ed., *Mapping the Frontier: Charles Wilson's Diary of the Survey of the 49th Parallel, 1858-1862, while Secretary of the British Boundary Commission* (Toronto: Macmillan, 1970), 7.

21 Ibid., 8–9.

22 Vin Coyne, "Letter, Number, or Name? How Our Streets Got Their Names," *Semiahmoo Sounder,* n.d., White Rock Museum and Archives, Vin Coyne Collection.

23 In a journal entry dated June 25, 1859, British Boundary Commission member Charles Wilson noted waking up "covered with mosquitoes," a problem that he solved by rushing "frantically into the river." Stanley, *Mapping the Frontier,* 54; G. Fern Treleaven, *Roads, Rivers, and Railways: 100 Years of Transportation in Surrey* (Surrey: Surrey Museum and Historical Society, 1981), 10.

24 McIntosh, *The Collectors,* 194.

25 Stanley, *Mapping the Frontier,* 10.

26 Lorraine Ellenwood, *Years of Promise: White Rock, 1858-1958* (White Rock, BC: White Rock Museum and Archives Society, 2004), 28.

27 "Reclaimin' Our History," *Peace Arch News,* October 16, 1995.

28 Ellenwood, *Years of Promise,* 28.

29 Hastings, *Along the Way,* 48.

30 Ellenwood, *Years of Promise,* 33.

31 Margaret Lang Hastings, "The Ropers among First Families to Develop Area," *White Rock and District Mercury,* January 7, 1970.

32 Hastings, *Along the Way,* 88–89.

33 Margaret Lang Hastings, "At 85, Fred Johnson Storehouse of Memories," *White Rock Sun,* January 16, 1964.

34 Margaret Lang Hastings, "Along the Way," *Peace Arch News,* September 28, 1985.

35 "Reclaimin' Our History," *Peace Arch News,* October 16, 1995; Ted Colley, "Natives Celebrate Return of Land," *Surrey Leader,* July 5, 1997.

36 Blaine was originally known as Semiahmoo, then "Concord." Lottie Roeder Roth, *History of Whatcom County, Volume I* (Seattle: Pioneer Historical, 1926), 794.

37 Writers' Program of the Work Projects Administration in the State of Washington, *Washington: A Guide to the Evergreen State* (Portland: Binfords and Mort, 1941), 472.

38 Marie Arbuckle et al., *A Symbol of Our Heritage, the Old Fir Tree: Blaine Centennial History, 1884–1984* (Blaine, WA: Profile Publications, 1984), 15.

39 James G. Blaine was popular in the Pacific Northwest partly because his main platforms included western development and Chinese exclusion. H. Draper Hunt, "The Plumed Knight at Home: An Intimate Sketch of James G. Blaine," *Maine Historical Society Quarterly* 28, 1 (1988).

40 "Fires, Border Play Important Role in History of Blaine," *Blaine Journal,* July 30, 1959.

41 Margaret Stewart Interview, British Columbia Archives, File 326: 1–2, Accession Tape No. 326, Tape No. 1, Track No. 1.

42 Ellenwood, *Years of Promise,* 40.

43 Ibid.

44 Ibid., 40–41.

45 "Hendry, John," in *Dictionary of Canadian Biography Online,* http://www.biographi.ca/en/bio.php?id_nbr=7438.

46 Jack Berry, "The History of the Port of Pacific Highway, BC," Reference Files, Canada Customs, Surrey Archives.

47 Arbuckle et al., *A Symbol of Our Heritage,* 16.

48 Jack Brown, "The Blaine–Point Roberts Salmon Fisheries," http://www.surreyhistory.ca/fisheries.html.

49 "Worth Noting by Farmers of Valley," *British Columbian,* July 1, 1913.

50 Hastings, *Along the Way,* 161.

51 "Fires, Border Play Important Role in History of Blaine," *Blaine Journal,* July 30, 1959; *Thirteenth Census of the United States 1910, Volume 4: Reports by States, Nebraska–Wyoming* (Washington, DC: Government Printing Office, 1912–14).

52 Olive Bell Wilson Interview, Surrey Archives, Acc. No. SMA90.021; Hastings, *Along the Way,* 120.

53 Treleaven, *Roads, Rivers, and Railways,* 65; Al Carder Memoirs, Surrey Archives, Reference Files.

54 In his memoirs, Surrey resident Al Carder remembers this low-lying land with its black peat soil being excellent for farming but subject to flooding during the winter. Al Carder Memoirs, Surrey Archives, Reference Files.

55 Barrie Sanford, *Railway by the Bay: 100 Years of Trains at White Rock, Crescent Beach, and Ocean Park, 1909–2009* (Vancouver: National Railway Historical Society, 2009), 20.

56 Vin Coyne, "Vintage White Rock: A Life of Firsts," *Peace Arch News,* January 15, 2000.

57 "White Rock before the Railway" (display), White Rock Museum and Archives, August 2009.

58 *Henderson's British Columbia Gazetteer and Directory* (Vancouver: Henderson, 1910), 676; Margaret Lang Hastings, "The White Rock Story," White Rock Museum and Archives, Hastings Collection, Box 13.

59 "White Rock's First Hotel" (display), White Rock Museum and Archives, August 2009.

60 Sanford, *Railway by the Bay,* 49.

61 In August 1913, the New Westminster-based *British Columbian* sought solace for the city's own construction slowdown by pointing out similar reductions in other major Canadian communities, from Winnipeg to London to Montreal. "City Not Alone in Building Decrease," *British Columbian,* August 26, 1913.

62 The *Semiahmoo Gazette,* originally a monthly newspaper, referred to White Rock as the Bay of Naples in its first edition, March 1913. "Winter Scene, Semiahmoo Bay," *Semiahmoo Gazette,* March 1913. A census carried out by the Great Northern Railway in early 1914 found just forty-eight families and 200 permanent residents at White Rock. However, locals were outraged at the number and performed their own census, which found 430 winter residents. Locals estimated that this population increased to roughly 3,500 during the summer months. "White Rock Incensed," *British Columbian,* February 17, 1914.

63 "Connect with Big Highway," *Blaine Journal,* April 28, 1911.

64 "Empire Day Railway Rates" and "Summer Railway Rates," *Semiahmoo Gazette,* May 18, 1914.

65 "Winter Scene, Semiahmoo Bay," *Semiahmoo Gazette,* March 1913.

66 "Subway Plans Drawn for White Rock," *British Columbian,* December 17, 1912; Editorial, *Semiahmoo Gazette,* February 5, 1914.

67 In December 1914, the *Semiahmoo Gazette* praised Taylor and MacKenzie for helping the development of White Rock by "obtaining government appropriations for main trunk roads connecting White Rock with outside points." "Pioneer Work Is Appreciated," *Semiahmoo Gazette,* December 15, 1914.

68 Surrey Council reportedly paid nearly $6,000 toward improving White Rock roads in 1913 alone. "Surrey Finances and Expenditures," *British Columbian,* December 9, 1913.

69 Completed in 1915, the pier was funded almost entirely by the dominion government. "Government Will Build Wharf at White Rock," *Semiahmoo Gazette,* June 20, 1914; "Wharf at White Rock," *Semiahmoo Gazette,* April 28, 1915.

70 "Wealthy Conscription Applied Literally Would Paralyze Production and Trade," *Semiahmoo Gazette,* December 6, 1917.

71 "British Columbia and the G.N. Railway," *Semiahmoo Gazette,* July 29, 1914.

72 "Great Northern Railway Company and the Laws of Canada," *Semiahmoo Gazette,* July 29, 1914.

73 "Great Northern Officials Inspect Crossings," *Semiahmoo Gazette*, August 15, 1914.
74 "A Case for the Inspector of Municipalities," *Semiahmoo Gazette*, October 27, 1914.
75 Newspaper evidence suggests that Blaine more frequently engaged with Lynden and Ferndale, Washington, when it came to sports. White Rock residents, meanwhile, tended to compete with people from New Westminster, Crescent Beach, and Barnet, British Columbia, when it came to athletic activities. "High School Notes," *Blaine Journal*, January 15, 1915; "Local Notes," *Blaine Journal*, May 28, 1915; "Sports Were Well Attended," *British Columbian*, August 5, 1913; "White Rock Baseball Team Compete with Barnet Athletic Association" and "Basketball – White Rock Plays Crescent," *Semiahmoo Gazette*, October 15, 1913; "Baseball," *Semiahmoo Gazette*, May 18, 1914; "Semiahmoo Athletics vs. Barnet Blue Sox," *Semiahmoo Gazette*, August 15, 1914.
76 Ellenwood, *Years of Promise*, 99.
77 "Fire Threatens Cottages," *Blaine Journal*, September 2, 1910; Margaret Lang Hastings, "Along the Way," *Peace Arch News*, December 28, 1978; Vin Coyne, "When the Siren Sounds," *Semiahmoo Sounder*, September 1991.
78 Ellenwood, *Years of Promise*, 111.

Chapter 5: "God Save the King"

1 The *Semiahmoo Gazette* was published in New Westminster until May 1915, when Sands moved the newspaper's main offices to White Rock. In October of that year, it formally changed its name to the *Surrey Gazette*, though Sands made the name change in the paper itself the previous June. The newspaper remained a bimonthly until September 1917, when it became a weekly until it ceased publication for financial reasons in May 1918. Margaret Lang Hastings, "History of the *Semiahmoo Gazette*," White Rock Museum and Archives, Hastings Collection, Box 13.
2 "British Columbia and the G.N. Railway," *Semiahmoo Gazette*, July 29, 1914.
3 "War Clouds Hang All Over Europe," *Blaine Journal*, July 31, 1914.
4 "Editorial Notes," *Semiahmoo Gazette*, April 1913.
5 Ibid.
6 "The British Navy Protects Canada," *Semiahmoo Gazette*, April 14, 1914.
7 "Empire Day," *Semiahmoo Gazette*, May 18, 1914.
8 "What Canada Has Done since 1867," *Semiahmoo Gazette*, June 20, 1914.
9 "The Hour Has Struck," *Semiahmoo Gazette*, August 15, 1914.
10 "War Eliminates Factions," *Windsor Evening Record*, August 6, 1914; "Size of Our Soldiers," *Windsor Evening Record*, August 8, 1914.
11 "Christendom's Day," *Semiahmoo Gazette*, December 15, 1914.
12 "Volunteers from White Rock," *Semiahmoo Gazette*, August 15, 1914.
13 "Imperial Veterans' As'sn, No. 2," *Semiahmoo Gazette*, August 15, 1914.
14 Members of White Rock's Imperial Reserve took their role of defending their community seriously. In December 1914, Henry Thrift invited a Prince Rupert drill instructor to the seaside resort town, where the latter trained reservists throughout the winter. "Local Notes," *Semiahmoo Gazette*, September 21, 1914, and December 15, 1914.
15 "Recruits Drill in Armories Tonight," *Windsor Evening Record*, November 24, 1914, 1; "Views of Readers – Men on Guard Duty," *Windsor Evening Record*, April 5, 1917; "Home Guard Unit Idea Abandoned," *Detroit Free Press*, May 25, 1917, 22.
16 "Patriotic Meeting," *Semiahmoo Gazette*, September 21, 1914.
17 Jo Labadie to Clarence M. Burton, March 18, 1917, Detroit Public Library, Burton Historical Collection, Clarence M. Burton Papers, Box 11.
18 W.E. Johnson Interview, March 1963, British Columbia Archives, Imbert Orchard Records, Tape 1.

19 Ibid., Tape 2.
20 Margaret Stewart Interview, British Columbia Archives, File 326: 1–2, Accession Tape No. 326, Tape No. 1, Track No. 1.
21 Margaret Lang Hastings, *Along the Way: An Account of Pioneering White Rock and Surrounding District in British Columbia* (Cloverdale, BC: D.W. Friesen, 1981), 116–17.
22 Ibid., 121–22.
23 "Pioneers of Surrey Municipality – Mr. H.T. Thrift," *Semiahmoo Gazette,* January 5, 1914.
24 "White Rock Elementary 70th Anniversary, May 19th & 20th, 1984," White Rock Museum and Archives, W.R. Elementary 70th Anniversary File, 1993–30; Margaret Lang Hastings, "The White Rock Story," White Rock Museum and Archives, Hastings Collection, Box 13; Margaret Stewart Interview, British Columbia Archives, File 326: 1–2, Accession Tape No. 326, Tape No. 1, Track No. 1.
25 "Pier in Hand," *Peace Arch News,* July 12, 2000.
26 "Surrey Rate Payers Prepare for a Fight," *Blaine Journal,* November 14, 1913; "Our Neighbors After St. Leonard," *Blaine Journal,* September 12, 1913; "The Year that Is," *Semiahmoo Gazette,* February 15, 1914.
27 "Surrey Finances and Expenditures," *British Columbian,* December 9, 1913; "White Rock League Is Incorporated," *British Columbian,* March 19, 1918; "White Rock Volunteers," *British Columbian,* August 11, 1914; "White Rock News," *British Columbian,* March 31, 1914; "Local Exemption Tribunal, BC No. 53," *Surrey Gazette,* December 6, 1917.
28 "Surrey Council," *British Columbian,* June 11, 1918.
29 Hastings, *Along the Way,* 134.
30 In Windsor, the Essex chapter of the Orange Order celebrated the Battle of the Boyne with a parade in July 1916. However, the marchers received a mixed reaction from locals in a city where Catholicism was the dominant faith. The city's mayor also made the Orangemen take down a banner that read "One Flag, One Language, One School." The Orange Lodge is rarely mentioned in St. Stephen's newspaper, though it appears that some locals joined the St. George, New Brunswick, chapter for various events. "Battle of Boyne Is Celebrated by Orange Visitors," *Windsor Evening Record,* July 13, 1916; "The Glorious Twelfth Celebrated at St. George," *Saint Croix Courier,* July 18, 1918.
31 "L.O.L. Semiahmoo," *Semiahmoo Gazette,* May 18, 1914.
32 "The L.O.L. Entertains," *Semiahmoo Gazette,* November 24, 1914.
33 Headline unknown, *British Columbian,* July 18, 1916; "Happened Happenings," *Surrey Gazette,* August 1, 1916.
34 "Wounded Warrior Returns Home," *Surrey Gazette,* March 7, 1918; "Accord Reception to Lieut. MacKenzie," *Surrey Gazette,* April 4, 1918.
35 "L.O.L. Semiahmoo Annual Banquet," *Surrey Gazette,* November 15, 1915.
36 "Local Men Have Medals," *Surrey Gazette,* November 8, 1917.
37 "Local News," *Blaine Journal,* July 16, 1915.
38 "War Relief Association Notes," *Blaine Journal,* January 22, 1915.
39 In a May 1914 editorial, Sheets claimed that an abandoned barn near the local baseball diamond was being used as a "drinking place for a few booze thirsty during ball games." Editorial, *Blaine Journal,* May 15, 1914.
40 "White Rock News," *British Columbian,* February 23, 1915.
41 "Local News," *Blaine Journal,* April 23, 1915; "Local News," *Blaine Journal,* September 10, 1915.
42 "White Rock News," *British Columbian,* March 24, 1914; "Local News," *Blaine Journal,* January 25, 1917.
43 See, for example, "War News Bits," *Blaine Journal,* August 7, 1914; "Brief War News," *Blaine Journal,* October 2, 1914; and "Brief War News," *Blaine Journal,* April 9, 1915.

44 "Russians Defeat 400,000 Teutons," *Blaine Journal,* April 23, 1915; "Russian Losses Are Huge," *Blaine Journal,* April 23, 1915.

45 "Brief War News," *Blaine Journal,* July 21, 1916.

46 "British Refuse to Save Germans," *Blaine Journal,* February 18, 1916.

47 "Brief War News," *Blaine Journal,* May 7, 1915.

48 "White Rock Man Killed at the Front," *Semiahmoo Gazette,* May 1915.

49 See, for example, "Private 'Glad of Wound' at Ypres," *Detroit Free Press,* May 29, 1915; "Colonel Captured by Windsor Man at Ypres," *Detroit Free Press,* June 19, 1915; Editorial, *Calais Advertiser,* May 5, 1915.

50 "*Lusitania* Is Sunk by a Submarine," *Blaine Journal,* May 14, 1915; "Manufacture of Booze Cut Down Two-Thirds," *Blaine Journal,* May 14, 1915.

51 This article was originally published in the *Washington Call* and later reprinted by the *Blaine Journal.* Editorial, *Blaine Journal,* July 2, 1915.

52 See, for example, "Great Need for Christ's Kingdom" and "Earthly Wealth, Heavenly Riches," *Blaine Journal,* October 2, 1914.

53 Eventually, even Russell's supporters were banned from entering Canada. "Russellites Run Foul of Censor," *Windsor Evening Record,* February 28, 1918; M.J. Reid, Dominion Immigration Inspector, to A.G. McColl, Acting Canadian Immigration Inspector-in-Charge, White Rock, November 16, 1917, LAC, MF C-10429, File 774004.

54 "Blaine Remains Dry by Majority of 358" and "Washington Dry; Republicans Win," *Blaine Journal,* November 6, 1914.

55 Editorial, *Blaine Journal,* October 16, 1914.

56 Unlike the *Surrey Gazette,* the *Blaine Journal* thrived during the war, with its readership increasing substantially during the conflict. Editorial, *Blaine Journal,* December 15, 1916.

57 The *Blaine Journal* rarely published letters from local soldiers serving in the CEF, but there were exceptions, including a note from Private Justin Dorr, sent from France in December 1916. The letter mentioned several Blaine residents fighting with the Canadians. "Soldier Writes from France," *Blaine Journal,* February 2, 1917; "Former Blaine Boy Tells of 'Going Over the Top,'" *Blaine Journal,* April 26, 1918.

58 *Wrigley's British Columbia Directory, 1919* (Vancouver: Wrigley Directories, 1919), 1178; Barrie Sanford, *Railway by the Bay: 100 Years of Trains at White Rock, Crescent Beach, and Ocean Park, 1909-2009* (Vancouver: National Railway Historical Society, 2009), 33. Blaine Municipal Government, City Council Minutes, October 19, 1914, Washington State Archives, NW369-6-1; "South Surrey Conservatives Hold Session in White Rock," *Semiahmoo Gazette,* February 16, 1915.

59 "State Bank of Blaine, Wash.," "Wolten & Montfort," and "White Rock Beach Agates," *Semiahmoo Gazette,* April 14, 1914; "The Pastime Theatre of Blaine," *Semiahmoo Gazette,* February 16, 1915.

60 "Glass Houses," *Surrey Gazette,* June, 1915.

61 Ibid.

62 The community involvement of Sands: "Patriotic Meeting," *British Columbian,* September 15, 1914; "White Rock News," *British Columbian,* February 16, 1915; Edgar and Harold Sands in the military: "Corp. E.H. Sands Awarded Medal," *British Columbian,* October 23, 1917; "Local Notes," *Surrey Gazette,* April 15, 1916.

63 "Border Towns," *Surrey Gazette,* October 15, 1915.

64 The *Blaine Journal* noted that the town "practically closed up shop" on the afternoon of April 10 as "everyone who could went to Bellingham to either take part or witness in the big patriotic parade." "Local News," *Blaine Journal,* April 13, 1917.

65 Editorial, *Blaine Journal,* April 6, 1917.

66 On Allied victories: "Germans Abandon Lines to British," *Blaine Journal,* March 9, 1917; "Drive Germans on Wide Front," *Blaine Journal,* April 13, 1917; "French Launch Great Offensive," *Blaine Journal,* April 20, 1917; on condemnations of German actions during the war: "American Sailors Tell of Sufferings" and "Zimmerman Admits Plot against US," *Blaine Journal,* March 16, 1917.

67 "Victoria Day," *Surrey Gazette,* June 1, 1917.

68 "Local News," *Blaine Journal,* June 1, 1917.

69 "Many Visitors Here Flag Raising Day," *Blaine Journal,* May 25, 1917.

70 The following year White Rock's returned soldiers were invited to attend Blaine's Memorial Day exercises. "Memorial Service for the Grand Army," *Blaine Journal,* May 25, 1917; "Memorial Day," *Blaine Journal,* May 24, 1918.

71 For more on the Chautauqua, see Jennifer A. Brown et al., "Chautauqua and the Philosophical Origins of Social Reconstruction," *American Educational History Journal* 33, 2 (2006).

72 "Our Chautauqua," *Blaine Journal,* June 15, 1917.

73 "Chautauqua Is Highly Pleasing," *Blaine Journal,* June 29, 1917.

74 "Victoria Day," *Surrey Gazette,* June 1, 1917; "Extols Crescent's Summer Charms," *British Columbian,* July 31, 1917.

75 "The Stars and Stripes Are Now Worthy of Full Honours," *Surrey Gazette,* May 1, 1917.

76 White Rock was one of only a few BC communities to vote against prohibition that year. "British Columbia Dry by 8,000," *Blaine Journal,* September 22, 1916.

77 "Two Blaine Bootleggers Are Sent to Jail," *Blaine Journal,* June 1, 1917; "Autos and Booze Plenty Here on Labor Day," *Blaine Journal,* September 7, 1917.

78 The prerogative of the White Rock Improvement League in the latter stages of the war continued to be the town's development as a resort area. The league petitioned Surrey Council for funding to help with the improvement of roads, railway crossings, and other infrastructure. See Surrey Council Minutes, 1917 and 1918.

79 Curfew: October 16, 1916; Pool rooms: May 7, 1917; Pawn shops: August 19, 1918, Blaine Municipal Government, City Council Minutes, Washington State Archives, NW369-6-1.

80 Blaine Municipal Government, City Council Minutes, October 1, 1917, and February 18, 1918, Washington State Archives, NW369-6-1.

81 White Rock voted twenty-six to twenty-two against prohibition. "British Columbia Dry by 8,000," *Blaine Journal,* September 22, 1916.

82 See Surrey Council Minutes, August 11–25, 1917, http://www.surrey.ca/bylawsandcouncillibrary/August-11-1917-RC-71B3.pdf; June 8, 1918, http://www.surrey.ca/bylawsandcouncillibrary/June-8-1918-RC-3EoC.pdf.

83 "Surrey Second in the Valley," *British Columbian,* November 26, 1918; Lorraine Ellenwood, *Years of Promise: White Rock, 1858-1958* (White Rock, BC: White Rock Museum and Archives Society, 2004), 145.

84 Ellenwood, *Years of Promise,* 30.

85 "Blaine Rejoices Over Signing of Armistice," *Blaine Journal,* November 15, 1918.

Chapter 6: Booze and Bandits

1 The first piece of legislation designed to limit Chinese immigration was a fifty-dollar head tax imposed in 1885, the year that the CPR was completed. Although that represented a substantial sum of money at the time, it was deemed not enough by white British Columbians, who saw to its increase to $500 by 1903. Valerie Knowles, *Strangers at Our Gates: Canadian Immigration and Immigration Policy, 1540-2006* (Toronto: Dundurn Press, 2006), 71–73; Seema Sohi, "Race, Surveillance, and Indian Anticolonialism in the

Transnational Western US–Canadian Borderlands," *Journal of American History* 28, 2 (2011).

2 Knowles, *Strangers at Our Gates*, 72.

3 This was more of a perceived threat than a real one since, most of the time, Chinese labourers filled jobs considered undesirable by whites. Ninette Kelley and Michael J. Trebilcock, *The Making of the Mosaic: A History of Canadian Immigration Policy* (Toronto: University of Toronto Press, 1998), 94.

4 "1911 Census of Canada," Vancouver Public Library, http://guides.vpl.ca/ccg.

5 The US census pools these racial groups. *Thirteenth Census of the United States 1910, Volume 4: Reports by States, Nebraska–Wyoming* (Washington, DC: Government Printing Office, 1912–14).

6 R. Fawcett, Inspector, to Malcolm R.J. Reid, March 8, 1913, LAC, MF C-10429, File 774004.

7 For example, the immigration department removed the money qualification from May 1 to September 30, 1912. Memorandum from W.D. Scott, March 11, 1912, and March 28, 1912, LAC, MF C-10429, File 774004.

8 Circular from W.D. Scott to Port Agents and Boundary Inspectors, March 16, 1912, LAC, MF C-10429, File 774004.

9 In 1912, the IWW helped to organize strikes involving 8,000 workers employed by the Canadian Northern and Grand Trunk Pacific Railways. Although it was formed in Chicago in 1905, its base of power became the Pacific Northwest, where itinerant workers faced particularly harsh working conditions. For more, see Mark Leier, *Where the Fraser River Flows: The Industrial Workers of the World in British Columbia* (Vancouver: New Star Books, 1990), 53; A. Ross McCormack, "The Industrial Workers of the World in Western Canada: 1905-1914," Canadian Historical Association Historical Papers, 1975; and W.D. Scott to W.W. Cory, Deputy Minister of the Interior, February 12, 1912, LAC, MF C-10429, File 774004.

10 Circular letter from W.D. Scott to Boundary Inspectors, April 30, 1913, LAC, MF C-10429, File 774004.

11 R. Fawcett to Malcolm R.J. Reid, March 8, 1913, LAC, MF C-10429, File 774004.

12 In December 1917, Dominion Immigration Inspector M.J. Reid complained in a letter to a Great Northern Railway representative that the railway's schedule left literally no time for inspection at White Rock, with trains scheduled to arrive and leave the town at the same time. Malcolm R.J. Reid to Kenneth J. Burns, General Passenger Agent, Great Northern Railway, December 15, 1917, LAC, MF C-10429, File 774004.

13 Circular from Superintendent of Immigration W.D. Scott to Border Inspectors, January 13, 1913, LAC, MF C-10429, File 774004.

14 W.D. Scott to J.H. MacGill, December 22, 1911, and J.H. MacGill to W.D. Scott, December 27, 1911, LAC, MF C-10429, File 774004.

15 W.D. Scott to J.H. MacGill, February 18, 1912, LAC, MF C-10429, File 774004.

16 H.G. Lawrence to W.D. Scott, February 29, 1912, LAC, MF C-10429, File 774004.

17 "Origins of Peoples of Canada," *British Columbian*, April 15, 1913.

18 In comparison, in Vancouver, Chinese, Japanese, and East Indian peoples as a group accounted for one-eighteenth of the local population. *Fifth Census of Canada 1911: Religions, Origins, Birthplace, Citizenship, Literacy, and Infirmities, by Provinces, Districts, and Sub-Districts, Volume II* (Ottawa: C.H. Parmlee, 1913), Table VII, 170–71.

19 Ibid., 214–15.

20 In fact, the 1911 census reveals that just five Chinese and no Japanese lived in the entire county of Charlotte. Ibid., 178–79.

21 "Editorial Notes," *Semiahmoo Gazette*, April 3, 1913.

22 "White Rock News," *British Columbian*, April 21, 1914.

23 Margaret Lang Hastings, *Along the Way: An Account of Pioneering White Rock and Surrounding District in British Columbia* (Cloverdale, BC: D.W. Friesen and Sons, 1981), 215.

24 According to historian Edward P. Crapol, Blaine "was in the forefront to exclude ... Chinese immigration to the United States." As a senator in the 1870s, Blaine supported legislation designed to prevent Chinese labourers from entering the country. For some, his position on Asian immigration was surprising given his rather liberal attitudes toward equal rights for African Americans. Edward P. Crapol, *James G. Blaine: Architect of Empire* (Wilmington, DE: Scholarly Resources, 2000), 55–56.

25 Kristofer Allerfeldt, "Race and Restriction: Anti-Asian Immigration Pressures in the Pacific North-West during the Progressive Era, 1885-1924," *History* 88, 289 (2003).

26 Jack Brown, "The Blaine–Point Roberts Salmon Fisheries," http://www.surreyhistory.ca/fisheries.html.

27 Jean Barman, *The West Beyond the West: A History of British Columbia* (Toronto: University of Toronto Press, 1991), 119.

28 In the early twentieth century, smugglers allegedly charged fifty dollars for each Chinese person smuggled across the border. Ellenwood, *Years of Promise*, 142.

29 Ibid., 58.

30 Ibid., 142.

31 "Many Aliens Try to Cross Boundary," *Blaine Journal*, September 4, 1914.

32 "Local News," *Blaine Journal*, April 30, 1915.

33 "Pacific Highway Station Opened," *Blaine Journal*, July 18, 1913.

34 "Port of White Rock, BC," *Semiahmoo Gazette*, April 14, 1914.

35 In Windsor and Detroit, attitudes toward prohibition were fairly ambivalent. In February 1918, Mayor of Detroit Oscar Marx discouraged police from watching saloons and instead encouraged them to focus on catching "burglars" and "slayers." In Windsor, the *Evening Record* supported closing saloons but believed that locals should be allowed to drink alcohol in their homes. In St. Stephen and Calais, there was mutual support for prohibition. Liquor smuggling was rampant in all four towns but does not appear to have affected cross-border relations at the local level. "Lessen Watch on Bars – Marx," *Detroit News*, February 18, 1918; "Ontario Temperance Act," *Windsor Evening Record*, March 11, 1918; "Bone Dry Order," *Windsor Evening Record*, March 13, 1918; "As Others See Us," *Saint Croix Courier*, August 9, 1917; "Congratulations Extended from across the Stream," *Saint Croix Courier*, September 20, 1917. For more on prohibition in Detroit and Windsor, see Philip P. Mason, *Rumrunning and the Roaring Twenties: Prohibition on the Michigan-Ontario Waterway* (Detroit: Wayne State University Press, 1995).

36 City of Detroit, Journal of the Common Council, September 8 and 14, and October 6 and 13, 1914, Detroit Public Library, Burton Historical Collection.

37 "Local Notes," *Semiahmoo Gazette*, September 21 and December 15, 1914.

38 The bandits targeted Washington centres Sedro-Woolley, Granite Falls, and Elma, and BC towns Abbotsford and New Hazelton, before making their way to the White Rock area. Margaret Lang Hastings, "Sheriff's Posse Ends Tragic 1914 Shootout," *Peace Arch News*, October 1, 1986.

39 His family was from New Westminster, but Adams moved to White Rock upon being appointed customs officer at Pacific Highway in 1912. "Subway Plans Drawn for White Rock," *British Columbian*, December 17, 1912.

40 "Retribution Swift and Sure," *Semiahmoo Gazette*, October 27, 1914; "New Westminster Man Shot Dead by Russian Bandits," *British Columbian*, October 27, 1914.

41 The exact amount of said booty is not known, though authorities did report that, during the Sedro-Woolley robbery alone, the bandits made off with $12,000 in gold coins, silver,

and cash. A fraction of that sum, approximately $3,000, was found on the bodies of the dead robbers. Hastings, "Sheriff's Posse Ends Tragic 1914 Shootout."

42 "White Rock Hotel," *Semiahmoo Gazette,* June 20, 1914.

43 "Seek Hotel Proprietor," *British Columbian,* September 1, 1914.

44 "Kengyel Sends Farewell," *British Columbian,* September 8, 1914.

45 Malcolm R.J. Reid to W.D. Scott, September 25, 1914, LAC, MF C-10429; "Local News," *Blaine Journal,* April 30, 1915.

46 "Charge of Treason against Two Hall's Prairie Farmers," *British Columbian,* July 13, 1915; "Charged with Aiding Alien Enemies across Border," *British Columbian,* July 20, 1915; "Two Farmers Facing High Treason Charge," *Toronto World,* July 13, 1915; "Treason Charge Not Sustained," *Blaine Journal,* July 23, 1915.

47 According to the *British Columbian,* Martin often pointed to criticisms of Raymer's character in *Narodni List,* an independent Croatian newspaper published in the United States (though banned during the war by Canada). "Freed on Own Recognizance," *British Columbian,* November 9, 1915; "About *Narodni List,*" http://chroniclingamerica.loc.gov/lccn/sn83030217/.

48 All other evidence was hearsay, with immigration agents testifying to having heard that Hamel and Kitzel were smuggling Germans and Austrians across the border to Blaine. "Hamel-Kitzel Trial Opens," *British Columbian,* October 26, 1915; "Freed on Own Recognizance," *British Columbian,* November 9, 1915.

49 "Defence Wants Guarantee Witness Won't Be Interned" and "Hamel-Kitzel Trial Opens," *British Columbian,* October 26, 1915; "Freed on Own Recognizance," *British Columbian,* November 9, 1915.

50 "Obituary," *Blaine Journal,* July 5, 1918.

51 Lottie Roeder Roth, *History of Whatcom County, Volume II* (Seattle: Pioneer Historical, 1926), 900–1.

52 "Charged with Aiding Alien Enemies across Border," *British Columbian,* July 20, 1915.

53 Jack Berry, "The History of the Port of Pacific Highway, BC," Canada Customs, Surrey Archives, Reference Files.

54 A.L. Joliffe, Commissioner of Immigration, to W.D. Scott, September 17, 1918, LAC, MF C-10429, File 774004.

55 B.R. Whiteley, Immigration Inspector, to Malcolm R.J. Reid, September 12, 1916, and J.C. Cornish, Immigration Inspector, to Malcolm R.J. Reid, September 13, 1916, LAC, MF C-10429, File 774004.

56 "Heavier Duties for Border Officials," *Surrey Gazette,* April 25, 1918; "Much Traffic across the Border," *British Columbian,* June 11, 1918.

57 "British Columbia Day," *Blaine Journal,* October 5, 1917; Editorial, *Blaine Journal,* December 28, 1917.

58 "Government Is Not Consistent in Handling Booze Situation," *Blaine Journal,* July 20, 1917.

59 "Local News," *Blaine Journal,* October 25, 1918.

60 "The Oriental Invasion," *Surrey Gazette,* March 15, 1917; "Labour Battalions," *Surrey Gazette,* January 24, 1917.

61 When petitioning for government funding to construct a wharf at White Rock in 1913, local officials noted all businesses in town, including a "meat market." However, in 1918, the *Blaine Journal* noted that there was no meat market in White Rock. Johnson insisted that no such business could survive with Blaine meat priced so cheaply. "Pier in Hand," *Peace Arch News,* July 12, 2000; "Local News," *Blaine Journal,* August 23, 1918.

62 "Local News," *Blaine Journal,* August 23, 1918.

63 W.E. Johnson Interview, March 1963, British Columbia Archives, Imbert Orchard Records, Tape 2.

64 Hastings, *Along the Way*, 199–201.

65 "Views of Readers – The Lady Searcher," *Windsor Evening Record*, March 30, 1915; "Views of Readers – That Customs Raid," *Windsor Evening Record*, April 1, 1915, 4; "Great Differences between Understanding and Perception," *Saint Croix Courier*, May 9, 1918.

Conclusion

1 Robert Rutherdale, *Hometown Horizons: Local Responses to Canada's Great War* (Vancouver: UBC Press, 2004), xi.

2 "Canadian Contingent," *Windsor Evening Record*, August 1, 1914, 4; "Twenty-First May Be Asked to Send 100 Men to the Front," *Windsor Evening Record*, August 5, 1914.

3 "The Horrible Cost" and "Keep Neutrality All US Can Do," *Detroit News*, August 1, 1914; "What War Will Do," *Detroit Free Press*, August 3, 1914; "Believes Great War Will Be Long Drawn Struggle," *Detroit News*, September 2, 1914.

4 "Encampment Makes More Sacred Patriotism of Peace, Says Governor, in Welcome," *Detroit News*, September 2, 1914.

5 The "South Detroit" episode in Windsor in 1917 suggests that this might have been the case there. However, it would be wrong to suggest that social and economic ties to a nearby US community completely eradicated feelings of a cultural connection to Britain in either Windsor or St. Stephen. Brandon Dimmel, "South Detroit, Canada: Isolation, Identity, and the US–Canada Border, 1914–1918," *Journal of Borderlands Studies* 26, 2 (2011).

6 White Rock: the *Semiahmoo/Surrey Gazette* regularly promoted Conservative MP J.D. Taylor and MPP Frank J. MacKenzie. When Taylor appeared in White Rock in 1917, local political and business leader Henry Thrift referred to him as "the man who put White Rock on the map." White Rock was also home to the South Surrey Conservative Association. "Wealthy Conscription Applied Literally Would Paralyze Production and Trade," *Semiahmoo Gazette*, December 6, 1917; "South Surrey Conservatives," *Semiahmoo Gazette*, May 18, 1914.

7 The federal election of 1911 split Essex County, with Essex North voting Conservative and Essex South voting Liberal. In the provincial election of 1914, the Liberals swept Essex County despite resounding success for the Whitney Conservatives elsewhere. Neil F. Morrison, *Garden Gateway to Canada: One Hundred Years of Windsor and Essex County, 1854-1954* (Windsor: Herald Press, 1954), 240–43.

8 See Martin F. Auger, "On the Brink of Civil War: The Canadian Government and the Suppression of the 1918 Quebec Easter Riots," *Canadian Historical Review* 89, 4 (2008); and James M. Pitsula, *For All We Have and Are: Regina and the Experience of the Great War* (Winnipeg: University of Manitoba Press, 2008), 196.

9 "South Detroit," *Windsor Evening Record*, May 23, 1917; "Voice of Readers – Prefers 'Detroit, Canada,'" *Windsor Evening Record*, November 12, 1917.

10 Editorial, *Saint Croix Courier*, May 31, 1917; "The News from Calais," *Saint Croix Courier*, May 4, 1916; "Great Differences between Understanding and Perception," *Saint Croix Courier*, May 9, 1918.

11 When the war started, approximately 75 percent of federal revenue was based on customs and excise duties. By the Second World War, the share had dropped to 40 percent. Dave McIntosh, *The Collectors: A History of Canadian Customs and Excise* (Toronto: NC Press, 1984), 133.

12 See James W. Walker, "Race and Recruitment in World War I: Enlistment of Visible Minorities in the Canadian Expeditionary Force," *Canadian Historical Review* 70, 1 (1989).

13 Tim Cook, *At the Sharp End: Canadians Fighting the Great War, 1914–1916* (Toronto: Viking Penguin, 2007), 27.

14 See Anne-Marie Kinahan, "Transcendent Citizenship: Suffrage, the National Council of Women of Canada, and the Politics of Organized Womanhood," *Journal of Canadian Studies* 42, 3 (2008).

15 See Lara Campbell, "We Who Have Wallowed in the Mud of Flanders: First World War Veterans, Unemployment, and the Development of Social Welfare in Canada, 1929-1939," *Journal of the Canadian Historical Association* 11 (2000).

16 Carl Berger, *A Sense of Power: Studies in the Ideas of Canadian Imperialism, 1867-1914* (Toronto: University of Toronto Press, 1970), 264.

17 "Views of Readers – The Lady Searcher," *Windsor Evening Record,* March 30, 1915.

18 "Short Stories of Events in Town and Country," *Saint Croix Courier,* May 20, 1915.

19 Editorial, *Saint Croix Courier,* June 14, 1917.

20 "The Talk of the Town," *Saint Croix Courier,* May 21, 1914; "Victoria Day Observance for the Boys in Khaki," *Saint Croix Courier,* May 18, 1916.

21 "Victoria Day," *Surrey Gazette,* June 1, 1917.

Bibliography

PRIMARY SOURCES

Archival Materials

British Columbia Archives

"Blaine, Wash., the Peace Arch City." Pamphlet. NWp 979.731.

Margaret Stewart Interview. Imbert Orchard Records. T0326: 0001, 0002.

W.E. Johnson Interview. Imbert Orchard Records. T0765: 0001, 0002.

Calais Free Library

Calais Marriage Records, 1892–1955. Unpublished manuscript.

Charlotte County Archives

"Calais Schools: Yesterday and Today." Pamphlet. Box A796, 10–11.

"General Directory of Calais and St. Stephen, 1890–1891." City Directory. Box A792, 6–4 (2).

"House of Commons to F.M. Smith Esq., Town Clerk, Milltown, NB." May 16, 1916. Milltown Records Collection. Box A787, 1.20.

"Orphan's Friend Lodge." Pamphlet. Henry F. Eaton Steamer File. Box 9–12.

"Short's Shipyards." Pamphlet. Berla Short Collection. Box A787, 1.32.

Detroit Public Library

Burton, Clarence M. Papers. Burton Historical Collection Manuscripts Collection. Box 11.

Detroit Study Club Records. Lillian Johnson Collection. Papers. Burton Historical Collection Manuscripts Collection. Box 2:2.

Journal of the Common Council, City of Detroit, 1913–18. Burton Historical Collection.

Shattuck, Marquis E. Papers. Burton Historical Collection Manuscripts Collection. Series 2, Box 11:4.

St. Andrew's Society Records, 1850–1978. Burton Historical Collection Manuscripts Collection. Box 1:10, 20:13.

Library and Archives Canada

Department of Immigration Correspondence. RG76, Microfilm Reels C-10616, File 801552; C-10429, File 774004; C-10632, Files 804947, 805189, and 804948.

"Guards to Be Placed on United States End of International Bridges during War." RG25, Vol. 1160, File 312.

"Peace Centenary Celebration of One Hundred Years of Peace among English Speaking Peoples." RG25, Vol. 1116, File 1255.

"Protection of Frontiers." RG24, Vol. 4262, File C-13.

Talbot Mercer Papineau Fonds. MG30-E52, Vol. 03294.

New Brunswick Provincial Archives
St. Stephen Municipal Records, 1914–18. RS420, F581.

Saint Croix Public Library
"Biography of Rev. Duncan McColl." Pamphlet. Project Preservation Reel 2.
Canadian Club Minutes, 1913–18. Project Preservation Reel 2, Part 12.
"General Directory of Calais and St. Stephen, 1908–1909." City Directory.
Royal Canadian Legion, St. Croix Branch 9, Minutes, 1917–18. Reel F20266, F20269.

Surrey Archives
Berry, Jack. "The History of the Port of Pacific Highway, BC" Reference Files, Canada Customs.
Carder, Al. Memoirs. Reference Files.
Henderson's British Columbia Gazetteer and Directory. Vancouver: Henderson, 1910.
"How They Lived, as Told by Margaret M. Stewart." Biographical Files, Stewart 170.75.
Olive Bell Wilson Interview. Audio Recording. Accession Number SMA90.021.
Wrigley's British Columbia Directory, 1919. Vancouver: Wrigley Directories, 1919.

Washington State Archives
Blaine Municipal Government, City Council Minutes, 1914–18. NW369-6-1.

White Rock Museum and Archives
Margaret Lang Hastings Collection. Papers. Box 13.
"White Rock before the Railway" (museum display). August 2009.
"White Rock Elementary 70th Anniversary, May 19th & 20th, 1984." Pamphlet. W.R. Elementary 70th Anniversary File, 1993-30.
"White Rock's First Hotel" (museum display). August 2009.

Windsor Public Library Archives
Bowlby Estate Collection. Papers. Accession Number 1995/7.
Hallam Collection. Papers. MS 5.
Windsor City Council Committee Records and Reports, 1913–18. RG 2 AI-1, 2.
Windsor City Council Minutes, 1913–18. RG2 AI/V-1.

Government Publications
"Canadian Royal Labor Commission." In *Index to the Miscellaneous Documents of the House of Representatives for the First Session of the Fiftieth Congress, 1887–1888.* Washington, DC: Government Printing Office, 1889.
Fifth Census of Canada 1911: Religions, Origins, Birthplace, Citizenship, Literacy, and Infirmities, by Provinces, Districts, and Sub-Districts, Volume II. Ottawa: C.H. Parmlee, 1913.
Fourteenth Census of the United States 1920, Volume 3: Population 1920: Composition and Characteristics of the Population by States. Washington, DC: Government Printing Office, 1921.
Ninth Census of Canada 1951, Volume I. Ottawa: Queen's Printer and Controller of Stationery, 1953.
Sixth Census of Canada 1921, Volume I. Ottawa: F.A. Acland, 1924.
Sixth Census of Canada 1921: Age, Conjugal Condition, Birthplace, Immigration, Citizenship, Language, Educational Status, School Attendance, Blindness, and Deaf Mutism, Volume II. Ottawa: F.A. Acland, 1925.

Thirteenth Census of the United States 1910, Volume 3: Reports by States, Alabama–Montana. Washington, DC: Government Printing Office, 1912–14.

Thirteenth Census of the United States 1910, Volume 4: Reports by States, Nebraska–Wyoming. Washington, DC: Government Printing Office, 1912–14.

Newspapers

Blaine Journal
British Columbian
Calais Advertiser
Detroit Free Press
Detroit News
Ludington Daily News
New York Times
Saint Croix Courier
Semiahmoo/Surrey Gazette
Toronto World
Windsor Evening Record
Windsor Star

Other Primary Sources

"Address of the Sons of Liberty of Montréal to the Young People of the Colonies of North America, October 4, 1837." Ottawa: Institut Canadien de Microreproductions Historiques, 1983.

Borden, Henry. *Robert Laird Borden: His Memoirs.* Toronto: Macmillan, 1938.

Brown, William Wallace. "Pioneers of Calais." In *Calais Centennial, 1909.* Calais: St. Croix Historical Society, 2009.

McCully, Charles G. "Our Men and Women in the Past." In *Calais Centennial, 1909.* Calais: St. Croix Historical Society, 2009.

Scott, W.D. "The Immigration of Races, 1914." In *"A Country Nourished on Self-Doubt": Documents in Canadian History, 1867–1980,* edited by Thomas Thorner. Peterborough: Broadview Press, 1998.

Surrey Municipal Council Minutes, 1913–18. http://www.surrey.ca/city-government/5491.aspx.

SECONDARY SOURCES

Books and Articles

Aitken, Hugh G.J., and W.T. Easterbrook. *Canadian Economic History.* Toronto: University of Toronto Press, 1988.

Alcock, Donald G. "The Best Defence Is ... Smuggling? Vermonters during the War of 1812," *Canadian Review of American Studies* 20, 1 (1995).

Allan, Chantall. *Bomb Canada, and Other Unkind Remarks in the American Media.* Edmonton: Athabasca University Press, 2009.

Allen, Robert S. "His Majesty's Indian Allies: Native Peoples, the British Crown, and the War of 1812," *Michigan Historical Review* 14, 2 (1988).

Allerfeldt, Kristofer. "Race and Restriction: Anti-Asian Immigration Pressures in the Pacific North-West during the Progressive Era, 1885-1924." *History* 88, 289 (2003).

Altheide, David L., and R. Sam Michalowski. "Fear in the News: A Discourse of Control." *Sociological Quarterly* 40, 3 (1999).

"Ambassador Bridge Traffic Up Slightly in 2011 Compared to 2010." *Windsor Star,* January 4, 2012.

Anastakis, Dimitry. "From Independence to Integration: The Corporate Evolution of the Ford Motor Company of Canada, 1904-2004." *Business History Review* 78, 2 (2004).

Anderson, Fred. *The War that Made America: A Short History of the French and Indian War.* New York: Penguin, 2006.

Annis, Matthew. "The 'Chinese Question' and the Canada-US Border, 1885: 'Why Don't Governor Squire Send His Troops to Semiahmoo to Prevent the Twelve or Fifteen Thousand Pagans from Crossing Our Borders into British Columbia?'" *American Review of Canadian Studies* 40, 3 (2010).

Antal, Sandy, and Kevin R. Shackleton. *Duty Nobly Done: The Official History of the Essex and Kent Scottish Regiment.* Windsor: Walkerville Publishing, 2006.

Arbuckle, Marie. *A Symbol of Our Heritage, the Old Fir Tree: Blaine Centennial History, 1884–1984.* Blaine, WA: Profile Publications, 1984.

Armstrong, Frederick. *The Forest City: An Illustrated History of London, Canada.* Burlington, ON: Windsor Publications, 1986.

–. "James Dougall and the Founding of Windsor, Ontario." *Ontario History* 76, 1 (1984).

Artibise, Alan F. "Cascadian Adventures: Shared Visions, Strategic Alliances, and Ingrained Barriers in a Transborder Region." In *Holding the Line: Borders in a Global World,* edited by Heather M. Nicol and Ian Townsend-Gault. Vancouver: UBC Press, 2005.

Astore, William J. "Gentle Skeptics? American Catholic Encounters with Polygenism, Geology, and Evolutionary Theories from 1845 to 1875." *Catholic Historical Review* 82, 1 (1996).

Auger, Martin F. "On the Brink of Civil War: The Canadian Government and the Suppression of the 1918 Quebec Easter Riots." *Canadian Historical Review* 89, 4 (2008).

Barman, Jean. *The West Beyond the West: A History of British Columbia.* Toronto: University of Toronto Press, 1991.

Bartholomew, Robert. "Phantom German Air Raids on Canada: War Hysteria in Ontario and Quebec during the First World War." *Canadian Military History* 7, 4 (1998).

Bell, William. "Reno Gang's Reign of Terror." *Wild West Magazine,* February 2004.

Bellamy, Matthew. "Beer Wars." *Beaver* 89, 2 (2009).

Bellfy, Phil. "Cross-Border Treaty Signers: The Anishnaabeg of the Lake Huron Borderlands." In *Lines upon the Water: First Nations and the Great Lakes Borders and Borderlands,* edited by Karl Hele. Waterloo: Wilfrid Laurier University Press, 2008.

Berger, Carl. *A Sense of Power: Studies in the Ideas of Canadian Imperialism, 1867–1914.* Toronto: University of Toronto Press, 1970.

–. *The Writing of Canadian History: Aspects of English-Canadian Historical Writing: 1900–1970.* Toronto: Oxford University Press, 1976.

Bernard, Jean-Paul. "The Rebellions of 1837 and 1838 in Lower Canada." In *Quebec since 1800: Selected Readings,* edited by Michael D. Behiels. Toronto: Irwin Publishing, 2002.

–. *Rebellions of 1837 and 1838 in Lower Canada.* Historical Booklet No. 55. Ottawa: Canadian Historical Association, 1996.

Bernier, Gerald, and Daniel Salée. "A Discourse of Protest: The Patriotes Decade (1828-1838)." In *Reappraisals in Canadian History, Pre-Confederation,* edited by C.M. Wallace, R.M. Bray, and A.D. Gilbert. Scarborough: Prentice Hall, Allyn and Bacon Canada, 1999.

Berton, Pierre. *Vimy.* Toronto: Pierre Berton Enterprises, 1986.

Bigony, Beatrice A. "A Brief History of Native Americans in the Detroit Area." *Michigan History* 61, 2 (1977).

Billington, Ray Allen. *Westward Expansion: A History of the American Frontier.* New York: Macmillan, 1982.

Blackett, R.J.M. *Divided Hearts: Britain and the American Civil War.* Baton Rouge: Louisiana State University Press, 2001.

Blanchard, Jim. *Winnipeg's Great War: A City Comes of Age.* Winnipeg: University of Manitoba Press, 2010.

Boileau, John. *Half-Hearted Enemies: Nova Scotia, New England, and the War of 1812.* Halifax: Formac, 2005.

Boyd, Edward, ed. "The Days before Yesterdays in the St. Croix Valley." Manuscript, St. Croix Public Library, 2001.

Bradbury, Susan L., and Daniel E. Turbeville III. "Are Enhanced Trade and Enhanced Security Mutually Exclusive? The Western Canada–US Borderland in a Post-9/11 World." *American Review of Canadian Studies* 38, 3 (2008).

Brebner, John Bartlett. *The Neutral Yankees of Nova Scotia: A Marginal Colony during the Revolutionary Years.* Toronto: McClelland and Stewart, 1939.

Brebner, John Bartlett, and Marcus Lee Hansen. *The Mingling of the Canadian and American Peoples.* New York: Arno Press, 1940.

Brooks, Stephen. *Public Policy in Canada: An Introduction.* Toronto: Oxford University Press, 1998.

Brown, Jennifer A., Karen L. Riley, and Ray Braswell. "Chautauqua and the Philosophical Origins of Social Reconstruction." *American Educational History Journal* 33, 2 (2006).

Brown, Robert Craig, and Ramsay Cook. *Canada, 1896–1921: A Nation Transformed.* Toronto: McClelland and Stewart, 1974.

Brown, Robert Craig, and Donald Loveridge. "Unrequited Faith: Recruiting the CEF, 1914-1918." *Revue internationale d'histoire militaire* 51, 54 (1982).

Brown, Wallace. "Victorious in Defeat: The American Loyalists in Canada." In *Reappraisals in Canadian History: Pre-Confederation,* edited by C.M. Wallace, R.M. Bray, and A.D. Gilbert. Scarborough: Prentice Hall, Allyn and Bacon Canada, 1999.

Bukowczyk, John J. "Migration, Transportation, Capital, and the State in the Great Lakes Basin, 1815-1890." In *Permeable Border: The Great Lakes Basin as Transnational Region, 1650–1990,* edited by John J. Bukowczyk. Pittsburgh: University of Pittsburgh Press, 2005.

–. "Trade, War, Migration, and Empire in the Great Lakes Basin, 1650-1815." In *Permeable Border: The Great Lakes Basin as Transnational Region, 1650–1990,* edited by John J. Bukowczyk. Pittsburgh: University of Pittsburgh Press, 2005.

Burton, Clarence Monroe. *When Detroit Was Young: Historical Studies.* Detroit: Burton Abstract and Title, 1950.

Campbell, Lara. "We Who Have Wallowed in the Mud of Flanders: First World War Veterans, Unemployment, and the Development of Social Welfare in Canada, 1929–1939." *Journal of the Canadian Historical Association* 11 (2000).

Carroll, Francis M. "Drawing the Line." *Beaver* 83, 4 (2003).

Carter-Edwards, Dennis. "The War of 1812 along the Detroit Frontier: A Canadian Perspective." *Michigan Historical Review* 13, 2 (1987).

"Cascading Across the Line." *Surrey/North Delta Leader,* May 28, 1999.

Cavendish, Richard. "The Founding of Detroit." *History Today* 51, 7 (2001).

Clark, Charles E. *Maine: A History.* New York: W.W. Norton, 1976.

Coates, Ken S. "Border Crossings: Patterns and Processes along the Canada–United States Boundary West of the Rockies." In *Parallel Destinies: Canadian-American Relations West of the Rockies,* edited by Ken S. Coates. Seattle: University of Washington Press, 2002.

Colley, Ted. “Natives Celebrate Return of Land.” *Surrey Leader,* July 5, 1997.

Conrad, Margaret, and Alvin Finkel. *History of the Canadian Peoples: 1867 to Present.* Toronto: Pearson Education Canada, 2005.

Cook, Tim. *At the Sharp End: Canadians Fighting the Great War, 1914–1916.* Toronto: Viking Penguin, 2007.

–. *Shock Troops: Canadians Fighting the Great War, 1917–1918.* Toronto: Viking Penguin, 2008.

Copp, Terry. “The Military Effort, 1914–1918.” In *Canada and the First World War: Essays in Honour of Robert Craig Brown,* edited by David Mackenzie. Toronto: University of Toronto Press, 2005.

Costrell, Edward. *How Maine Viewed the War, 1914–1917.* Orono: University of Maine Press, 1940.

Coyne, Vin. “Letter, Number, or Name? How Our Streets Got Their Names.” *Semiahmoo Sounder,* n.d.

–. “Vintage White Rock: A Life of Firsts.” *Peace Arch News,* January 15, 2000.

–. “When the Siren Sounds.” *Semiahmoo Sounder,* September, 1991.

Crapol, Edward P. *James G. Blaine: Architect of Empire.* Wilmington: Scholarly Resources, 2000.

Creighton, Donald. *The Empire of the St. Lawrence.* Boston: Houghton Mifflin, 1958.

Cruikshank, Ken. “The Intercolonial Railway, Freight Rates, and the Maritime Economy.” In *Farm, Factory, and Fortune: New Studies in the Economic History of the Maritime Provinces,* edited by Kris E. Inwood. Fredericton: Acadiensis Press, 1993.

Crump, Jennifer. *Canada under Attack.* Toronto: Dundurn Press, 2010.

Daniels, Roger. *Coming to America: A History of Immigration and Ethnicity in American Life, Second Edition.* New York: Perennial, 2002.

Davies, Aubrey G. “International Frontier Week.” In “The Days before Yesterdays in the St. Croix Valley,” edited by Edward Boyd. Manuscript, St. Croix Public Library, 2001.

Davis, Harold. *An International Community on the St. Croix, 1604–1930.* Orono: University of Maine Press, 1950.

Den Otter, A.A. *The Philosophy of Railways: The Transcontinental Railway Idea in British North America.* Toronto: University of Toronto Press, 1997.

Diamond, Jared M. *Guns, Germs, and Steel: The Fates of Human Societies.* New York: W.W. Norton, 1997.

Dickason, Olive Patricia, and William Newbigging. *A Concise History of Canada's First Nations.* Toronto: Oxford University Press Canada, 2010.

Dimmel, Brandon. “Shutting Down the Snake Ranch: Battling Booze at the BC Border, 1910-1914.” In *Beyond the Border: Tensions across the Forty-Ninth Parallel in the Great Plains and Prairies,* edited by Kyle Conway and Timothy Patsch. Montreal: McGill-Queen's University Press, 2013.

–. “South Detroit, Canada: Isolation, Identity, and the US–Canada Border, 1914–1918.” *Journal of Borderlands Studies* 26, 2 (2011).

Dixon, Muriel H. “The Story of Indian Island.” *Saint Croix Courier,* October-November 1977.

Dougherty, Doug. *St. Stephen Yesteryear.* St. Stephen, NB: Parsons Printing, 2000.

Douglas, R. Alan. *Uppermost Canada: The Western District and the Detroit Frontier, 1800–1850.* Detroit: Wayne State University Press, 2001.

Drache, Daniel. *Borders Matter: Homeland Security and the Search for North America.* Halifax: Fernwood Publishing, 2004.

–. "The Canadian Bourgeoisie and Its National Consciousness." In *Close the 49th Parallel: The Americanization of Canada*, edited by Ian Lumsden. Toronto: University of Toronto Press, 1970.

Duguid, A. Fortescue. *Official History of the Canadian Forces in the Great War, 1914–1918.* Ottawa: J.O. Patenaude, 1938.

Dunning, Thomas P. "The Adventures of Patriot Hunters: Danger, Place, Memory, and Virtue at the Windmill." *Canadian Review of American Studies* 29, 1 (1999).

Eagan, Bill. *Woven in Time: An Oral History of the Milltown (St. Croix) Cotton Mill.* Bayside, NB: Korby, 2004.

Ellenwood, Lorraine. *Years of Promise: White Rock, 1858–1958.* White Rock, BC: White Rock Museum and Archives Society, 2004.

Ellis, James H. *A Ruinous and Unhealthy War: New England and the War of 1812.* New York: Algora, 2009.

Errington, Jane. *The Lion, the Eagle, and Upper Canada: A Developing Colonial Ideology.* Montreal: McGill-Queen's University Press, 1987.

Estes, Todd. "John Jay, the Concept of Deference, and the Transformation of Early American Political Culture." *Historian* 65, 2 (2002).

Ettinger, Patrick. *Imaginary Lines: Border Enforcement and the Origins of Undocumented Immigration, 1882–1930.* Austin: University of Texas Press, 2009.

Ewan, Christopher. "The Emancipation Proclamation and British Public Opinion." *Historian* 67, 1 (2005).

Fazio, John C. "Intrepid Mariners." *Civil War Times* 46, 1 (2007).

"Fires, Border Play Important Role in History of Blaine." *Blaine Journal*, July 30, 1959.

Folster, David. *The Chocolate Ganongs of St. Stephen, New Brunswick.* Toronto: Macmillan, 1990.

Forkey, Neil S. "Anglers, Fishers, and the St. Croix River: Conflict in a Canadian-American Borderland, 1867-1900." *Forest and Conservation History* 37, 4 (1993).

Franklin, Deborah. "The Boar War." *Smithsonian* 36, 3 (2005).

Fraser, Marian Botsford. *Walking the Line.* Vancouver: Douglas and McIntyre, 1989.

Ganong, William Francis. *Champlain's Island: St. Croix (Dochet).* Saint John: New Brunswick Museum, 1945.

Gastil, Raymond D., and Barnett Singer. *The Pacific Northwest: Growth of a Regional Identity.* Jefferson, NC: McFarland, 2010.

Gattinger, Monica, and Geoffrey Hale. *Borders and Bridges: Canada's Policy Relations in North America.* New York: Oxford University Press, 2010.

Gerson, Noel B. *Mr. Madison's War: 1812: The Second War for Independence.* New York: Julian Messner, 1966.

Gervais, C.H. *The Border Police: One Hundred and Twenty-Five Years of Policing in Windsor.* Windsor: Penumbra Press, 1992.

Gillis, R. Peter, and Thomas R. Roach. *Lost Initiatives: Canada's Forest Industries, Forest Policy, and Forest Conservation.* Westport, CT: Greenwood Press, 1986.

Glazebrook, G.P. de T. *A History of Transportation in Canada.* Toronto: Ryerson Press, 1938.

Goutor, David. "Constructing the 'Great Menace': Canadian Labour's Opposition to Asian Immigration, 1880–1914." *Canadian Historical Review* 88, 4 (2007).

Granatstein, J.L. *Yankee Go Home: Canadians and Anti-Americanism.* Toronto: HarperCollins, 1996.

Granatstein, J.L., and Desmond Morton. *Marching to Armageddon: Canadians and the Great War, 1914–1918.* Toronto: Lester and Orpen Dennys, 1989.

Graybill, Andrew R., and Benjamin H. Johnson. *Bridging National Borders in North America: Transnational and Comparative Histories.* Durham: Duke University Press, 2010.

Green, Michael D., and Theda Perdue. *North American Indians: A Very Short Introduction.* New York: Oxford University Press, 2010.

Greer, Allan. "1837–38: Rebellion Reconsidered." *Canadian Historical Review* 76, 1 (1995).

Gregg, Michael L. "Archaeological Complexes of the Northeastern Plains and Prairie-Woodland Border, A.D. 500-1500." In *Plains Indians, A.D. 500–1500: The Archaeological Past of Historic Groups,* edited by Karl H. Schleiser. Norman: University of Oklahoma Press, 1994.

Groβ, Gerhard P. "There Was a Schlieffen Plan: New Sources on the History of German Military Planning." *War in History* 15, 4 (2008).

Gwyn, Sandra. *Tapestry of War: A Private View of Canadians in the Great War.* Toronto: HarperCollins, 1992.

Haas, Ernst B. *Beyond the Nation-State: Functionalism and International Organization.* Stanford: Stanford University Press, 1964.

Harrison, Charles Yale. *Generals Die in Bed: A Story from the Trenches.* Toronto: Annick Press, 2002.

Hastings, Margaret Lang. "Along the Way." *Peace Arch News,* December 28, 1978.

–. "Along the Way." *Peace Arch News,* September 28, 1985.

–. *Along the Way: An Account of Pioneering White Rock and Surrounding District in British Columbia.* Cloverdale, BC: D.W. Friesen, 1981.

–. "At 85, Fred Johnson Storehouse of Memories." *White Rock Sun,* January 16, 1964.

–. "The Ropers among First Families to Develop Area." *White Rock and District Mercury,* January 7, 1970.

–. "Sheriff's Posse Ends Tragic 1914 Shootout." *Peace Arch News,* October 1, 1986.

Hawkes, Arthur. *Canadian Nationalism and the War.* Montreal: n.p., 1916.

Haycock, Ronald G. *Sam Hughes: The Public Career of a Controversial Canadian, 1885–1916.* Waterloo: Wilfrid Laurier University Press, 1986.

Haynes, Sam W. *James K. Polk and the Expansionist Impulse.* New York: Longman, 1997.

Higham, John. *Strangers in the Land: Patterns of American Nativism, 1860–1925.* New Brunswick, NJ: Rutgers University Press, 1955.

Holton, F.J., D.H. Bedford, and Francis Cleary. *History of the Detroit and Windsor Ferries.* Detroit: University of Michigan Library, 1918.

Hunt, H. Draper. "The Plumed Knight at Home: An Intimate Sketch of James G. Blaine." *Maine Historical Society Quarterly* 28, 1 (1988).

Innis, Harold A. *The Diary of Simeon Perkins, Vol. 1: 1766–1780.* Toronto: Champlain Society, 1948.

Inwood, Kris E. "Maritime Industrialization from 1870 to 1910: A Review of the Evidence and Its Interpretation." In *Farm, Factory, and Fortune: New Studies in the Economic History of the Maritime Provinces,* edited by Kris E. Inwood. Fredericton: Acadiensis Press, 1993.

Jacobs, Major James Ripley, and Glenn Tucker. *The War of 1812: A Compact History.* New York: Hawthorn Books, 969.

Janelle, Donald G. "The Maine Connection: Quebec to New Brunswick." In *Borderlands: Essays in Canadian-American Relations.* Toronto: ECW Press, 1991.

Joe, Philip, and Louis Miranda. "How the Squamish Remember George Vancouver." In *From Maps to Metaphors: The Pacific World of George Vancouver,* edited by Robin Fisher and Hugh J.M. Johnston. Vancouver: UBC Press, 1993.

Kaufman, Jason. *The Origins of Canadian and American Political Differences.* Cambridge, MA: Harvard University Press, 2009.

Kaufman, Scott, and John A. Soares, Jr. "Sagacious beyond Praise? Winfield Scott and Anglo-American–Canadian Border Diplomacy, 1837-1860." *Diplomatic History* 30, 1 (2006).

Kealey, Gregory S. "State Repression of Labour and the Left in Canada, 1914-20: The Impact of the First World War." *Canadian Historical Review* 73, 3 (1992).

–. "The Surveillance State: The Origins of Domestic Intelligence and Counter-Subversion in Canada, 1914–21." *Intelligence and National Security* 7, 3 (1992).

Kelley, Ninette, and Michael J. Trebilcock. *The Making of the Mosaic: A History of Canadian Immigration Policy.* Toronto: University of Toronto Press, 1998.

Keshen, Jeffrey. *Propaganda and Censorship during Canada's Great War.* Edmonton: University of Alberta Press, 1996.

Kinahan, Anne-Marie. "Transcendent Citizenship: Suffrage, the National Council of Women of Canada, and the Politics of Organized Womanhood." *Journal of Canadian Studies* 42, 3 (2008).

Kitchen, Martin. "The German Invasion of Canada in the First World War." *International History Review* 7, 2 (1985).

Klug, Thomas. "The Detroit Labor Movement and the United States–Canada Border, 1885-1930." *Mid-America* 80, 3 (1998).

–. "The Immigration and Naturalization Service (INS) and the Making of a Border-Crossing Culture on the US–Canada Border, 1891–1941." *American Review of Canadian Studies* 40, 3 (2010).

–. "Residents by Day, Visitors by Night: The Origin of the Alien Commuter on the US-Canadian Border during the 1920s." *Michigan Historical Review* 34, 2 (2008).

Knowles, Valerie. *Strangers at Our Gates: Canadian Immigration and Immigration Policy, 1540–2006.* Toronto: Dundurn Press, 2006.

Knowlton, Isaac Case. *Annals of Calais, Maine and St. Stephen, New Brunswick Including the Village of Milltown, Me., and the Present Town of Milltown, N.B.* Calais, ME: Sears, 1875.

Konrad, Victor, and Lauren McKinsey. *Borderlands Reflections: The United States and Canada.* Orono, ME: Borderlands Project, 1989.

LaDow, Beth. *The Medicine Line: Life and Death on a North American Borderland.* New York: Routledge, 2001.

–. "Sanctuary: Native Border Crossings and the North American West." *American Review of Canadian Studies* 31, 1–2 (2001).

Landau, Henry. *The Enemy Within: The Inside Story of German Sabotage in America.* New York: Van Rees Press, 1937.

Landon, Fred. *Western Ontario and the American Frontier.* Toronto: Ryerson Press, 1941.

Lawson, Philip. *The Imperial Challenge: Quebec and Britain in the Age of the American Revolution.* Montreal: McGill-Queen's University Press, 1989.

Laxer, James. *The Border: Canada, the US, and Dispatches from the 49th Parallel.* Toronto: Anchor Canada, 2004.

Leacock, Stephen. *Canada: The Foundations of Its Future.* Montreal: Seagram, 1941.

Leier, Mark. *Where the Fraser River Flows: The Industrial Workers of the World in British Columbia.* Vancouver: New Star Books, 1990.

Leonard, Thomas C. "Mistaking Eugenics for Social Darwinism: Why Eugenics Is Missing from the History of American Economics." *History of Political Economy* 37 (2005).

Little, J.I. *Loyalties in Conflict: A Canadian Borderland in War and Rebellion, 1812–1840.* Toronto: University of Toronto Press, 2008.

Lochbiler, Don. *Detroit's Coming of Age: 1873 to 1973*. Detroit: Wayne State University Press, 1973.

Longo, Julie. "Consuming Freedom: The International Freedom Festival as Transnational Tourism Strategy on the Windsor–Detroit Border, 1959–1976." *Michigan Historical Review* 34, 2 (2008).

Loyal She Remains: A Pictorial History of Ontario. Toronto: United Empire Loyalists' Association of Ontario, 1984.

Lutz, Stuart. "Terror in St. Albans." *Civil War Times Illustrated* 40, 3 (2001).

MacDonald, Cheryl. "Spring Ahead." *Beaver* 81, 2 (2001).

Mack, Sharon Kiley. "New Calais Border Crossing Opens." *Bangor Daily News*, November 16, 2009.

–. "Two Cities in Two Countries with One Emergency-Response Mission." *Bangor Daily News*, March 26, 2011.

Malcolmson, Robert. *Capital in Flames: The American Attack on York, 1813*. Montreal: Robin Brass Studio, 2008.

Marchildon, Gregory P. "From Pax Britannica to Pax Americana and Beyond." *Annals of the American Academy of Political and Social Science* 538 (1995).

Mason, Philip P. *Rumrunning and the Roaring Twenties: Prohibition on the Michigan-Ontario Waterway*. Detroit: Wayne State University Press, 1995.

Masters, Donald C. *The Reciprocity Treaty of 1854: Its History, Its Relation to British Colonial and Foreign Policy and to the Development of Canadian Fiscal Autonomy*. Toronto: McClelland and Stewart, 1963.

McCallum, Margaret. "Separate Spheres: The Organization of Work in a Confectionery Factory: Ganong Bros., St. Stephen, New Brunswick." *Labour/Le travail* 24 (1989).

McClintock, Thomas C. "British Newspapers and the Oregon Treaty of 1846." *Oregon Historical Quarterly* 104, 3 (2003).

McCormack, A. Ross. "The Industrial Workers of the World in Western Canada: 1905-1914." *Canadian Historical Association Historical Papers* (1975).

McCoy, Charles A. *Polk and the Presidency*. Austin: University of Texas Press, 1960.

McIntosh, Dave. *The Collectors: A History of Canadian Customs and Excise*. Toronto: NC Press, 1984.

Mead, Gary. *The Doughboys: America and the First World War*. New York: Overlook Press, 2000.

Miller, Ian Hugh Maclean. *Our Glory and Our Grief: Torontonians and the Great War*. Toronto: University of Toronto Press, 2002.

Moore, Stephen T. "Refugees from Volstead: Cross-Boundary Tourism in the Northwest during Prohibition." In *The Borderlands of the American and Canadian Wests: Essays on the Regional History of the 49th Parallel*, edited by Sterling Evans. Lincoln: University of Nebraska Press, 2006.

Morgan, Carl. *Birth of a City: Commemorating Windsor's Centennial, 1992*. Windsor: Benchmark, 1991.

Morgan, Cecilia. "Of Slender Frame and Delicate Appearance: The Placing of Laura Secord in the Narratives of Canadian Loyalist History." *Journal of Canadian Historical Association* 5 (1994).

Morrison, Neil F. *Garden Gateway to Canada: One Hundred Years of Windsor and Essex County, 1854–1954*. Windsor: Herald Press, 1954.

Morton, Desmond. *Fight or Pay: Soldiers' Families in the Great War*. Vancouver: UBC Press, 2004.

–. *When Your Number's Up: The Canadian Soldier in the First World War*. Toronto: Random House, 1993.

Mount, Graeme. *Canada's Enemies: Spies and Spying in the Peaceable Kingdom.* Toronto: Dundurn Press, 1993.

–. "Drums along the St. Mary's: Tensions on the International Border at Sault Ste. Marie." *Michigan History* 73 4 (1989).

Mount, Graeme, John Abbott, and Michael J. Mulloy. *The Border at Sault Ste. Marie.* Toronto: Dundurn Press, 1995.

Mowat, Grace Helen. *The Diverting History of a Loyalist Town: A Portrait of St. Andrews, New Brunswick.* Fredericton: Brunswick Press, 1953.

Neal, Frederick. *The Township of Sandwich, Past and Present.* Windsor: Record Printing, 1909.

Ngai, Mae M. "The Architecture of Race in American Immigration Law: A Reexamination of the Immigration Act of 1924." *Journal of American History* 86, 1 (1999).

Nicholson, G.W.L. *Canadian Expeditionary Force, 1914–1918: Official History of the Canadian Army in the First World War.* Ottawa: Roger Duhamel, Queen's Printer and Controller of Stationery, 1962.

–. *The Gunners of Canada: The History of the Royal Regiment of Artillery.* Toronto: McClelland and Stewart, 1967.

Nicol, Eric. *Vancouver.* Toronto: Doubleday Canada, 1978.

Norrie, Kenneth, Douglas Owram, and J.C. Herbert Emery. *A History of the Canadian Economy.* Toronto: Nelson, 2002.

Olbey, Christian. "Unfolded Hands: Class Suicide and the Insurgent Intellectual Paraxis of Mary Ann Shadd." *Canadian Review of American Studies* 30, 2 (2000).

Open Canada: A Global Positioning Strategy for a Networked Age. Toronto: Canadian International Council, 2010.

Orth, Samuel P. "The Alien Contract Labor Law." *Political Science Quarterly* 22, 1 (1907).

Oxford, William. *The Ferry Steamers: The Story of the Detroit–Windsor Ferry Boats.* Erin, ON: Boston Mills Press, 1992.

Pehl, Matthew. "The Remaking of the Catholic Working-Class: Detroit, 1919–1945." *Religion and American Culture* 19, 1 (2009).

Petrie, Joseph Richards. *The Regional Economy of New Brunswick: A Study Prepared for the Committee on Reconstruction.* Fredericton: n.p., 1944.

"Pier in Hand." *Peace Arch News,* July 12, 2000.

Pitch, Anthony S. *The Burning of Washington: The British Invasion of 1814.* Annapolis, NS: Naval Institute Press, 1998.

Pitsula, James M. *For All We Have and Are: Regina and the Experience of the Great War.* Winnipeg: University of Manitoba Press, 2008.

Plaut, Jonathan V. *The Jews of Windsor, 1790–1990: A Historical Chronicle.* Toronto: Dundurn Press, 2007.

Poitras, Jacques. *Imaginary Line: Life on an Unfinished Border.* Fredericton: Goose Lane Editions, 2011.

Poremba, David Lee. *Detroit: A Motor City History.* Chicago: Arcadia, 2001.

Power, Michael. "Bishop Fallon and the Riot at Ford City, 8 September 1917." Occasional Paper No. 3, Essex County Historical Society, 1986.

Prerau, David. *Seize the Daylight: The Curious and Contentious Story of Daylight Saving Time.* New York: Thunder's Mouth Press, 2005.

Prins, Harold E. "Children of Gluskap: Wabanaki Indians on the Eve of the European Invasion." In *American Beginnings: Exploration, Culture, and Cartography in the Land of Norumbega,* edited by Emerson W. Baker, Edwin A. Churchill, Richard D'Abate, Kristine L. Jones, Victor A. Konrad, and Harald E.L. Prins. Lincoln: University of Nebraska Press, 1994.

Ramirez, Bruno. *Crossing the 49th Parallel: Migration from Canada to the United States, 1900–1930*. Ithaca: Cornell University Press, 2001.

Rankin, Andrew. "Researchers in a Race against Time on Historic Island." *Toronto Star*, August 16, 2011.

Rawling, Bill. *Surviving Trench Warfare: Technology and the Canadian Corps, 1914–1918*. Toronto: University of Toronto Press, 1992.

"Reclaimin' Our History." *Peace Arch News*, October 16, 1995.

Rees, Ronald. *Historic St. Croix: St. Stephen–Calais*. Halifax: Nimbus, 2003.

Reid, John G. "An International Region of the Northeast: Rise and Decline, 1635–1762." In *The Northeastern Borderlands: Four Centuries of Interaction*, edited by Stephen J. Hornsby, Victor A. Konrad, and James J. Herlan. Fredericton: Acadiensis Press, 1989.

Reimer, Chad. "Borders of the Past: The Oregon Boundary Dispute and the Beginnings of Northwest Historiography." In *Parallel Destinies: Canadian-American Relations West of the Rockies*, edited by John M. Findlay and Ken S. Coates. Seattle: University of Washington Press, 2002.

Remarque, Erich Maria. *All Quiet on the Western Front*. Oxford: Heinemann, 1970.

Renshaw, Patrick. "The IWW and the Red Scare, 1917-1924." *Journal of Contemporary History* 3, 4 (1968).

Risberg, Erica. "The Hillbillies of Maine: Rural Communities, Radio, and Country Music Performers." *Maine History* 45, 3 (2010).

Robbins, Keith. *The First World War: The Outbreak, Events, and Aftermath*. Oxford: Oxford University Press, 1984.

Roberts, David. *In the Shadow of Detroit: Gordon M. McGregor, Ford of Canada, and Motoropolis*. Detroit: Wayne State University Press, 2006.

Roberts, Gillian, and David Stirrup. "Introduction to the ARCS Special Issue on Culture and the Canada–US Border." *American Review of Canadian Studies* 40, 3 (2010).

Romney, Paul. *Getting It Wrong: How Canadians Forgot Their Past and Imperilled Confederation*. Toronto: University of Toronto Press, 1999.

Roth, Lottie Roeder. *History of Whatcom County, Volume I*. Seattle: Pioneer Historical, 1926.

–. *History of Whatcom County, Volume II*. Seattle: Pioneer Historical, 1926.

Roy, Patricia E. *A White Man's Province: British Columbia Politicians and Chinese and Japanese Immigrants, 1858–1914*. Vancouver: UBC Press, 1989.

Russell, Peter. *Constitutional Odyssey: Can Canadians Become a Sovereign People?* Toronto: University of Toronto Press, 2004.

Rutherdale, Robert. *Hometown Horizons: Local Responses to Canada's Great War*. Vancouver: UBC Press, 2004.

Sanford, Barrie. *Railway by the Bay: 100 Years of Trains at White Rock, Crescent Beach, and Ocean Park, 1909–2009*. Vancouver: National Railway Historical Society, 2009.

Sassman, Richard. "A Borderline War." *American History* 35, 6 (2001).

Scee, Trudy Irene. *City on the Penobscot: A Comprehensive History of Bangor, Maine*. Charleston, SC: History Press, 2010.

Schillinger, Elisabeth Hupp. "British and US Newspaper Coverage of the Bolshevik Revolution." *Journalism Quarterly* 43, 1 (1966).

Sears, Edwin, and Vincent Short. *Sail and Steam: Along the Maine Coast*. Portland, ME: Bond Wheelwright, 1955.

Sellers, Charles. *James K. Polk, Continentalist, 1843–1846*. Princeton: Princeton University Press, 1966.

Senior, Hereward. *The Last Invasion of Canada: The Fenian Raids, 1866–1870*. Toronto: Dundurn Press, 1991.

Sharp, Paul. *Whoop-Up Country: The Canadian-American West, 1865–1885*. Minneapolis: University of Minnesota Press, 1955.

Smith, David R. "Structuring the Permeable Border: Channeling and Regulating Cross-Border Traffic in Labor, Capital, and Goods." In *Permeable Border: The Great Lakes Basin as Transnational Region, 1650–1990*, edited by John J. Bukowczyk. Pittsburgh: University of Pittsburgh Press, 2005.

Smith, Goldwin. *Canada and the Canadian Question*. London: Macmillan, 1891.

Smith, Marian. "The Immigration and Naturalization Service (INS) at the US–Canadian Border, 1893–1993: An Overview of Issues and Topics." *Michigan Historical Review* 26, 2 (2000).

Sohi, Seema. "Race, Surveillance, and Indian Anticolonialism in the Transnational Western US–Canadian Borderlands." *Journal of American History* 28, 2 (2011).

Stacey, C.P. "The Divine Mission: Mackenzie King and Hitler," *Canadian Historical Review* 61, 4 (1980).

Stanley, George F.G. *Mapping the Frontier: Charles Wilson's Diary of the Survey of the 49th Parallel, 1858–1862, while Secretary of the British Boundary Commission*. Toronto: Macmillan, 1970.

–. *The War of 1812: Land Operations*. Toronto: Macmillan in collaboration with the National Museum of Man, 1983.

Stoehr, Catherine Murton. "Nativism's Bastard: Neolin, Tenskwatawa, and the Anishinabeg Methodist Movement." In *Lines Drawn Upon the Water: First Nations and the Great Lakes Borders and Borderlands*, edited by Karle Hele. Waterloo: Wilfrid Laurier University Press, 2008.

Stokesbury, James L. *A Short History of World War I*. New York: William Morrow, 1981.

Strachan, Hew. *The First World War*. New York: Viking Penguin, 2004.

Stuart, Reginald. *Dispersed Relations: Americans and Canadians in Upper North America*. Baltimore: Johns Hopkins University Press, 2007.

Sugden, John. "Early Pan-Indianism: Tecumseh's Tour of the Indian Country, 1811–1812." *American Indian Quarterly* 10, 4 (1986).

Sugrue, Thomas. *The Origins of the Urban Crisis: Race and Inequality in Postwar Detroit*. Princeton: Princeton University Press, 1996.

Sutcliffe, John B. "Neoliberalism in a Small Canadian City? Windsor City Council and the Reform of the Detroit River Border Crossing." *American Review of Canadian Studies* 41, 3 (2011).

Swartz, Donald. "A Young Man's Benefit: The Independent Order of Odd Fellows and Sickness Insurance in the United States and Canada." *Labour/Le travail* 48 (2001).

Swettenham, John Alexander. *To Seize the Victory: The Canadian Corps in World War I*. Toronto: Ryerson Press, 1965.

Swyripa, Frances, and John Herd Thompson. *Loyalties in Conflict: Ukrainians in Canada during the Great War*. Edmonton: Canadian Institute of Ukrainian Studies, 1983.

Teaching with Documents: Using Primary Sources from the National Archives. Washington, DC: National Archives and Records Administration, 1989.

Thompson, John Herd. *The Harvests of War: The Prairie West, 1914–1918*. Toronto: McClelland and Stewart, 1978.

Thorner, Thomas. "General Introduction." In *A Few Acres of Snow: Documents in Pre-Confederation History*, edited by Thomas Thorner. Toronto: University of Toronto Press, 2009.

–. "Let Someone Else Have a Taste of Our Good Life: The Immigrant Experience." In *"A Country Nourished on Self-Doubt": Documents in Canadian History, 1867–1980*, edited by Thomas Thorner. Peterborough: Broadview Press, 1998.

Treleaven, G. Fern. *Roads, Rivers, and Railways: 100 Years of Transportation in Surrey.* Surrey, BC: Surrey Museum and Historical Society, 1981.

Tuchman, Barbara. *The Guns of August.* New York: Ballantine Books, 1962.

Tucker, Robert W. *Woodrow Wilson and the Great War: Reconsidering America's Neutrality, 1914–1917.* Charlottesville: University of Virginia Press, 2007.

Vance, Jonathan. *Death So Noble: Memory, Meaning, and the First World War.* Vancouver: UBC Press, 1997.

–. *A History of Canadian Culture.* New York: Oxford University Press, 2011.

Walker, James W. "Race and Recruitment in World War I: Enlistment of Visible Minorities in the Canadian Expeditionary Force." *Canadian Historical Review* 70, 1 (1989).

Whitehead, Don. *Border Guard: The Story of the United States Customs Service.* Toronto: McGraw-Hill Book, 1963.

Widdis, Randy. *With Scarcely a Ripple: Anglo-Canadian Migration into the United States and Western Canada, 1880–1920.* Montreal: McGill-Queen's University Press, 1999.

Willms, A.M. "Conscription 1917: A Brief for the Defence." In *Conscription 1917,* edited by Ramsay Cook, A.M. Willms, J.M. Bliss, and Martin Robin Willms. Toronto: University of Toronto Press, 1969.

Wilson, Barbara. *Ontario and the First World War, 1914–1918: A Collection of Documents.* Toronto: Champlain Society, 1977.

Wilson, Brian. "The Spirit of the Motor City: Three Hundred Years of Religious History in Detroit." *Michigan Historical Review* 27, 1 (2001).

Wise, S.F. *Canadian Airmen and the First World War.* Toronto: University of Toronto Press in cooperation with the Department of National Defence and the Canadian Government Publishing Centre, Supply and Services Canada, 1980.

Wood, Patricia K. "Borders and Identities among Italian Immigrants in the Pacific Northwest, 1880–1938." In *Parallel Destinies: Canadian-American Relations West of the Rockies,* edited by Ken S. Coates. Seattle: University of Washington Press, 2002.

Woon, Yuen-fong. "The Voluntary Sojourner among the Overseas Chinese: Myth or Reality?" *Pacific Affairs* 56, 4 (1983).

Writers' Program of the Work Projects Administration in the State of Washington. *Washington: A Guide to the Evergreen State.* Portland, OR: Binfords and Mort, 1941.

Wynn, Graeme. "New England's Outpost in the Nineteenth Century." In *The Northeastern Borderlands: Four Centuries of Interaction,* edited by Stephen Hornsby , Victor A. Konrad, and James J. Herlan. Fredericton: Acadiensis Press, 1989.

Zolberg, Aristide R. *A Nation by Design: Immigration in the Fashioning of America.* Boston: Harvard University Press, 2008.

Zunz, Olivier. *The Changing Face of Inequality: Urbanization, Industrial Development, and Immigrants in Detroit, 1880–1920.* Chicago: University of Chicago Press, 1982.

Website Articles

"1814: Battle of Lundy's Lane." Archives of Ontario, War of 1812, http://www.archives.gov.on.ca/en/explore/online/1812/niagara-1814.aspx.

"1911 Census of Canada." Vancouver Public Library, http://guides.vpl.ca/ccg.

"About Blaine." http://www.ci.blaine.wa.us/132/About-Blaine.

"About *Narodni List.*" http://chroniclingamerica.loc.gov/lccn/sn83030217/.

"About White Rock." http://www.whiterockcity.ca/EN/main/community/about-white-rock.html.

Brown, Jack. "The Blaine–Point Roberts Salmon Fisheries." http://www.surreyhistory.ca/fisheries.html.

"Building Fort Ponchartrain." History of Detroit, http://historydetroit.com/places/fort_ponchartrain.php.

"Calais Academy, Class of 1919." http://www.calaisalumni.org/class19.htm#Cobb.

"Canadian Border City Has First Homicide in 26 Months." http://www.cnn.com/2011/11/25/world/americas/canada-windsor-first-homicide/.

"Causes and Events of the War of 1812: A Timeline." http://www.warof1812.ca/1812events.htm.

"Census Metropolitan Area of Windsor, Ontario." Statistics Canada, http://www12.statcan.gc.ca/census-recensement/2011/as-sa/fogs-spg/Facts-cma-eng.cfm?LANG=Eng&GK=CMA&GC=559.

"Charlotte County Government." http://www.heritagecharlotte.com/documents/CharlotteCo-Government.pdf.

"Coercive Acts, The." Massachusetts Historical Society, http://www.masshist.org/revolution/coercive.php.

"Early French Settlements, 1605-1691." Statistics Canada, http://www.statcan.gc.ca/pub/98-187-x/4064812-eng.htm.

"Ganong, Gilbert White." *Dictionary of Canadian Biography Online*, http://biographi.ca/en/bio.php?id_nbr=7386.

"Hands across the Border Peace Arch Celebration." https://www.peacearchpark.org/.

"Hendry, John." *Dictionary of Canadian Biography Online*, http://www.biographi.ca/en/bio.php?id_nbr=7438.

"History: Chinese Immigration in Canada." Chinese Canadian National Council, http://www.ccnc.ca/cgi-sys/suspendedpage.cgi.

"History of a Peace Park, The." https://www.peacearchpark.org/.

"International Homecoming Festival." http://internationalhomecomingfestival.com/.

"Loyalist Burial Ground, King Street, St. Stephen, N.B." http://www.rootsweb.ancestry.com/~nbststep/loyalistcem/loyalistbg.htm.

"Michigan Central Station." Historic Detroit.org, http://www.historicdetroit.org/building/michigan-central-station/.

Niazi, Amil. "Border Stories: A Commuter's Journey." http://www.cbc.ca/news/canada/border-stories-a-commuter-s-journey-1.991906.

–. "Border Stories: St. Stephen, N.B., and Calais, Maine." http://www.cbc.ca/news/canada/border-stories-st-stephen-n-b-and-calais-maine-1.1011362.

"Pacific Scandal, The." Library and Archives Canada, http://www.collectionscanada.gc.ca/executive-decree/023004-3052-e.html.

"Populations of Various Ethnic Groups." History Detroit, 1701-2001, http://historydetroit.com/statistics/index.php.

"President Wilson's Proclamation Establishing Conscription, 28 May 1917." First World War.com, http://www.firstworldwar.com/source/usconscription_wilson.htm.

"River Raisin Battlefield." City of Monroe, http://www.co.monroe.mi.us/government/departments_offices/museum/docs/River_Raisin_Battlefield_Brochure.pdf.

"Sir John A. Macdonald, Canada's Patriot Statesman: The Policies." Library and Archives Canada, http://www.collectionscanada.gc.ca/023/013/023013-5000-e.html.

Smiley, Gene. "The US Economy in the 1920s." https://eh.net/encyclopedia/the-u-s-economy-in-the-1920s/.

"St. Stephen, New Brunswick." Statistics Canada, http://www12.statcan.gc.ca/mobile/92-591/table-eng.cfm?SGC=1302037.

"Town of St. Stephen: Event Display." http://www.town.ststephen.nb.ca/townevents/eventdisplay.php?id=332.

"Transcontinental Timeline: PBS' American Experience." http://www.pbs.org/wgbh/americanexperience/features/timeline/tcrr-timeline/.
"Vanishing City: The Story behind Detroit's Shocking Population Decline." http://newsfeed.time.com/2011/03/24/vanishing-city-the-story-behind-detroit%E2%80%99s-shocking-population-decline/.
"War of 1812: From Colony to Country." A Reader's Guide to Canadian Military History, Library and Archives Canada, http://www.collectionscanada.gc.ca/military/025002-2000-e.html.
"Welcome to the City of Calais." http://calaismaine.org/.

Theses and Dissertations

Dimmel, Brandon. "Domestic Diplomacy: The Relationship between Windsor and Detroit during the First World War, 1914–1918." MA Research Paper, University of Windsor, 2006.
Morrison, Neil F. "Essex County, Province of Ontario: A Geographical Study." PhD diss., University of Michigan, 1944.
Smylie, Eric. "Americans Who Did Not Wait: The American Legion of the Canadian Expeditionary Force, 1915–1917." MS thesis, University of North Texas, 1996.

Index

Note: (i) after a page number indicates a photograph, map, or figure

Studies in Canadian Military History

John Griffith Armstrong, *The Halifax Explosion and the Royal Canadian Navy: Inquiry and Intrigue*

Andrew Richter, *Avoiding Armageddon: Canadian Military Strategy and Nuclear Weapons, 1950–63*

William Johnston, *A War of Patrols: Canadian Army Operations in Korea*

Julian Gwyn, *Frigates and Foremasts: The North American Squadron in Nova Scotia Waters, 1745–1815*

Jeffrey A. Keshen, *Saints, Sinners, and Soldiers: Canada's Second World War*

Desmond Morton, *Fight or Pay: Soldiers' Families in the Great War*

Douglas E. Delaney, *The Soldiers' General: Bert Hoffmeister at War*

Michael Whitby, ed., *Commanding Canadians: The Second World War Diaries of A.F.C. Layard*

Martin Auger, *Prisoners of the Home Front: German POWs and "Enemy Aliens" in Southern Quebec, 1940–46*

Tim Cook, *Clio's Warriors: Canadian Historians and the Writing of the World Wars*

Serge Marc Durflinger, *Fighting from Home: The Second World War in Verdun, Quebec*

Richard O. Mayne, *Betrayed: Scandal, Politics, and Canadian Naval Leadership*

P. Whitney Lackenbauer, *Battle Grounds: The Canadian Military and Aboriginal Lands*

Cynthia Toman, *An Officer and a Lady: Canadian Military Nursing and the Second World War*

Michael Petrou, *Renegades: Canadians in the Spanish Civil War*

Amy J. Shaw, *Crisis of Conscience: Conscientious Objection in Canada during the First World War*

Serge Marc Durflinger, *Veterans with a Vision: Canada's War Blinded in Peace and War*

James G. Fergusson, *Canada and Ballistic Missile Defence, 1954–2009: Déjà Vu All Over Again*

Benjamin Isitt, *From Victoria to Vladivostok: Canada's Siberian Expedition, 1917–19*

James Wood, *Militia Myths: Ideas of the Canadian Citizen Soldier, 1896–1921*

Timothy Balzer, *The Information Front: The Canadian Army and News Management during the Second World War*

Andrew B. Godefroy, *Defence and Discovery: Canada's Military Space Program, 1945–74*

Douglas E. Delaney, *Corps Commanders: Five British and Canadian Generals at War, 1939–45*

Timothy Wilford, *Canada's Road to the Pacific War: Intelligence, Strategy, and the Far East Crisis*

Randall Wakelam, *Cold War Fighters: Canadian Aircraft Procurement, 1945–54*

Andrew Burtch, *Give Me Shelter: The Failure of Canada's Cold War Civil Defence*

Wendy Cuthbertson, *Labour Goes to War: The CIO and the Construction of a New Social Order, 1939–45*

P. Whitney Lackenbauer, *The Canadian Rangers: A Living History*

Teresa Iacobelli, *Death or Deliverance: Canadian Courts Martial in the Great War*

Graham Broad, *A Small Price to Pay: Consumer Culture on the Canadian Home Front, 1939–45*

Peter Kasurak, *A National Force: The Evolution of Canada's Army, 1950–2000*

Isabel Campbell, *Unlikely Diplomats: The Canadian Brigade in Germany, 1951–64*

Richard M. Reid, *African Canadians in Union Blue: Volunteering for the Cause in the Civil War*

Andrew B. Godefroy, *In Peace Prepared: Innovation and Adaptation in Canada's Cold War Army*

Nic Clarke, *Unwanted Warriors: The Rejected Volunteers of the Canadian Expeditionary Force*

David Zimmerman, *Maritime Command Pacific: The Royal Canadian Navy's West Coast Fleet in the Early Cold War*

Cynthia Toman, *Sister Soldiers of the Great War: The Nurses of the Canadian Army Medical Corps*

Daniel Byers, *Zombie Army: The Canadian Army and Conscription in the Second World War*

J.L. Granatstein, *The Weight of Command: Voices of Canada's Second War Generals and Those Who Knew Them*

Douglas E. Delaney and Serge Marc Durflinger, eds., *Capturing Hill 70: Canada's Forgotten Battle of the First World War*

Colin McCullough, *Creating Canada's Peacekeeping Past*

Studies in Canadian Military History

Published by UBC Press in association with the Canadian War Museum.